MONTESQUIEU

MONTESQUIEU

Pioneer of the
Sociology of Knowledge

by

W. STARK
M.A., DR RER. POL., DR JUR.

UNIVERSITY OF TORONTO PRESS
TORONTO 1961

"Les causes morales forment plus le caractère général d'une nation et décident plus de la qualité de son esprit que les causes physiques."

*Essai sur les Causes
qui peuvent affecter les Esprits
et les Caractères*

CONTENTS

PREFACE

IN THE PREFACE to my recent book, *The Sociology of Knowledge*, I expressed the hope that I had not only provided an introduction to, and reappraisal of, the subject which is known under that name, but also laid the foundations for a systematic study of its history. Indeed, I went even further: I said that I had already made a beginning to this study myself and analysed and assessed the contribution of one of its prime pioneers, the Baron de Montesquieu. My intention at that time was to incorporate this investigation of Montesquieu's doctrine into a more broadly conceived work on "The Origins of the Sociology of Knowledge". This plan I have now abandoned. An adequate discussion of the beginnings of the sociology of knowledge would presuppose a time-consuming search for its ultimate roots in both the empiricist and the rationalist traditions of philosophy as well as an account of at least Vico and Comte in addition to that of the Baron de la Brède. A book dealing thoroughly with this broad field—and, needless to say, nothing but a thorough investigation would ever satisfy me—would take years to write, run to something like 600 pages and prevent me from making, for a very long time, any contribution to the more topical discussions going on in the social sciences. I have therefore decided to publish my study of Montesquieu on its own, and here it is. I intend it in all modesty to be a kind of model or rather pattern on which parallel analyses of other classical authors could be built, and I should like to express the hope that hands will not be wanting to carry on the work and provide monographs which will do for other significant figures what I have tried to do for Montesquieu. The task is not easy; the sociology of thought is, in all the earlier thinkers at any rate, intertwined with the sociology of action, and a total assessment of the extant literature, coupled with a most careful separation of what belongs to the one division of sociology and what to the other, is needed in every case to achieve a satisfactory result. But if the task is not easy, it is at the same time a pleasant one. I have enjoyed my reading of Montesquieu and my writing on him, and such work as I have done on, e.g., Vico and Comte has convinced me that they, too, have much to give to him who steeps himself in their minds and searches for their opinions on the great problems which fall within the framework of a sociology of knowledge.

The fact that I have decided to reduce my contribution to the descriptive history of the subject (which, I acknowledge, has to be put down on the debit side) is to some extent counterbalanced by some inquiries, albeit minor in scope, which I have made, or still intend to make, into other aspects. I have, for instance, tried to correct the widespread conviction that the sociology of knowledge as a whole, and not only the doctrine of ideology, is the child of revolutionary sentiment. I have shown in a lecture which I gave at Harvard in March, 1958, that there exists beside the revolutionary tradition of Voltaire and Marx also a conservative tradition which we find in such writers as Johann Gottfried Herder, the Vicomte de Bonald, and others of the pre-romantic and romantic periods. This paper is soon to appear in *Kyklos*. I have pursued the topic further in two lectures in the University of Zürich during July, 1959. My title was: *Die idealistische Geschichtsauffassung und die Wissenssoziologie* and my subject mainly the Spanish thinker Juan Donoso Cortès. This study is to be published in the *Philosophisches Jahrbuch der Görres-Gesellschaft*.

Another avenue which I am endeavouring to open up is more in the nature of an empirical application of the sociology of knowledge. One way of bringing the observable facts of history into the framework of this branch of learning is to take the basic concepts of Tönnies, community and association, and ask whether mental structures can be identified which are regularly associated with, and understandable as outgrowths and complements of, the forms of life known by these terms. A first move in this direction was the paper I submitted to the Fourth World Congress of Sociology at Stresa in September 1959: "The Sociology of Knowledge and the Problem of Ethics". What I tried to show was that there is a definite communal ethic and an equally definite but diametrically opposed associational ethic, and that certain far-reaching developments, such as the growing secularisation of life and thought since the end of the Middle Ages, are largely due to this dichotomy in moral conceptions and the shifts which have occurred with regard to it. Other fields in which this dichotomy could be shown to be both present and significant are legal thought and judicial practice, æsthetic thought and artistic practice, the theory and practice of education, etc. etc. My Aquinas lecture of 1956 (published under the title "The Contained Economy" as Aquinas Paper no. 26) in a sense also belongs here, for what makes St Thomas's economics so different from modern economics is the fact that he has his mental roots in community, whereas modern economists speak about, and think and feel in terms of, association.

If I have succeeded, in these various papers, in opening one or two windows, much yet remains to be done. My earlier book, large as it is, has little in it on the proper method of the sociology of knowledge, and this topic will also have to be discussed one day. But I do not wish to speak of the future here. All I have at heart at the moment is to explain why this study of Montesquieu is launched in an independent form, and so to justify my action in this respect.

In view of the enormous literature already existing on the Baron de Montesquieu, it is something of a responsibility to add yet another item to the list. My excuse must be that I have asked the great man some questions which have not been put to him before; those questions which, in a more general manner, have been formulated in the second half of *The Sociology of Knowledge*. In my search for the answers, I have willy-nilly become involved in all the difficulties of Montesquieu scholarship and interpretation. Was he essentially a rationalist, or was he a romantic before his time? The problem has been discussed over and over again, without tangible result. Well might Montesquieu address to those who have studied him, and quarrelled about him, the words of Conrad Ferdinand Meyer: "I am no thought-out book of fiction. I am a man. I have my contradiction." Still, little is done by acknowledging the *double entendre* of his work; assuming that he belonged to both worlds at the same time, the further question, to what extent he was a rationalist and to what extent a pre-romantic, unavoidably arises and demands a solution. I can do no more here than record that I see him as a forerunner rather than as a camp-follower, a progressive man and mind, a pioneer. Why I have come to this conclusion will appear from my text, even though I have not made the elucidation of this issue my main concern.

Once again I have a pleasant debt of gratitude to discharge. This time it is to Dr Alison Hanham who has searched my book for infelicities of style and errors of expression. My readers ought to be as thankful to her as I am myself.

This study is essentially a sequel to *The Sociology of Knowledge*, and so offers me a welcome opportunity to say how happy I am about the overwhelmingly favourable reception which that book has received at the hands of colleagues, readers and reviewers. May this minor investigation be equally fortunate! I desire no more.

Manchester,   W. STARK
December 1959.

I

THE CONQUEST OF CARTESIANISM

MONTESQUIEU, or to give him his full name, Charles Louis Joseph de Secondat, Baron de la Brède et de Montesquieu, was born in the year 1689 and thus belonged to the generation whose keenest and most independent minds reacted against the Cartesian philosophy which had dominated French thinking up to the end of the seventeenth century. His eye was turned towards the concrete, not, like that of Descartes, towards the abstract. He was a lover of facts and not of speculation: speculation seemed to him pale, anæmic, a plaything for listless intellects, facts colourful, real, vital, the proper concern of the social philosopher. It is true that a careful analysis can discern some traces of the Cartesian outlook even in his work; but they are few and far between, accidental rather than essential, and certainly not, as some writers have tried to make out, characteristic of his total achievement.

For Descartes himself, Montesquieu had all due respect. In one connection he calls him the man "who has overcome the darkness of the old philosophy" (I, 1314[1]), i.e. the man who has destroyed the deadening influence of the degenerate scholasticism which had ruled before his day; in another he notes that the defenders of religion, after having attacked Descartes and accused him of atheism, had been forced to fall back on his very arguments for the defence of the theistic position (II, 1165 *seq*.); and in a third he goes so far as to say that it was Descartes who first convincingly demonstrated the true distinction between body and soul (I, 1557)—a very bold assertion indeed. But in the passage in which Montesquieu pays

[1] All references are to Roger Caillois' edition of the *Oeuvres Complètes* in the *Bibliothèque de la Pléiade*, 1949–51. The translations are my own.

Cartesius the greatest compliment, he also emphasises that he is not his disciple: "Descartes has taught those who have come after him, to discover his very errors. I compare him to Timoleon who said: 'I am happy that, through me, you have received freedom to oppose my wishes'." (I, 1548).

While he was thus not disrespectful to the master, he had great fun in ridiculing the disciples. There are several *Lettres Persanes* in which the latter-day Cartesians are the butt of Montesquieu's devastating wit. Writing to the holy dervish Hassein, Usbek reports about a group of philosophers who have undertaken to explain the whole of the divine creation by means of a simple mechanism, who regard two pretended laws as the key to all nature, and who, by using five or six truths, seem to have worked as many marvels and miracles as the prophets of Islam (I, 274 *seq.*). Even more aggressive and wounding is Rica's letter to Usbek in which he describes his encounter with a typical absent-minded "geomètre" on the Pont-Neuf. This man had steeped himself so deeply in the Cartesian world-view that he saw no more than lines and curves where other people beheld things of a thousand-and-one qualities. A castle was for him nothing but a body sixty foot long and thirty-five foot wide; the bombardment of a town nothing but so many trajectories through the air; and all that the visit to magnificent gardens had wrung from him was the remark that it would have been a good thing if they had been laid out in such a way as to make the alleyways appear throughout equally wide (I, 320 *seq.*[1]). There is a deeper meaning in these light-hearted skits. Montesquieu makes it quite plain in his playful fashion that he regards Cartesian formalism as a philosophy that narrows and empties and even cripples the mind.

M. Barckhausen has rightly remarked[2] that Montesquieu was interested in everything *bar* mathematics, that, indeed, mathematics was his blind spot, and nothing can prove more convincingly that his total mental habit was altogether different

[1] Cf. also letters CXXXV (333 *seq.*) and especially CXLV (357 *seq.*), the latter particularly amusing. That the *savant* held up to disdain here, is a Cartesian, is clear from the fact that he describes dogs as *automates*. Cf. furthermore the unfavourable judgment of Leibniz in *Correspondance de Montesquieu*, ed. Gebelin and Morize, I, 1913, 275.

[2] M. Barckhausen, *Montesquieu, Ses Idées et ses Oeuvres*, 1907, pp. 5, 303, 322.

from the Cartesian than this simple fact. There are only very few stray remarks concerning mathematics in Montesquieu's collected *Pensées*, and they are all informed by a certain hostility against the science and the art of figures. "The methods of the geometricians," Montesquieu writes, "are chains which tie them up and prevent them from moving freely" (I, 1181). Mathematicians know only two concepts, "true" and "false"; they do not know (what is yet so important, at any rate in human affairs) that there is a middle realm, the realm of the probable, of the more or less probable (*ib*). Another fragment is even more pointed: "I don't give more esteem to a man who has devoted himself to one science than to a man who has devoted himself to another, if both have brought to their studies the same spirit and the same good sense. All sciences are valuable and assist each other. I know nobody who would dispute about the dignity and the preferability of his art except [foolish people like] the dancing master and the fencing master in Molière. I say this," Montesquieu concludes, "against the geometricians" (I, 1181 *seq.*). But even this passage is not the most outspoken. Another evinces even greater ill-will: "When a man is a good geometrician and acknowledged as such, he has still to prove that he has *esprit*" (I, 1296).

Barckhausen conjectures that this hostility against mathematics as a pursuit and mathematicians as a tribe may have been due to an inability on Montesquieu's part to master their subject. Perhaps so; but the explanation thus offered is at best partial. Montesquieu had a better and, so to speak, more respectable reason for fighting the claim of the exact sciences to be on a higher level than all other branches of learning. He notes that it is one of the natural tendencies and enjoyments of the human spirit to formulate general propositions (I, 1295), and that this applies more particularly to petty minds (II, 882). But in politics, nothing can be more dangerous than to act and to rule on the basis of general, abstract principles: life is too manifold, too complex, and too tender for such treatment. After reading some book on medicine, he jots down the following observation: "One must avoid introducing geometry into medical science, because the former concerns the *quantum* and the latter the *quale*" (II, 1403 *seq.*). But this surely applies even more to the study and to the handling of the body social than to the study and the healing of the body physical. The science and the art of politics, too, tend to be corrupted by the introduction of alien methods. But it was perhaps less the corruption of the social disciplines that Montesquieu feared than their neglect—a neglect which he was resolved to remedy. "Among the Greeks and the Romans," he writes, "admiration for political and moral knowledge was carried to a kind of cult. Today, we have appreciation only for the physical sciences, we occupy ourselves exclusively with them, and political good and evil is among us a sentiment rather than an object of learning. Thus, not having been born in the century that would have suited me, I have decided to become a follower of that excellent man, the Abbé de Saint-Pierre, who has written so much on Politics in our days," and to make a contribution to that subject. Perhaps, Montesquieu adds half jokingly, half earnestly, "there may appear, in seven or eight centuries from now, some nation to whom my ideas will be very useful . . ." (II, 1039 *seq.*; cf. also *ib.*, fragment 199). Can there be a better proof than these words that Montesquieu was out of sympathy with his Cartesian environment, and that he was determined to swim against the stream?[1]

[1] There are two special fields in which Montesquieu's often underestimated hostility against the Cartesian tradition can also be seen: epistemology and æsthetics. In epistemology Montesquieu denies that we carry within us the concept of infinity as an inborn idea. That concept can only be built up in and through experience, by an analysis "of the universality of things" (I, 1177; cf. also Dedieu, *Montesquieu*, 1913, 279 *seq.*). Furthermore, the act of cognition is not to Montesquieu, as it is to the rationalists, exclusively or even predominantly an act of the intellect. "The soul knows through its ideas and through its feelings; for, though we may contrast idea and feeling, yet, when [the soul] perceives a thing, it feels it [at the same time]; and there are no concepts so purely intellectual that the spirit cannot perceive them, or, at least, believe itself to perceive them, and thus to feel them." (II, 1243). So far as æsthetics is concerned, Montesquieu claimed that Cartesianism had a deadening influence on the sense of beauty. "What manages to ruin the sense of the sublime among us . . . is the new philosophy which speaks to us only of general laws . . . That philosophy weakens the taste which men spontaneously have for poetry" (I, 1019). In more concrete terms, Montesquieu attacked the preference for geometrical designs which, under the influence of Cartesianism, had crept into e.g. house-building and landscape gardening: "Excessive regularity is sometimes, and indeed often, disagreeable. There is nothing so beautiful as the sky; yet it is covered with stars without order. The houses and the gardens around Paris have . . . the fault of being too much alike: they are perpetual copies of Le Nôtre . . ." (I, 1265). "The principles of geometry are very true; but if one were to apply them to matters of taste, one would rob reason itself of its reasonableness" (II, 1165). Cf. also *Essai sur le Goût*, II, 1240 *seq.*, esp. 1244.

However, the main question must be whether there are evidences of Cartesian influence in Montesquieu's *magnum opus, De l'Esprit des Lois,* and several authors, foremost among them Lanson, have claimed to discover the Cartesian method at the very root of Montesquieu's argument there.[1] Montesquieu starts by *defining* the three basic forms of government: republic, monarchy, and despotism; that is to say, in his manner of speaking, by describing their "nature", and then he proceeds to indicate their "principle", i.e. their general character, the springs of human action which are more particularly at work in each of them. And he claims that between "nature" and "principle", between definition and vital inspiration, there is a simple logical concatenation so that the latter can be deduced from the former. "I have said that the nature of republican government consists in this, that the people in a body, or certain families, have the sovereign power; that of monarchical government, that the prince has the sovereign power but will exercise it according to established laws; that of despotic government, that a single person rules according to his sweet will and caprices. I need no more in order to find their three principles; they derive naturally therefrom" (II, 251). This certainly looks like a piece of pure Cartesianism. But appearances are deceptive. Whatever Montesquieu may have fancied himself to have done, what he did do in point of fact was to find the life-principles of the three forms of government in reality, that is, he gained them through the study of facts, inductively and not deductively. His picture of the republican way of life is quite obviously and unmistakably based on the history of Rome, of Athens and of Venice; his idea of the limited monarchy on medieval France and the feudal order in general; and his sketch of despotism on the accounts of contemporary travellers, above all on their description of Persia and Turkey. If Montesquieu had really reached his conception of the three archtypes by deductive reasoning from a basic, initially posited definition, he would have shown us in detail how effect proceeds from cause, how consequence arises from antecedent. But he does nothing of the kind. He simply tells us what he knows about democracy, constitutional monarchy, and dicta-

---

[1] Cf. *Revue de Métaphysique et de Morale,* 1896, 540 *seq.* Cf. also Dedieu, *Montesquieu,* 1913, 83 *seq.* and 90 *seq.*

torship: but what he knows he knows from his study of the sources and from his personal observations in the years of his travels. The passage which we have quoted is no more than careless and irresponsible talk; or perhaps it is a programme which Montesquieu meant to fulfil but never did. Be this as it may—the fact remains that *De l'Esprit des Lois* is a book of description, not of reasoning, an application of the Baconian method rather than of the method of Descartes. Dedieu rightly emphasises that Montesquieu is more empirical than even the avowed empiricist Locke: "Locke deduces liberty from the initial formula of English government as a logician deduces the consequence from a principle. He assumes a contract between sovereign and subjects, a delegation of power, which leaves sovereignty in the hands of the people, to whom it should return in the form of political and civil freedoms safeguarding the rights of the subjects against encroachments by the central government. Montesquieu omits this original contract which is beyond the possibility of observation. He bases himself on the real circumstances of the English constitution".[1] Here as everywhere Montesquieu builds on the bedrock of facts: nowhere does he spin, *more Cartesiano*, formal definitions from his brain. Indeed, he shows a healthy contempt for formal definitions. To discover them, he says, "the idea which the least educated people have, will suffice" (II, 239).

Thus, while Montesquieu may have thought it desirable to bring his factual knowledge into the framework of a formal scheme and to hook his concrete observations on to abstract definitions, the substance of his work is decidedly empirical. And we know from his own pen that science and empiricism were to him more or less the same thing. Not long before his death, he read Charles Bonnet's book *Recherches sur l'Usage des Feuilles dans les Plantes* and wrote to the author: "This book has given me constant pleasure, because you lead us from observation to observation."[2] He could think of no greater praise of a scientist's or a scholar's work than to say that he had kept close to reality.

The impressions which we have gained from the preceding investigation of Montesquieu's relation to the Cartesian

---

[1] *Montesquieu, L'Homme et l'Oeuvre*, 1943, 86.
[2] Cf. *Correspondance de Montesquieu*, ed. Gebelin and Morize, II, 1914, 510.

tradition will be confirmed in a more positive manner when we study his attitude to the general approach initiated by Bacon. In his younger years, Montesquieu was a keen naturalist and amateur scientist, and the papers which have survived from this period, though they undoubtedly show a tendency towards pan-determinism and pan-mechanism, are yet in essence based on the twin techniques of exact experience and experiment. The Academy of Bordeaux to which he belonged was a centre of scientific research in this specific meaning of the term. The schooling which he received there, remained with him all his life. Even the *Lettres Persanes*, though no more than a piece of frivolity and a protracted joke, show a definite element of acute observation of contemporary reality. Rhédi did what Montesquieu knew every educated person should do. Writing to Usbek from Venice, he says: "I instruct myself in the secrets of commerce, in the interests of the princes, in the form of their government; even the European superstitions I do not neglect; I apply myself to medicine, to physics, to astronomy; I study the arts . . ." And thus, Rhédi concludes, one can get clear of the clouds which cover one's eyes (I, 177). Montesquieu acted on this principle himself when, in 1728, he set out on his travels. They were more than a simple sight-seeing tour. What Montesquieu really wanted was to see the different types of government at work. He had ransacked the books; they could give him no more; he had to go and see things for himself. Several details are highly revealing. Why, for instance, did the Baron de la Brède go to Hungary? Because Hungary was a backward country, a country of survivals, and Montesquieu hoped to catch there an impression of feudalism as it must have been all over Europe at an earlier time. To China he could not go, but he did the next best thing: he frequented a person who had lived there for quite a while—Monsignor Fouquet, the missionary. Always there is an effort to get at the facts, to get as near to the facts as may be humanly possible. Nor is experiment forgotten over observation. "A prince could undertake a nice investigation," Montesquieu writes. "Feed three or four infants like animals, with goats or deaf-and-dumb wet-nurses. These infants would make a language for themselves. This language could be examined. One could see nature left to itself and untrammelled by the prejudices of education; one

7

could know from them, after their instruction, what they had thought; one could stimulate their mind by giving them all the things necessary for invention . . ." (I, 1213). Only the thoughts of a genuine disciple of Bacon could travel in such a direction: there is Baconian method in Montesquieu's mad little scheme!

However, it must be admitted that there were obstacles and limitations to Montesquieu's empiricism. One was his passion for antiquity, what one could call his classical humanism. It is true that he gives a warning to politicians not to take their Tacitus too seriously: the circumstances under which he worked are not likely ever to return (I, 1421). Yet Montesquieu is never happy, unless he has, as it were, the Romans on his side. Their wisdom seems to him wisdom *par excellence*. Then there is a sort of *esprit de système* in Montesquieu, a desire to marshal and master the facts in a certain order—one could almost say, to bring them under a certain discipline. While keenly, even passionately interested in all facts, even the oddest ones, he was yet a little impatient with them when they threatened to upset his system. He claims that the constitutional monarchy occurs regularly in territories of medium size, but he does not admit that Spain was in her finest hour a country on which the sun never set. He sees the earth's vast expanses of open space as the natural home of despotism, but he omits to mention that the kingdom of Achim (in the northern part of Sumatra), with its comparatively narrow local confines, was a flagrant exception to this rule. The facts, clearly, are not always allowed to have it all their own way. Finally, there are Montesquieu's practical and political preoccupations, especially his overwhelming love of liberty. As soon as he speaks about liberty, he tends to become a special pleader. This is noticeable, for instance, in his discussion of England, the country he is holding up to the world, because of its free institutions, as a kind of model. Inconvenient features in the English set-up are passed over in silence or so interpreted, or rather misinterpreted, as to fit in with the drift of the argument. Discussing the judicial power, he puts criminal justice into the foreground, civil justice into the background; and why? Because he prefers speaking about the jury, the twelve good men and true, to speaking about judges nominated by the Crown. Nor was it quite legitimate on his part to call the House of Commons, as it then was, a body representing the people. It was not democratically elected, and it was shot through by aristocratic agents and influences. In general, Montesquieu closes his eyes to the strongly oligarchical nature of the English constitution. Again, the facts are not allowed to have it all their own way.

These certainly are blemishes, weaknesses, faults from the empiricist point of view. But they are not mortal. In spite of them, Montesquieu remains, and deserves to be called, a Baconian spirit. Whenever he criticises others, he criticises them for their failure to follow the facts and to see reality in all its manifold colours. Thus he says that he cannot approve of contemporary French historiography. The historians do not try to form a systematic conspectus *after* having read the sources; they begin with a system and only look for their proofs afterwards (I, 1382 *seq.*)—an unreasonable and illicit procedure. Contemporary political scientists seemed to the Baron de la Brède to fall into a similar ditch. They discuss what is better, monarchy, aristocracy or the popular state. But there exists in the world "an infinite number of kinds of monarchy, aristocracy, and popular state", and so the question which they raise is much too vague to be capable of a sensible answer (I, 1428). Let it not be said that Montesquieu is here preaching what he does not practise; that he sees the mote in his brother's eye and not the beam in his own. A perusal of book XXIX of the *Esprit des Lois* would alone be sufficient to overthrow such an accusation. It is remarkable for its insistence on the concrete, the tangible and the individual. How much care does he not take here to show that often things that look alike are not in truth alike; that form must not cover up fact; that reality must be seen in depth, and not only in its surface appearances!

It can, of course, be argued against the interpretation of Montesquieu's work here put forward, that the word "Reason" occurs in many key sentences of his books, and that he often demands that reality ought to be brought into line with reason, so that he must have been very near the rationalist position after all. For instance: "Law, in general, is human reason in so far as it rules all the peoples of the earth; and the political and civil laws of each nation should be nothing else but particular cases in which that human reason has found application" (II, 237). This certainly sounds like a rationalist credo on Montesquieu's part. And, living as he did at the end of the seventeenth and in the first half of the eighteenth century, it would have been almost miraculous if he had not spoken the language of rationalism—indeed, if he had been quite free from the rationalist prejudice. But what is the concept of reason with which he works? When he demands that reality ought to be brought into line with reason, he does not mean to say that it ought to be made logical. He only calls for that reasonableness which is moderation, justice, and indeed charity. Anybody calling Montesquieu a rationalist, should add at once that he was a rationalist with a difference. "Since I am in Europe, my dear Rhédi," Usbek writes from Venice in *Lettre Persane* LXXX (I, 252), "I have seen many forms of government. Things are not here as in Asia, where the rules of politics are everywhere found the same. I have often inquired which would be the government most in conformity with reason. It seems to me that the most perfect is the one which fulfils its purpose at the smallest expense; so that the one which guides men in the manner which is best suited to their [natural] leanings and inclinations is the most perfect. If, under a mild government, the people is as well controlled[1] as under a severe government, the former is preferable because it is more in harmony with reason . . ."[2] It is not the logician, the mathematician, the Cartesian, the rationalist who speaks in this passage and in other, similar, ones. It is the humanist, the humanitarian, and the friend of the people. We have admitted that Montesquieu's empiricism was not perfect; but we should do him less than justice if we were to assert that he tried to press the world into an abstract Procrustean scheme. He was much too much impressed by, and much too much enamoured of, its over-whelming variety. Nor was he unaware of the fundamental irrationality of human conduct so often overlooked or argued

---

[1] *"aussi soumis"*.

[2] Cf. also the *Essai sur le Goût*, II, 1260 *seq*. Montesquieu says here that what is meant to cause us pleasure should be based on reason, or should depart from reason as little as possible. But his examples make it quite clear that he calls for reason in the sense of reasonableness and not for reason in the sense of rationality. The Roman Marius should not be made to say on the stage that he does not fear the hostility of the House of Lords if only he has the favour of the House of Commons, or that he values virtue higher than all the gold of Potosi. Montesquieu simply fights stupidity and absurdity here: he does not call in art for any *sentiment de rationalité*.

away by the votaries of rationalism among both active statesmen and theoretical writers. "It is rare," he writes, "that great
politicians know men [as they really are]. As they themselves
have subtle and clever opinions, they believe that all other men
have them also. But it is far from true that all men are subtle:
on the contrary, men act almost always from whim or passion,
or they act simply in order to act and in order to avoid the
reproach that they are not acting" (I, 115). This awareness of
the irrationality of human life must have been an additional
incentive in Montesquieu's mind to study life as it really is.

It appears from all this that Montesquieu, though to some
extent suffering from the after-effects of the rationalism which
was slowly going out in his time, was yet, by and large, a
typical protagonist of that sober empiricism that was slowly
coming in. We can see this even in his sociology of knowledge.
As we shall find later on, Montesquieu surmised that men's
mode of thinking may be determined by their physical apparatus; and that their physical apparatus may depend, in turn, on
the physical environment within which it is placed and to
which it must adjust itself. In a cold country, for instance, the
imagination will be less active than in a warm climate because
the nerves will only report a sensation to the brain if it is fairly
strong, and so stimulation will be lacking which will be
comparatively abundant in the south. It is characteristic of
Montesquieu that he looked for both experiential and experi-
mental confirmation of this hypothesis. "I have observed the
exterior tissue of a sheep's tongue," he reports, "in the place
where it seems to the naked eye covered with little papillæ. I
have seen with a microscope on these papillæ tiny hairs or a
kind of down; between the papillæ were pyramids which
formed at their tips as it were small brushes. There is great
likelihood that these pyramids are the main organ of taste. I
have frozen half the tongue and I have found with the naked
eye the papillæ considerably diminished; some stretches of
papillæ had even retired into their protective skin. I have
examined their tissue with the microscope, and I have seen no
more pyramids. As the tongue became unfrozen, the papillæ
appeared to the naked eye to raise themselves up again; and,
under the microscope, the small tufts began to reappear. This
observation confirms what I have said, that in cold countries

the nervous tufts are less expanded; they are ensconced in their cover where they are withdrawn from the action of external objects. Hence the sensations are less vivid" (II, 476). Can anything be more in line with the Baconian spirit than this approach? And Montesquieu was not satisfied with one observation. He wanted further controlled experimenting. On a piece of paper which has come down to us, he noted: "Make an experiment on a sinew, on a nerve. Put it lengthwise into a long glass tube stopped by two plugs. Place it on ice. See if the nerve contracts under the influence of the ice" (II, 1481). It is clear that Montesquieu was moving in a blind alley; it is obvious that the sociology of knowledge cannot be furthered by such investigations. But this is not the point here. Here we are concerned with the general character of his mind; here we are endeavouring to show, and indeed hope to have shown, that he belonged to the realistic rather than to the rationalistic school, to the school of Bacon rather than to that of Descartes. His love of experiment—so dear to Bacon's spirit and so alien to Descartes'—should clinch our argument.

But we have not done with Cartesianism yet. What we have said about Montesquieu so far concerned the mature Montesquieu, whose portrait we tried to elaborate and to fix in the readers' mental eye. It does not apply to the young Montesquieu, the Montesquieu of the early twenties of the eighteenth century, the Montesquieu as yet immature. We would willingly pass over that temporary phase in his development, were it not that it found expression in a specific sociology of knowledge which a book like the present must not neglect.

Now, the young Montesquieu, the young Secondat before his grand tour, had a much larger dose of Cartesianism in his intellectual make-up than the older man, the man who had returned from abroad after seeing a good deal of the world. There were three inter-connected tendencies in his mind; a tendency towards rationalism in general; a tendency towards determinism; and a tendency towards sociological mechanism. If they had not, all of them, been overcome in due time, they would have produced a Montesquieu of very different intellectual habit from the man we know.

The general tendency towards rationalism can best be traced in the *Lettres Persanes* of 1721. Letter XLVI from Usbek

to Rhédi argues about religion, and the main submission of
Usbek, or rather of Montesquieu, is this, that the only valuable
part of religion is its moralising effect. Ceremonies are useless
and absurd. But not only the rites of Christianity are condemned, the dogmas, too, are reduced to dust and ashes. We
know nothing about the attributes of that great X which is
behind reality and which men in their ignorance call God. We
know indeed that He is; but we do not know what he is (I,
1176). The theologians are involved in insoluble contradictions.
How could they ever hope to resolve the contradiction between
God's foreknowledge and His justice which they equally
assert? Or that between God's supposed immutability and the
dogma of a creative act in time, since if creation has in fact
taken place in time, there must have been an anterior period
when God either could not or would not create, which implies
that He is not immutable (I, 238 *seq.* and 298 *seq.*). Such clever
argument is typical of the rationalist temper and shows (as
indeed do all the *Lettres Persanes*) that the young Montesquieu
was a forerunner of the scoffers and the atheists, the Voltaires,
Diderots, and D'Alemberts. Indeed, in one passage he even
formulates their basic philosophy, namely the demand that all
phenomena of existence must be reduced to natural causes so
that the preternatural and the supernatural are effectively
pushed out of court. Writing to a Jewish doctor, Nathanael
Lévi, Rica upbraids him for maintaining that in some cases it is
impossible to explain why a certain general should have won a
battle, rather than his adversary without having recourse to
supernatural aids. "I", Rica says, "I will tell you that you must
be wilfully blind if you do not find in the lay of the land, in the
number or in the courage of the soldiers, or in the experience of
the captains sufficient causes for the production of the effect of
which you pretend not to know the cause." And Rica adds, by
way of principle: "In order to make sure that an effect which
might have been produced by a hundred thousand causes is
supernatural, it is first necessary to discover whether one of
these causes has not been active: but that is impossible". Rica
has only contempt and pity for obscurantists like Lévi: "Men
are so unhappy! They alternate eternally between false hopes
and ridiculous fears, and, instead of taking their stand on reason,
they make for themselves monsters which frighten them or

phantoms which lead them astray" (I, 353 *seq.*). This rationalism even tends to form itself, in Montesquieu's mind, into an
epistemological principle of typically rationalist import: "The
soul, preoccupied by the action which it is going to take, the
motive which determines it, the danger which it is about to
avoid, does not see properly . . . because passion causes us to
feel and never to see [clearly]" (II, 136).[1]

Of these rationalistic, even libertinist convictions little
remained in the older Montesquieu except a certain anti-
clericalism. Certainly, he did not love black soutanes, at any
time of his life. But he edged progressively nearer to the religious
position and even made some basic tenets of orthodox theology
his own. To *Lettre Persane* LXIX, which had insisted so strongly
on the unresolved perplexities of theological speculation, he
added in 1754 a new paragraph which showed how far he had
travelled in the intervening thirty-three years: "God is so high
that we do not even see his clouds. We know him well only in
his commandments. He is immense, spiritual, infinite" (I, 240).
These words are perhaps still capable of a deistic, rather than
fully Christian, construction, but there is plenty of other
evidence that the Baron de la Brède had lived himself away,
clearly and decisively, from the deism of his youth. In *De
l' Esprit des Lois* the necessity of dogma is conceded in religion
(II, 730), everything in Christianity, "up to the resurrection of
the body, leads us to spiritual ideas". A revelation, too, is now
seen to be indispensable, given the nature of man as we actually
find it. "What convinces me of the necessity of a revelation, is
the insufficiency of natural religion in view of the fear and
superstition of men: for, if, today, you were to place men in the
pure state of natural religion, tomorrow they would fall again
into some crude superstition" (I, 1550). These are deep words.
And deeper still are the following sentences in which M.
Dedieu rightly discerns a true Pascalian ring:[2] "If the Christian
religion is not divine, it is certainly absurd. Why then did
it appeal to those very philosophers who had abandoned
paganism precisely on account of its absurdity? What! Those

---

[1] Cf. with this quotation the passage from II, 1243, quoted above on p. 4
(footnote) which, coming from the pen of the very old Montesquieu, implies an
entirely different epistemology—an epistemology that is not rationalist.

[2] *Montesquieu*, 1913, 286.

philosophers who maintained that paganism was offensive to the majesty of the Deity, accept the idea of a crucified God, after they had taught men the immutability, the immensity, the spirituality, the wisdom of God? What a revolting idea is the execution of a God!" But, as if that were not enough, it is the pariah nation of the Jews from which the Messiah springs, Jews are his followers, Jews are his witnesses. And yet "the Gospels are published, and they are accepted by the Pyrrhonists who say that one must doubt everything; by the Naturalists, who believe that everything is the effect of figures and movements; by the Epicureans who deride all the miracles of paganism; indeed, by all the enlightened people, by all philosophical sects!" Truly, "if the establishment of Christianity among the Romans were no more than [an event] within the order of the things of this world, it would . . . be the most extraordinary thing that has ever happened" (I, 1558 *seq.*). This, indeed, is Pascal's mode of thinking and of argumentation. But we have even better proof of Montesquieu's change of heart. He makes himself the apologist of the faith and crosses swords with its enemies, Spinoza and Bayle (I, 1138 *seq.*, and II, 715, 719). Gone are the days when Montesquieu, with the deists, put all religions into one pot; and even more the days when he had tended, with the scoffers, to equate religion and superstition: "Phryné's joke is well known. She took part in a great feast; the game was played where each guest in turn can order the others to do what he likes. She had noticed that the women who were at the feast wore paint. She called for water to be brought, took a towel and washed her face with it. The [other] women [who had to follow her example] appeared ugly and full of wrinkles; Phryné [alone] remained in the splendour of her natural beauty. *Voilà la Religion et la Superstition*" (II, 1096).[1]

Somewhat more difficult to prove than this change of mind in religion is Montesquieu's abandonment of rationalist philosophy in the more technical sense of the word. But he wrote in his closing days to his grandson that "it is not our intellect[2] but our soul which leads us", and that a cultivated sentiment is more important than cleverness, knowledge and

---

[1] It should also be mentioned that Montesquieu accepted the last rites of the Church with great devotion.

[2] "*esprit*".

enlightenment (I, 994). Obviously one must not make too much of these words; but they may serve as a straw in the wind.

The determinism which ran in harness as it were with Montesquieu's early rationalism can best be studied in the essay *De la Politique* of 1722 or 1723. The thesis of this *opusculum* is that every political effort men may make, be they even great and powerful men like Henry VIII or Philip II, will be unavailing, that there can be no art of politics as everything depends on causes which we cannot gauge and which we cannot, consequently, mould. The Regency in France under the minority of Louis XV was bound to be successful. If the opposite had been done to what was done, it would still all have ended happily; indeed, "if, one after the other, fifty other princes had taken on the government and had each behaved in his own way, they would, all the same, have brought that regency to a happy conclusion." Minds, things, conditions and interests were such, that this end result had to emerge. On the other hand, Charles I was doomed to fail. "If this king had not offended his subjects in one way, he would have offended them in another. It was destined in the order of causes that he should be wrong" (I, 114 *seq.*).

This determinism lasted an even shorter time and disappeared even more completely than the general rationalism with which it was linked. Already in 1725, in a lecture to the Academy of Bordeaux, Montesquieu throws it energetically overboard. "Those who say that a blind fatality has produced all the effects which we see in the world, talk great nonsense; for what greater absurdity can there be than a blind fatality which has produced beings who are not subject to blind fatality?" (I, 109).[1] Henceforth, a belief in human freedom accompanies Montesquieu through life, a belief none the less decisive for the fact that he regards free will as an imperfection in man—a perfect being would never need to vacillate (I, 1542).

It will be useful to follow this matter up a little further because it will lead us fairly deep into our author's general sociological conceptions. In the *Considérations sur les Causes de la Grandeur des Romains et de leur Décadence*, there are two passages which still seem to savour of determinism. "It is not fortune that rules the world: one can ask the Romans, who had a

[1] Cf. also II, 232 and 1124.

continuous train of prosperity when they directed themselves according to a certain plan, and an uninterrupted chain of ill success when they comported themselves according to another. There are general causes, either moral or physical, which are active in each monarchy, which raise it up, maintain it, or overthrow it; all accidents are subject to these causes; and if the chance of a battle, that is to say, a special cause, has ruined a state, there was a general cause which brought it about that that state had to perish by a single battle: in a word, the main tendency carried with it all the particular accidents." Not long before this passage there occurs another which seems similar in drift. "The errors which statesmen commit are not always free; often they are necessary consequences of the situation in which they find themselves . . ." (II, 172 *seq.*). Surely, here universal determinism is, in principle, abandoned: men are not always free; hence they are at any rate sometimes free. But this conclusion, justified as it is on the face of Montesquieu's text, does not by any means go far enough. If it can be shown that the "cause" that leads to people's discomfiture, is their own moral or rather immoral mode of action, then determinism is, properly speaking, abandoned altogether: a cause that is posited by men themselves is not a cause that determines them *ab extra*. Now, it is true that Montesquieu, in the passage which we have quoted, speaks of a physical as well as of a moral cause. But that physical cause is not in evidence throughout the *Considérations*, whereas the moral "cause" is. We see this already on the same pages. Continuing his argument, Montesquieu writes: "For nearly two centuries, the troops of Denmark have almost always been beaten by those of Sweden: it must be assumed that, independent of the courage of the two nations and the vicissitude of arms, there is in the Danish government, military or civil, an internal vice which has produced this effect." An internal vice: the cause here mentioned (anarchy, political indiscipline) is a cause of man's own fashioning, and hence no necessary cause at all.

Here again it is much more fruitful to observe what Montesquieu does, than what he says. As he moves down the corridor of history from Romulus to Romulus Augustulus, he notes at every crucial point how it is men's action—men's responsible action—that determines good and ill success. What caused

Rome's early prosperity? The greatness of her kings (II, 70). What was responsible for her revival after the disaster of Cannæ? The iron will and the wisdom of her senators (80 *seq.*). What accounts for her glory after Titus and Nerva? The advent of Trajan, "a noble, great, and beautiful soul" (153). What "re-established the empire on the point of collapse?" The rule of Claudius, Aurelius, Tacitus and Probus, "four great men" (164). It is surely permissible to interpret Montesquieu by saying that, though in the days of these emperors all objective tendencies made for the destruction of the empire, it was the mettle of her rulers that inhibited and indeed inverted these tendencies. When he comes to the triumphs of Belisarius, he says so himself. "It is in the qualities of this great man that we can find the principal causes of his successes. Under a general who had all the principles of the first Romans, there formed an army such as the ancient Roman armies had been. Great virtues usually hide themselves or are lost in servitude; but the tyrannical government of Justinian could not suppress the greatness of that soul, nor the superiority of that genius" (186).[1] Belisarius at any rate was the master of fate and not its tool.

In the *Esprit des Lois*, there are not only passages which give concrete examples of the responsibility and self-determination of men, like the chapter on Charles XII of Sweden;[2] but the whole matter is raised to the level of abstract discussion. Unfortunately, Montesquieu expressed himself in a manner which could be, and was, misunderstood. But not only do we have his own authoritative elucidations of the decisive text in his *Défense de l'Esprit des Lois*; we can also see that a sympathetic reader could have no doubt of his belief in free will from the very beginning. The passages which seem to countenance a fatalistic interpretation of Montesquieu occur in the opening considerations of the work, in the preface and in chapter 1 of book one. In the preface Montesquieu expresses the opinion that an examination of men must lead to the conviction "that they are not led exclusively by their fancies". And Montesquieu continues: "I have posited [certain] principles, and I have seen the particular cases falling into line with them as of their own

[1] Cf. also II, 302 *ad finem*.

[2] "Neither nature nor fortune ever worked so strongly against him as he did himself" (II, 387; cf. also I, 1408 *seq.*).

accord; the histories of all the nations are nothing but their consequences; and each particular law is connected with another law or depends on another that is more general" (II, 229). This sounds like an assertion of universal determination, but it is nothing of the kind. For what does Montesquieu mean by "principle"? Which are the "principles" which, once posited, draw certain consequences after them? They are no impersonal laws or tendencies, nor yet innate or physical urges on the part of men, but simply the modes of moral action, of our free moral deportment, which are at the root of our fate. What Montesquieu asserts, is this: that *if* men have embraced a certain principle of conduct, if they have, for instance, given their state a certain form, *then* they must also face the implications and consequences of their decision. Certainly, definite basic resolutions necessitate definite ulterior developments; everything is connected, indeed, permeated by a certain logic; but at the inception there stands man's will and man's responsibility. Only an interpretation of this kind can really do justice to Montesquieu's argument. How would we explain otherwise that he repeats in chapter 1 (p. 232) the diatribe quoted above (p. 16) against the believers in a blind fatality? And it is a similar spirit in which we must approach the understanding of the first paragraph of the first chapter. "Laws, in the widest meaning [of the term], are the necessary interrelations which derive from the nature of things: and in this sense all beings have their laws; the Deity has its laws; the material world has its laws; the intelligences above man have their laws; the animals have theirs; man has his laws" (II, 232). The question which this passage at once prompts, and which has been raised all too rarely by the Baron's interpreters, is this: what are the laws that govern God, angels, and men? And the answer to this question (which, indeed, Montesquieu himself gives in so many words) must be: they are self-imposed laws, laws which are not incompatible with freedom and responsibility, but rather their spontaneous expression (II, 233 *seq.* and 1124 *seq.*). There is good evidence, then, that the determinism of *De la Politique* was a youthful error on the part of Montesquieu rather than a lasting conviction.

The same applies to the slight tendency towards sociological mechanism which a careful reading of his earlier work will reveal. *Lettre Persane* CII brings it out best. Monarchies, in the true sense of the word, are rare and transitory formations, Montesquieu says. They tend to degenerate either into despotisms or democracies. "Power can never be equally divided between People and Prince; the equilibrium is too difficult to preserve. It is unavoidable that power should decrease on the one side while it increases on the other . . ." (I, 281). This is a typically mechanistic statement. And in the preliminary notes to the *Traité des Devoirs* there is a passage which shows that around 1725 Montesquieu was also thinking in terms of a social contract, hence embracing the social theory which was tending to grow out of the basic panmechanism of that post-Newtonian, post-Cartesian period (I, 1129 *seq.*).

But this mechanism is short-lived in Montesquieu's mind. It is true that its language tends to persist (cf. II, 257, 603, 968, 977), but where, in later life, there is talk of "balance" or of the counter-balancing of political forces, there are no deeper implications, there is simply use made of a convenient mode of expression, of a metaphor which we all are inclined to employ.

It is at this point that our interpretation of the author of *L'Esprit des Lois* is most likely to run into resistance because the picture we are sketching of Montesquieu's mind is somewhat at variance with the currently accepted image. Montesquieu is best known for his theory of the separation of powers, and this theory is usually formulated by saying that he demanded that the legislative, the executive and the judicial powers should be kept separate and should be made to countercheck and to counterbalance each other. In this formulation, the doctrine seems indeed a mechanistic one.[1] But the mechanism lies more

---

[1] Edward Caird wrote this about Montesquieu: He committed an error "when he supposed that the great security of a free State lay in the separation of the legislative, executive, and judicial powers—i.e. in treating the different organs through which the common life expresses itself as if they were independent organisms. He forgot that if such a balance of power was realised, the effect must either be an equilibrium in which all movement would cease, or a struggle in which the unity of the State would be in danger of being lost. The true security," Caird goes on, ". . . must lie, not in giving them independent positions . . . but in subordinating them to the organic unity of the whole society . . ." (*The Social Philosophy and Religion of Comte*, 1893, 207). In so far as this passage is supposed to be a criticism of Montesquieu, it is completely abortive. As the text will show, Montesquieu demanded the very same integration of the three powers for which Caird is calling. But Caird's "summary" of Montesquieu's doctrine represents a view of our philosopher which is very widely held even today.

in the formula of its summariser than in the argument of its author. The decisive locus classicus is chapter 6 of book XI of the *Esprit des Lois*, and it is a simple fact that in that chapter not even the *language* of mechanistic sociology is used. Montesquieu sums up his theory in the following sentences: "The legislative body being [in England] composed of two parts, the one will control the other by their faculty of mutual restraint. Both will be bound by the executive power which will itself be bound by the legislative. These three powers should form a [system of] repose or inaction. But as, by the necessary movement of things, they are constrained to move along, they will be forced to move in harmony" (II, 405). In this absolutely central passage, there is not only no reference to a balance of power or influences; what is more, there is internal evidence of an entirely non-mechanistic mode of vision. A mechanist always is, and logically must be, an atomist; things can only counterbalance each other if they are separate. But Montesquieu does not demand the separation of powers in the mechanical sense of the word.[1] In fact, such a separation would have seemed to him disastrous. He demands much rather their harmonious integration. Now, harmony certainly implies balance, but not a mechanical balance, because the features that are set off against each other are linked by virtue of their common inherence in a superimposed whole. The balance of, and in, the healthy state is the balance of a beautiful face rather than the equilibrium of a lever; it is, in a word, organical rather than mechanical. It is not claimed here that Montesquieu was an organicist rather than a mechanist; that would be a bad over-statement of the case. On pp. 424–426 the word "balance" crops up several times. But the text on p. 426 clearly shows that the *unity* of government is as important in Montesquieu's mind as the separation of its branches. He stood, after he had out-grown his bairns' troubles, if not within, at any rate as near the organical tradition as the mechanistic. A string of quotations can prove it. In his *Considérations sur les . . . Romains*, in which the doctrine under discussion sometimes comes to the surface, we read: "The laws of Rome had wisely divided the public

---

[1] Barckhausen rightly insists that the term "separation of powers" is misleading. One should rather speak of their *"non-confusion"* (*Montesquieu, ses Idées et ses Oeuvres*, 1907, 95).

power into a great number of magistratures which supported, arrested and tempered each other" (II, 124 *seq.*). Granted that the word "arrest" smacks of checks and balances and half belongs in the orbit of mechanistic thought, the other two terms have a definite organological flavour. Functionaries who support, sustain, maintain each other are organs of a whole, not independent elements between whom there can be a trial of strength or a tug of war. Influences which temper each other are influences which harmonise each other, which move towards each other, not influences which pull in different directions. This is no fancy interpretation of the word "*tempérer*" or "*modérer*" as used by Montesquieu, it is his own. "In order to form a moderate government," the *Esprit des Lois* teaches, "it is necessary to combine the [three] powers, to regulate, to temperate them . . ." (II, 297), and in another context (II, 428) the "harmony of the three powers" is held up as the essential thing (cf. also II, 412 and 424). All this is organicism according to the spirit; but there is sometimes even organicism according to the letter. An occasional note runs as follows: "The great evil of the revocation of the Edict of Nantes was that it deprived the kingdom of a whole class of people, such as workmen, merchants etc." The damage would have been less great if the emigrants had come from all social strata, for "it is less pernicious to take [some] blood from the whole body than to cut off a member" (II, 1331).

As the matter is of great moment in the interpretation of Montesquieu's thought, it may still be permitted, and is indeed advisable, to look at chapter 4 of book XII of the *Esprit des Lois* where an opportunity for an instructive comparison between our supposed mechanist and the true mechanist Jeremy Bentham offers itself. Bentham maintains that there is, in the criminal, an unbalance between the expected pleasure yielded by a contemplated crime, and the estimated pain assumed to be connected with it. This unbalance must be corrected, and the necessary balance secured, by weighting more heavily, through the criminal law, the scale of pain or rather pain-apprehension. Montesquieu thinks differently. He does not demand that the quantity of the punishment should be brought into line with the quantitative configuration of the crime or criminal intention; what he demands is that the quality of the penance should correspond to the quality of the sin: he who has broken the rules of chastity, should be deprived of the advantages which society has attached to the observance of these rules; he who has violated the security of other peoples' possessions, should suffer himself in his possessions, etc. The contrast between the two thinkers is obvious; it is not a superficial contrast but one which indicates a deeper divergence in the direction of thought, a difference in mental type.

We can best end this discussion of Montesquieu's ill-named doctrine of the "separation" and "balance" of powers which is so important for a proper understanding of his transition from a mechanistic to a semi-organical social theory (and, remotely at least, for the proper understanding of the general transition, soon to come, from the rationalistic eighteenth century to the romantic nineteenth) by putting it into the framework of his whole life and endeavour. In doing so, we must emphasise first of all that the theory was developed after the travels: in other words, in spite of its bookish antecedents in such writers as Aristotle and Locke, it was drawn from experience rather than from reading.[1] Not only life in England, but a preceding stay in Holland seem to have inspired Montesquieu in this respect. But this new inspiration was only so powerful because it was met and reinforced by a drift and drive which had been in the Baron de la Brède, as we can here more appropriately call him, from the first moment of his life. Montesquieu was a nobleman who had the feudal spirit in his blood and bones; and he was *Président* of one of those provincial *Parlements* who regarded themselves as the very bulwarks of the ancient liberties of the French and the Franks. When Montesquieu speaks, he speaks with the voice of one who wants to check both the encroachments of a Crown tending to become despotic and of a peasantry ready to turn rebellious. Safety and liberty reside for him in the intermediary classes—those *"corps intermédiaires"* of whom he speaks often and with considerable warmth; they are in the keeping of the peers of the realm, and nowhere else will they be in appropriate hands.[2] The *notables* are the main moderating force in a monarchy: take their privileges away, and in a short time you will be under the rule either of a despotic or of

[1] Cf. in this sense Dedieu, *Montesquieu*, 1913, 152 *seq.*, *q.v.* for the detail.

[2] Cf. *loc. cit.* 4, 157 *seq.*, 159 *seq.*

popular government (II, 247). Even in the famous chapter 6 of book XI where the English constitution is discussed, the same feudal spirit shows itself. This is hardly ever sufficiently emphasised. "Of the three powers" Montesquieu writes, "that of judging is in a manner void. Thus there remain only two; and as they stand in need of a regulating influence which would temper them, that part of the legislative body which is composed of noblemen is very well fitted to fulfil this function" (II, 401). Here we do not get the picture of a pair of scales in one of which lies the Crown, and in the other the People; but rather of a chain whose middle link, the House of Lords, must be strong in order to be able to hold the two others down and to hold them together. Far from thinking in terms of an atomistic society in which a general equilibrium would secure equal opportunity for each and equal security for all—the key thought of the typical eighteenth century mechanists and rationalists—the Baron de la Brède thinks in terms of a hierarchical order, of the feudal monarchy which is to him the social utopia to be venerated and to be pursued. But a feudal, hierarchical society is, almost by definition, an organic society: the feudal age was, characteristically, also the age of sociological organicism. Hence Montesquieu's political striving stems from an ultimately organological ideal, and in this organological ideal even the doctrine of the "separation" and "balance" of powers has its beginning and its roots.

II

MONTESQUIEU'S FIRST SOCIOLOGY OF KNOWLEDGE

PERHAPS it was this attachment of Monsieur de la Brède to the vision of a well-integrated, but socially articulated human order (an attachment both intellectual and emotional) which explains why the rationalistic, deterministic and mechanistic period in his career as a social thinker was so transitory and so short. But however transitory and short it may have been, it spanned a few years of his life, and during these years there formed in his mind a specific sociology of knowledge which is interesting and appears to the historian looking back upon it as a halt on the road between Machiavelli and Holbach or Diderot. The first entry into Montesquieu's *Spicilège* or commonplace-book, inspired by some such book as *La Pratique du Jardinage*, reads as follows: "The burning bush. This shrub is all red and appears from a distance to be all on fire. It was in this bush that God appeared to Moses, but the bush was not in flames" (II, 1267). Of similar character is this later entry: "A fragment of Megasthenes informs us that Babylonia was an inundated country which was later reclaimed by its kings who, in order to achieve this, changed the course of the Euphrates and Tigris; it is apparently from this [historical fact] that there sprang [the legend of] the flood" (II, 1316; cf. also 1315 *sub* 349). Still in the same spirit, though concerning a different matter, is Montesquieu's explanation of the custom of blessing a man or wishing him good health after sneezing. Sneezing, he says, is a sign of health, "a purgation of the brain", and hence there is a natural cause for congratulation (II, 1280). Perhaps our last example from the *Spicilège* is slightly less flatly

25

rationalistic, but it, too, belongs into the same category as the three foregoing: "As the ancients made demi-gods out of heroes, so they transformed tyrants into monsters: the serpent Python, for instance, which was killed by Apollo, was a tyrant of Delphi" (II, 1314). In an early dissertation written for the Academy of Bordeaux which Montesquieu later tore up because, as he said, "it was worth nothing", the ancient story concerning the Satyrs is accounted for as follows: "All these troops of Satyrs, which the first men took for gods, and which the historians afterwards took for people, were merely [the zoological species of] monkey-goat (*aegophithecus*)".[1] One is reminded, in reading these explanations, if explanations they can be called, of the typical attitude of all rationalists from the *philosophes* à la D'Alembert to the scientists à la Spencer in the face of the unusual, the inexplicable, the irrational: there must be a perfectly simple way of accounting for what happened or happens; behind the unusual must be found the commonplace, behind the extraordinary the perfectly ordinary, behind the irrational the rational. If the facts appear in a distorted form— and behind all thought-contents there are facts—there must be error in the mind that reflects them; most probably the mental mirror is clouded by superstition so that it does not do its work properly. This attitude, which must kill a true understanding sociology of knowledge in the very root, stands out in all its crudity in *Lettre Persane* XVII. Why has the Prophet declared certain things impure, defiled, mystically tabu? There is really no mystery at all: the things put under a ban, such as pork, the flesh of that dirty animal, the pig, are simply repulsive to our senses, and this is the hard and sufficient core of all the religious folklore woven about this tabu. Why does the Moslem keep away from corpses? because they stink. Is that not reason enough? Montesquieu at once draws the natural rationalistic inference: the folklore is not needed; it only obfuscates the matter; wipe it away and return to reason! "The senses, divine Mollak," Usbek-de la Brède writes to Méhémet-Hali, "the senses ought to be the sole judges of the purity or impurity of things" (I, 156).

[1] For the short extract of the paper on the *Dieux Animaux* which alone has survived, and for the above quotations from it, cf. *Oeuvres Complètes de Montesquieu*, ed. André Masson, II, 1950, 665 *seq.*

It is certain that Montesquieu was confirmed in this attitude by his intercourse with Fontenelle, whom he met in the salon of his protectrix, the aged Marquise de Lambert. We are fortunate in having a note concerning one of their discussions which shows what manner of man Fontenelle was and how far young Montesquieu went with him, but also, what is more important, that there were already then, around 1722, sounder ideas budding in Montesquieu's head. The subject under discussion was divination. Why did the Romans, when they were about to choose a place for the founding of a colony, watch the contortions of the entrails of the beasts they had just sacrificed to the gods? Because, Fontenelle suggested, these contortions told them whether they found themselves in a healthy or an unhealthy location. Why did they watch the flight of the birds? Because birds fly where there is plenty of food, where consequently the grain can be expected to grow. Montesquieu seems to have acquiesced in these rationalistic ravings of his friend. But he had a contribution to make himself, and this is decidedly on a higher level. "I said: 'There is yet another reason for the killing of victims: those war-like nations . . . naturally imagined[1] a God who resembled them, who took pleasure in blood, who was cruel as they were, who demanded the blood of victims, of enemies, of citizens' " (I, 1573). This is half a step as it were, in the direction of the type of sociology of knowledge which, in my book "The Sociology of Knowledge", I have called cœnonic-holistic: the assumption is that the idea of the character of the deity, as it formed in the minds of men, was inspired by, and in its content corresponded to, the real character of the social life which these men were carrying on at the time on the level of action, on the level of unreflecting policy and practice.

If this attitude on the part of Montesquieu in his discussion with Fontenelle, which we may date *circa* 1722 or 1723, shows him already slightly receding from the extreme rationalistic position, the *Dissertation sur la Politique des Romains dans la Religion*, read before the Academy of Bordeaux on June 18, 1716, shows him right on or in it. Here again, the reader feels himself forcefully reminded of the great rationalists and materialists, of Machiavelli, Diderot and Spencer. Like them,

[1] "*. . . ont dû imaginer . . .*"

27

Montesquieu regards the religion established at Rome as essentially a tool in the hands of a small clique of crafty leaders who, by this means, cleverly turned the credulity and stupidity of the masses to the advantage of the state. "Pagan theology", he writes, summarising the gist of the essay in his *Discours sur Cicéron*, "was established in the beginning by the *politique* of the magistrates in the midst of a rude people . . ." (I, 94). It had its uses; but it was degrading all the same and became the more so, the more coarseness gave way to refinement and blindness to an enlightened attitude and outlook.

This implication, and even insistence, that religion has its uses among a brutish people but is degrading to a nation that has become enlightened, gives Montesquieu's early sociology of knowledge a definitely critical, "debunking" drift and character. The Roman legislators who established the Roman religion, had no exalted aim; they did not wish to reform manners or underpin morality; all they wanted to do was "to inspire a people which feared nothing, with the fear of the gods, and to use that fear in order to lead them according to their [own] fancies" (I, 81). The soothsayers who followed the armies were mouthpieces of the generals rather than of the gods; at home the *auspicia* were always so managed as to fit in with the designs of the upper classes; and if, by chance, the entrails of a sacrificial beast did not behave as they should have done, another was offered up until the magistrate-managers got what they wanted. Montesquieu seems convinced that their technique was perfect.[1] Indeed, he is full of admiration.[2] How clever they

[1] The details of this technique as described by young M. Secondat need not detain us here, but there is just one point which deserves mention, firstly because it shows Montesquieu's understanding of a specific social and sociological problem, and secondly because it gives us one more valuable insight into the dynamics of his mind. Unlike the Egyptians, the Romans did not allow the development of a separate priestly class but kept the sacred rites firmly in the hands of the secular magistrates—a fact which, among others, accounts for the strength of the Roman commonwealth (I, 89 *seq.*). Montesquieu puts his finger here on an important practical problem which can be seen in almost all periods of history—the relationship between the military and religious élites in a society. But whereas, as a young man, Montesquieu approved of the concentration of political and religious functions in the same set of hands, he later moved towards the position classically stated by Comte, according to which an independent clergy is useful in a state as constituting a salutary check on the all-too-powerful secular oligarchy (Cf. I, 1161, II, 715 *seq.*, and often).

[2] Cf. his critique of the religious policy of the native rulers of Mexico and Peru, such as Montezuma and Atahualpa, who mismanaged everything, in I, 1134 *seq.*

were, those masters of deception! They were on their guard even against their own weaknesses. If the cult had been semi-rational, they might have fallen into their own trap; they might have begun to believe themselves what they preached to their inferiors; so they made the popular religion as absurd as they possibly could: the salvation of the republic was made dependent on such things as the sacred appetite of a chicken! By rendering the rites so utterly ridiculous, the senators made sure that they would always keep their proper mental distance to them, that they would constantly bear in mind both the absurdity of this opium for the people and its political utility. As for the masses, they were so benighted as to believe anything: their "credulity . . . is always stronger than absurdity and extravagance". Indeed, "the more a thing was contrary to human reason, the more it appeared to them divine". Like all rationalists, Montesquieu shows here the cloven hoof of his kind. Rationalism, starting from the conviction of the inherent rationality of man *quâ* man, has ever had a dismal tendency to turn aristocratic and to despise the greater part of the human race (92, 82 *seq.*).

Anyone who takes this line, who maintains that the head of the Roman plebeians was filled with all manner of nonsense stuffed into it by the purposeful propaganda of the patricians, must, if he wants to be consistent, raise the question, what determined the thought-processes of the patricians themselves? *Quis custodiet custodes ipsos* is, after all, a query on which many changes can be rung, and which has a mental as well as a physical and political side to it. It speaks for the systematic character of Montesquieu's thought and for the tidiness of his mind that he does ask this question and tries to answer it. His answer is most revealing. The rulers of Rome were rationalists, deists in religion. They followed in their ideas the dictates of timeless reason. Behind the motley pantheon of the people they saw a hidden deity of many facets and manifestations, and they could, without degrading themselves, take part in the cult established for the masses, by adoring their little gods and goddesses, not in and for themselves, as the proletarians did, but as powers of the one hidden Power; of the one hidden World-Soul or X which even the eighteenth century has to acknowledge. Venus was not to them a goddess, not a supernal lady, but "the passive power of nature, in so far as it is capable of all generation"; Sol, or the Sun, was not to them a god or lord of the heavens, but the Supreme Being "in so far as it animates vegetation and renders the earth fruitful by its warmth" (I, 87). Montesquieu quotes the Stoic Balbus in proof of his contention and claims that the lost book of Asclepiades called *The Harmony of all Theologies* would have told us more about all this. He also calls in the aid of his Cambridge fellow-rationalist Ralph Cudworth; but he implies all along that the matter is quite clear from the study of all the sources, and does not stand in need of detailed demonstration.

The whole argument is a splendid proof of the fact that a rationalistic sociology of knowledge is, strictly speaking, impossible; that any attempt to move along these lines towards a theory of the genesis of ideas is bound to lead into a *cul-de-sac*. The Montesquieu who speaks through the *Dissertation sur la Politique des Romains dans la Religion* obviously believes that there is only one source of all ideas, and that is the human intellect, that *ratio* which is timeless and inborn in man and has produced all cleverness from mathematics to political management—in a word, the *ratio Cartesiana*. In the patricians this *ratio* expressed itself in their reasonable, deistic belief which held good in the second century B.C. as it is holding good in the eighteenth century A.D., the intervening two millenia notwithstanding. The patricians it dominated directly; the plebeians it dominated indirectly. For what they thought also flowed from the *ratio*, except that this *ratio* was not theirs but that of their betters, and that it was not allowed to shine in its purity but was deflected and decomposed by being made to pass through the prism of politics. Even the prejudices of the proletarians of Rome were no growth but an artefact, a manufactured article. There is no problem here which a sociology of knowledge would have to unravel. Cleverness is the key to everything.

A further field within which Montesquieu's early sociology of knowledge found fairly clear formulation was that of art criticism. All the students of his development, practically without exception, have emphasised that it was his period of foreign travel which weaned him from his youthful, narrowly rationalist philosophy of life and made of him that open-minded and generous student of history and human geography with whom we are familiar. But the first impressions he received when he crossed the borders of his native France confirmed rather than converted him in his opinions. Standing before the bronze doors of the famous Battistero at Florence, he remarks how superior the two of Ghiberti are to the one by Andrea Pisano—superior not because Ghiberti happened to be a more able artist, but rather because he lived a century after Pisano's day. He calls Pisano's work *un ouvrage gothique* and rude (*grossier*), but of Ghiberti's work he uses epithets like natural, correct and rational (*naturel, juste, sensible*) and reports with approval Michelangelo's dictum that Ghiberti's doors would be fit to be the gates of paradise (I, 951). This is not a stray judgment but fully characteristic of his deeper convictions at this particular time. There is, indeed, a well-developed art theory at the bottom of it.

This art theory is best reflected in a fragment which the editors of the Bordeaux edition have called *De la Manière Gothique*. In it, two styles are sharply contrasted: the *manière gothique* which is equated with bad taste, and *grâce* which is equated with good taste. This gothic manner is characterised by the cold and hard, as it were frozen, attitude of the human figures depicted on canvas or in stone; *grâce* on the other hand achieves, as the name indicates, gracefulness, that is to say, movement, life and unforced naturalness. In its early stages and in its days of decay art invariably conforms to the "gothic" pattern, but when it is at its heights, its works show forth all the glories of natural grace (I, 966).

The "gothic" type of art has in this way little to do with the nation of the Goths. In giving it this label, Montesquieu merely wishes to convey that here we have before us something primitive, something in a manner barbarian. Grace is, in contrast, something specifically civilised, something Greek. The Greeks first demonstrated what true art was and what all art should be. They set, not only a standard, but even a model, a model which is, in the nature of things, absolutely valid. It is as binding on the moderns as it ever was on the ancients. "The rules of Aristotle," Montesquieu writes, "are still the [right] rules for us today, and in spite of all the change in *mores* we cannot deviate from them" (I, 971). In another context he enthuses about such sculptures as the Venus of Medici and the Apollo of Belvedere. "These statues," he says, "cannot be sufficiently admired: for it is on them that the moderns have based their proportions, and one could almost assert that they have given us back art" (I, 927). The Renaissance, as one can see from these remarks, was for Montesquieu truly a re-nascence, a coming to life again of what once had been. All art is like Greek art, or it is not worthy of its name.

In contrast to classical art properly so called, and to the renewed classical art of the Renaissance which followed the same ideals, the gothic manner is specifically medieval. In a letter of this period, Montesquieu calls the Middle Ages "a time of barbarism",[1] and he explains the gracelessness of all the works of chisel and brush in those centuries by the general pre-dominance of ignorance. "We laboured vainly," he writes, "from the barbaric invasions until Giotto. Some Greek priests gave to Cimabue and to Giotto some feeble idea of what art is. Things remained in this state until the discovery of antiquity opened the mind of Michelangelo and his contemporaries. The Greeks achieved alone what we could only achieve through their assistance" (I, 957).

Who would not recognise in this simple black-and-white picture a reflection of that crude rationalistic prejudice which the intellectuals of the eighteenth century inherited from the humanists of the sixteenth and shared with them? Indeed, who would not recognise in it an expression of that typically ration-alistic superiority-complex which condemns out of hand all that does not conform to a certain narrowly defined pattern as ugly, stupid and despicable? For the Montesquieu of this period, *grâce* is the art of the educated, *la manière gothique* the art of the vulgar. Calling the latter "the taste of ignorance", he goes on to say, mainly with a view to gothic architecture with its statuary and turrets and pinnacles: "If one does not know true beauty, one imagines that a great number of ornaments will give grace and that beauty increases in proportion to the number of things which enter into the composition of the whole. In this way the lower classes would smother a young bride under ornaments, if expense would allow them to provide them. In this way women and children love knicknacks. Only the refined (*les beaux génies*) are capable of appreciating great simplicity" (I, 925). It is clear that from such a point of view there is no

[1] *Correspondence, loc. cit.*, I, 275.

road to the understanding of the glories of medieval art. The Montesquieu who first visited Florence had still a lot to learn.

Nevertheless, even the scattered notes from the grand tour contain here and there the promise of better things to come. There is in particular one passage which presages the total revolution soon to redirect all Montesquieu's thought. Here it is: "It seems to me that those *mores* and customs of nations which are not contrary to morality cannot be regarded as superior one to the other. For where is the rule by which they could be judged? They have no common measure, unless it be that each nation makes a principle out of its own *mores* and judges all the others by it" (I, 767). These words reveal an attitude which, unlike radical rationalism, does not close the mind to the meaning and rationality of the apparently meaningless and irrational, but on the contrary opens it and lets in the light.

And not only is there this first indication of Montesquieu's future attitude, there are also a few passages which foreshadow the main themes of his later researches. One or two concern the possible influence of religious conceptions on the genesis and character of artistic forms. If the Greeks had artistry and the Persians none, one of the reasons is that the Greeks imagined their gods in human shape, whereas the Persians did not (I, 956 and 968 *seq.*). In more recent times, Catholicism with its cult of the saints has favoured the flourishing of the creative arts, whereas Protestantism has had an adverse effect on them. "If the Protestant religion had prevailed in Europe, of how many beautiful things should we have been robbed?" (I, 970; cf. also 865 *seq.*). The geographical factor, too, makes its appearance. The same religious orders, for instance the Carthusians, are said to produce different human types and experiences in the north and in the south, in France and in Italy (I, 701 *seq.*). And in one clear-cut statement, the basic idea of Montesquieu's final sociology of knowledge is put forward with considerable punch: "The kings [of the kind of Antiochus and Seleucus] call *majesty* an exterior appearance which inspires fear. The [Roman] republicans, on the other hand, called *majesty* an exterior appearance which inspires love" (I, 593). As we shall see, words such as these could well serve as a motto to the mature Montesquieu's theory concerning the genesis of ideas. But in 1728, when they were written, that grand theory was as yet of the future.

III

THE TURN FROM RATIONALISM TO
REALISM

IT goes without saying that if Montesquieu had persevered
in the mode of thinking characteristic of the *Dissertation sur
la Politique des Romains dans la Religion* (and of the fragment
De la Manière Gothique), he would not have found a place in a
book such as the present. But in 1722, at the age of 33, he was,
as we have seen, already different from what he had been in
1716, and in 1734 he had moved again a good deal in the
direction of a non-rationalistic, even anti-rationalistic sociology
of knowledge. In the latter year he published his *Considérations
sur les Causes de la Grandeur et de la Décadence des Romains*, a book
in which the originally supposed "cause" for the greatness of
Rome would have loomed very large if it had still played the
same part in Montesquieu's thought as it had done eighteen
years before. But there is only one relative clause in which the
politique dans la religion is as much as mentioned (II, 113) and
little or nothing is made of it. In this fact we have yet another
indication of the deep dislocations in Montesquieu's thought
which took place over the period of his travels between 1728
and 1731. In *De l'Esprit des Lois* of 1748, chapter 4 of book XXV
allows us to look into Montesquieu's mature mind. The priests
now no longer appear as ideologists of the upper classes and
stultifiers of the lower: their function is now seen as a function of
society as a whole. As long as religious sacrifices are simply
offerings of the fruits of the fields, no priestly class is needed.
But "the natural desire to please the deity multiplied the
ceremonies"; permanent temples developed which had to be
maintained like private dwelling-places; and an increasing

attention to the demands of cleanliness produced the desire to have a clergy set apart and kept undefiled expressly for the purest of all services, the religious services (II, 739 *seq.*): thus there arose a religious class or caste simply through the unfolding of the division of labour. A spirit informs these considerations which is obviously very different from the one that had inspired the *Dissertation* of 1716. But the essential point is that Montesquieu dropped the division of society so near and so dear to the rationalistic thinkers, into a rationalistic upper class and a cowed, stupid, superstition-ridden lower class kept in its place by artificial, force- and fraud-inspired ideologies. In a passage which is difficult to place but which, as the reader can see must have been penned after Montesquieu's stay at Naples, he writes as follows: "What M. Van Dale says [in his *De Oraculis Veterum Ethnicorum*, on which Fontenelle later very largely based his *Histoire des Oracles*] concerning the knavery of the priests about the oracles does not appear to me proved in any way. There is every indication that they were deceived themselves. I judge of this by the miracle of the blood of St. Januarius which I can prove to be no swindle. The priests are of good faith; Naples is in good faith; and it could not be otherwise" (I, 1572). Montesquieu also rejects a suggestion put forward by Gaspard Schott according to which the mysterious sounds heard at Delphi were due to the passing of the mountain winds through some gadget or machine in the form of a tripod which could be regulated at will. "This would be impossible in any century" (*ib*). The priestess was seduced rather than a seducer, a victim of error rather than its engineer. The salient implication of these sentences is that irrational beliefs in the foreground are not the wilful products of rational wire-pullers in the background, but a growth and hence a problem. Here is the attitude, so signally lacking in 1716, out of which a genuine sociology of knowledge could arise.

One could bring this aspect of Montesquieu's mental development into a short formula by saying that whereas, as a young man, he saw world-views distinguished vertically, i.e. between the contemporary upper social strata and the lower social strata, the rational minority and the foolish multitude, he later saw them distinguished horizontally, i.e. between generations or periods or ages along the line of the flow of history. In other words, a historical element enters in, incompatible with the original rationalism, since for rationalism true rationality is potentially present in any age and irrationality in principle never necessary and never justified. But from historicism to relativism is only a short step, and Montesquieu logically took it. As M. Dedieu has pointed out, certain authors he read must have helped him on along this road.[1] There was, for instance, Gravina, whose *Origines Juris Civilis* (1701–1713) strongly fore-shadow tendencies that came to full fruition only in the romantic age. Gravina calls, in the style of his age, the laws fruits of a *ratio communis*, but only to add, almost in the same breath, that they grow out of a *ratio specialis* rather than out of a *ratio generalis*. Reason, he recognised, was time-bound and local, not universal and perpetual: it had to form under differing circumstances, physical, moral, traditional and so on, and was thus understandably different from society to society. The wisest legislators, he says, have adapted these laws "to the morals of the country and the century. Hence, although nature has given men the same idea of honesty, the aspect which it assumes is not the same with all [nations]. The laws of the different peoples are different from each other because they do not draw their utility[2] from the same sources, and though they [all] have need of good government, they could not [all] be well governed in the same fashion" (cit. Dedieu, 1913, 49). Doria's *Vita Civile* led in the same direction. The laws of a country arise from and depend on a complex of facts, such as the general mental habit of the population, the nature of the territory, the number of inhabitants, the kinds of their occupations. Such books taught Montesquieu not to look at the phenomena of the mind from above, from the empyrean of pure reason, but from below, from their roots in the soil and subsoil of reality. But life taught Montesquieu more than even the best books. We are once again face to face with a deep effect of his travels. When he left France, he was convinced that the best and, indeed, the only good form of government was the government of "gothic" France, the feudal order with its all-important *corps intermédiaires*. When he returned from England, he knew this was a mistake. He had seen across the Channel a form of government which was also good,

[1] *Montesquieu*, 1913, 48 *seq.*; *Montesquieu, L'Homme et L'Oeuvre*, 1943, 94 *seq.*
[2] "*avantage*".

even excellent, although its goodness and excellence were different from the goodness and excellence of the feudal organisation. Goodness and excellence, he now recognised, were essentially relative. Those who believe that Montesquieu only accepted a new ideal in order to drop his old love have little true knowledge of his mind. He never abandoned his preference of the ancient French constitution for France; he would never have imported English constitutionalism into his own country; but neither would he have tried to sell French feudalism to the British. His conviction after, say, 1730, was that the principles of public life are home-grown phenomena, not export articles. He had become a relativist. "The government most in keeping with nature", says the *Esprit des Lois*, is (not the one most rational in the absolute, quasi-mathematical sense of the word, but) "the one whose particular disposition is best related to the disposition of the people for which it is established" (II, 237).

Once in possession of the principle of relativism, Montesquieu quickly developed and exploited it. "I don't know how it happened," says a note, probably of fairly early date, "but a Turk found himself one day in the company of a Cannibal. 'You are very cruel', said the Mohammedan. 'You eat the prisoners you have taken in war.' 'What do you do with yours?' answered the Cannibal. 'Ah! We kill them. But we do not eat them when they are dead.' It seems," Montesquieu comments, "that there is no people which has not got its own particular cruelty; that each nation is moved only by that of the other nations, as if barbarity were a matter of habit, like fashions and clothes" (I, 1327). To this relativism Montesquieu was to hold fast for the rest of his life. If he says occasionally that "men are the same at all times" (II, 1375), what he means is not that they have an absolutely fixed nature beyond the grip of history or geography or other relativising forces, but only that they are always evil, always evil in some way or in some sense, always under the shadow of original sin—a fact which does not exclude relativity since sinfulness (e.g. cruelty) can appear in innumerable manifestations and forms according to circumstances. Our philosopher comes very near to expressing this himself. "As men have had at all times the same passions," he writes in his *Romains*, "the occasions which produce great changes are different, but the causes are ever the same" (II,

71). Perhaps this passage is not as strongly in favour of our argument here as we should wish; but the fundamental thought is there. The root evil of men's impious passions is always behind reality; but reality refracts it as the prism does the ray of light, and so we get motley appearances which depend in their concreteness on the refracting medium—on circumstances.

For the rest, relativism is to the mature Montesquieu not only a theoretical principle and problem, but also a practical demand. The good man will live according to it. "I am a good citizen," Montesquieu writes. "But in whatever country I had been born, I should have been a good citizen all the same" (I, 982). Man, he sums up in the *Esprit des Lois*, is a flexible being who bends himself, in society, to the ideas and impressions of those around him (II, 230). We must see and understand him in his concrete determination, not in his abstract perfection, in which alone the rationalists deign to consider him. There is, Montesquieu implies in the following passage, which shows that he is no longer the young Secondat of the *Dissertation sur la Politique des Romains dans la Religion*, nothing more futile than to apply to past man the yardsticks of present man: "To transport back into remote centuries all the ideas of the century in which one lives, is the most prolific of all sources of error. To the people who would [as it were] modernise all the ancient centuries, I should say what the priests of Egypt said to Solon: 'O Athenians! You are but children!' " (II, 902).[1]

This relativism produced in Montesquieu, as it must in any discerning and active mind, a corresponding effort to interpret the past in, and out of, its particularity. In a paragraph destined for the *Traité des Devoirs*, he had written round about 1725: "The historians are the severe investigators of the actions of those who have appeared upon this earth, and they are a replica of those judges of Egypt who called [before them] in judgment the souls of all the dead" (I, 1133). This desire to judge, to allot praise and blame, gives way to a desire to understand. Many are the passages in and through which this new desire speaks. "I do not embrace any opinions," a fragment runs, "bar those of the books of Euclid" (I, 982). And, more positively: "I never condemn men because of what they have done or what they have not done in virtue of the prejudices of

[1] On Montesquieu as a historian, cf. Dedieu, 1943, 121 *seq*.

their age. Most great men were subject to them ... They have not [even] seen, most of the time, the prejudices of their age ..." They only deserve blame if they have added to the prejudices of their society faults and errors of their own (I, 997). More positively still: "To judge of the beauties of Homer, it is necessary to place oneself in the camp of the Greeks, and not in a French army" (I, 1023). In general, "we shall never judge men well if we do not allow them the prejudices"—i.e. the specific predilections—"of their time" (I, 1340). Here we have already a principle of historical interpretation closely akin to the typical attitude of the sociologist of knowledge. It holds good even as between succeeding generations. "There is an astonishing unfairness in peoples' judgments: we accuse our fathers of having little spirit because they cried when they saw the little Regulus [on the stage in Pradou's play]; we believe that they cried because they had no common sense. No! They had as much spirit as we, neither more nor less; but their *moeurs* were different, their hearts differently disposed. It is for this reason that they cried and we do not cry" (I, 1250). To find an explanation for men's behaviour, and more particularly for their strange and irrational behaviour, was now Montesquieu's constant preoccupation and scholarly ambition. "Whenever a law appears odd, and it is not clear what interest the law-giver can have had in formulating it in this way, one should assume that it is more reasonable than it looks, and [in fact] that it is based on a sufficient reason. The law of Genghis Khan forbade the Mongols to go near to water during thunder. He wanted to prevent the Mongols who, in a country where thunder is very frequent, immediately jumped into water, from getting drowned" (II, 1111). Let us admit without subterfuge that Montesquieu's explanation smacks of rationalism, of that general rationalistic tendency which tries to find a reasonable cause behind all unreasonable appearances, which tends to make utility the core of every human action. Nevertheless, to have asked this question is in itself a significant move. It points forward, even if it does not wholly attain its end, towards a future sociology of knowledge.[1]

[1] Cf. also II, 145 *seq.*, where Montesquieu manfully strives to explain some apparently quite inexplicable happenings under the Roman emperors.—Where he finds himself confronted with phenomena, which he absolutely cannot comprehend, e.g. the strange doings of the Pythagoreans, he assumes that we are insufficiently informed about them and have, so to speak, lost the key (I, 1545).

Indeed, it is this effort, in evidence on many pages, to understand, by entering into an alien life-situation, the phenomena
flowing from it, that makes the reading of Montesquieu's work
so stimulating and shows us the mettle and the measure of the
man. And if he sometimes falls into the easy ways of the rationalists and propounds facile interpretations and explanations,
there are other occasions when he is far, far in advance of his
age. He notes that Homer is criticised because he shows us his
hero-kings cooking, thus exposing them to ridicule. But though
it would be a degrading spectacle to see a *roi-soleil* of the age of
absolutism cooking, the situation in heroic times was apt to
inspire an entirely different sentiment. The act of cooking was
then closely connected in men's minds with the act of religious
sacrifice; he that slew the victim had also to prepare a sacred
meal from its meat. Hence to the Greeks a king engaged in
cooking was not a king incongruously doing a menial job; he
was much rather a priest at a sacramental task (I,1236). Solon
is accused of great folly because one of his laws declared in-
famous those who, in a sedition, did not enter the lists on either
side. But Solon was living in a society composed of city states;
the danger was that in a period of political fermentation the
cool-hearted and clear-headed would keep aloof from politics
and the party leaderships fall into the hands of the hotbloods
and things thus be driven to an extremity. What Solon wanted
was to ensure that moderation should prevail, that the prudent
citizens should be brought into action and steady the course of
the zig-zagging ship of state. This recipe is a good one for a
petty community. If we regard it as extravagant today, it is
because we live in a society of a different type, in a spacially
and numerically more extended state where different methods
of political pilotage are indicated. Montesquieu's insight goes
at this point fairly deep. "In the seditions which occurred in
those petty states, the majority of the city entered into the
quarrel or carried it on. In our great monarchies, the parties
are composed of a few, and the people at large prefer to live in
[political] inactivity. In this [latter] case, it is natural to lead
the seditious back to the majority of citizens, and not [to drive]
the majority of the citizens [forward] towards the seditious: in
the other case, it is necessary to make the small number of wise
and quiet people join the seditious, for it is thus that the

fermentation of one liquor may be arrested by one single drop of another" (II, 866 *seq.*). Polybius, Plato, Aristotle, Theophrastus, Plutarch and Strabo, all agree that (as Plato has it) "one cannot introduce a change in music which would not also be one in the political constitution". Whence this queer conviction which seems to us *primâ facie* utterly artificial? The Greeks, Montesquieu explains, educated their young nobles for war. But such an education necessarily leads to crudeness and rudeness. The martial spirit had to be tempered, but in such a way that the refinement introduced did not give rise to softness and effemination. Music was the answer to the problem; music stimulates all the passions; hence it appeals to and evokes the gentle ones without destroying those that are not so gentle (II, 270 *seq.*). In the *leges barbarorum*, little attention is paid to parricide and little severity shown with regard to it. Montesquieu found an explanation of this fact, so repugnant to modern sentiment and so incomprehensible to the modern mind, in a feature of their social tradition. Procopius reports, in his book on the Gothic War, that if someone among the Heruleans became sick or decrepit, he appealed to his kinsmen to put him out of his misery, and this was arranged with the help of a stranger. Hence parricide was not conceived as a crime; it was much rather a custom, though a custom receding and increasingly fading as the barbarians became romanised, i.e. entered a different social tradition (II, 1116 *seq.*).

Montesquieu makes his greatest effort sociologically to comprehend the apparently incomprehensible when he discusses such "gothic" institutions as the ordeal, "the judgment of God". What more irrational—indeed what more repellent to reason—than the proofs "by fire" or "by water" or "by combat"?—"proofs which proved nothing, and which were related neither to innocence, nor to the crime". Montesquieu notes first of all, and rightly, the general warlike background of these institutions. They had grown out of, and continued, the practice of the feud. The ordeal was an attenuated sort of feud, and better than the feud properly so-called only in this, that it was controlled and supervised. He emphasises, furthermore, that a warlike nation, which thinks it natural that the issue of public affairs should depend on fighting and the outcome of fighting, will tend to develop, because of the basic unity of its world-view, the opinion that in private affairs too, the luck of arms should decide the issue. But he goes on to argue that the ordeal by combat was not, perhaps, entirely a matter of luck, a game of chance, a kind of blind man's buff. He distinguishes two cases: firstly, the case where the party accused is weak, say a woman; and secondly, the case when the party concerned is strong, a warrior, a man. If a woman challenged to combat does not find a champion and loses her cause, she must have been unpopular, distrusted and even despised; in the circumstances she really loses because she is known to the community as one who does not deserve to win. If a man is challenged and does not accept the challenge, and even if he accepts and is defeated, it is assumed that he is the less trustworthy individual of the two combatants, the socially less valuable person. "In a nation exclusively devoted to war, cowardice implies other vices; it proves that a man has resisted the education which he has received, and that he has not been sensible to the honour, nor guided by the principles, which have governed other people; it shows that he does not fear their contempt and that he does not think highly of their esteem: if only he has been born a person of quality,[1] he will not in the ordinary way lack the adroitness which should go together with strength, nor the strength which should combine with courage; because, setting great store by his honour, he will all his life have trained himself in the things without which it cannot be attained. Furthermore in a warlike nation where strength, courage and prowess are held in high esteem, the truly odious crimes are those which spring from trickery, slyness and guile, that is to say, from cowardice" (II, 811 *seq.*; cf. also I, 1474 *seq.*). The proof by the burning-hot iron and the boiling-hot water are explained in a similar vein: the man ready to touch them is the man more in harmony with the ideal of the time; medieval man's hands were—unless he was effeminate and hence despicable in terms of the code of chivalry—hard and horny, so that no permanent damage to them was really to be apprehended; only the skin of a person unused to handling the broadsword would show signs of the ordeal three days after it when the bandages were commonly removed, whereas the true warrior's callous palm would appear unmarked; hence the test was

[1] "... *pour peu qu'on soit bien né.*

essentially a test of character (*ib*). Even if these explanations do not hold water, they are greatly to Montesquieu's credit: whatever the value of the results to which he comes, his method is unexceptionable. It is the true method of the sociology of knowledge—to comprehend the meaning of individual pheno-mena by relating them to the total life situation out of which they arise and within which they function, to see the genesis of customs and ideas in their essential connexion with the social background and underground in which they are rooted. A man who could thus apply the method of the sociology of knowledge, was almost certain to be also interested in its theory—to attempt, that is to say, to develop such a theory. To this central aspect of Montesquieu's work we shall now turn our attention.

Let us only notice, in taking leave of the study of M. de la Brède's mental development and in taking up the more syste-matic analysis of his doctrine of the determination of ideas, that his desire to understand thoughts alien to his own, the desire basic to his sociology of knowledge, finally and irrevocably sets him apart from the rationalistic tradition through which he had passed in his youth. We have convincing testimony of this from the pen of one who was well qualified to give it. "What the Devil does he want to teach us by his treatise on fiefs?" Helvétius wrote to Saurin concerning Montesquieu. "Is this a matter which a wise and reasonable spirit should seek to disentangle? What legislation could grow out of that barbarous chaos of laws which force had established, which ignorance had respected and which will for ever be opposed to a good order of things?" (cit. Alengry, *La Sociologie chez Auguste Comte*, 1900, 389). The rationalists *à la Helvétius* worked in season and out of season with one pair of concepts—the concepts right and wrong, reasonable and unreasonable. All that was not reason-able and right was disregarded—the sharpest form of condem-nation. Montesquieu discarded this fatuous dichotomy on the threshold of his maturity. It is no exaggeration to say that in his mind there was already an inkling of the great truth which Hegel was to formulate two generations later when he said—what is real is reasonable; what is real has a *raison d'être*—"*quelque raison fondée sur l'expérience*" (I, 1474; II, 812)—which we must endeavour to find. In spite of his youthful rationalism, the Baron de Montesquieu stands before us as essentially a forerunner of the romantic age.

IV

MONTESQUIEU'S BASIC DOCTRINE OF MAN

MONTESQUIEU's sociology of knowledge can best be approached through his general sociology; his general sociology in turn must be seen in the light of his basic concept of man. Hence our investigation should begin with a study of what Kant would have called the Monsieur de la Brède's "anthropology".

This "anthropology" is not conceived by its author as a strictly scientific discipline. Prediction of human behaviour is out of the question; human conduct is so diverse as to make all generalisation problematic. Montesquieu himself certainly generalises from time to time; but, as M. Barckhausen has remarked, who has grasped this aspect of his thought better than anyone else, "it is only *sous bénéfice d'inventaire* that he generalises."[1] The rights of concrete experience against abstract generalisation must ever be reserved. Montesquieu manifestly thinks little of those Englishmen "who spend their life calculating events which, in view of the nature of things and the caprice of fortune, that is to say of men, are hardly subject to calculation" (II, 582). Not mathematics, but only observation can enlighten us about the nature of man.

Now, what does observation teach us? Montesquieu has no comforting doctrine. Experience shows us above all "the reality of our vices and the imperfections of our virtues" (I, 1276). It confirms, so we may understand the philosopher of La Brède, the sad story of the fall. He belongs to the school of Montaigne; he does not move one inch towards the position of

---

[1] Montesquieu, *Ses Idées et Ses Oeuvres*, 1907, 44 seq.

Rousseau.[1] Nor does he, with Leibniz, assume that the springs of human action are in the last analysis rational. Men act "out of caprice or out of passion" or simply in order to act (I, 115). For the rest, they follow their advantages as they see them, for "selfishness is the greatest ruler of the earth" (I, 288).

That Montesquieu really thought in terms of a fallen nature, in terms of total perversion even, can be seen from a string of passages which span his whole adult life from the *Lettres Persanes* of 1721 to the *Essai sur le Goût* of 1756. In the *Lettres Persanes* Usbek speaks of "the misery of the human condition": the stories of the desert saints are, rightly understood, an allegory of human life in general: temptations beset us on all sides, our passions never leave us in peace, our heart is full of monsters, our mind full of delusions: evil thrusts "into our very vitals" (I, 269). In the *Essai sur le Goût* the ageing Montesquieu refers, in exactly the same spirit, to "our natural malignity" (II, 1262). Men are evil; they tend to ruin everything; most of them will rather do a great deed than a good deed; in fact, "that heroism of which Morality can approve, impresses but few people. It is the heroism which destroys Morality which strikes us and evokes our admiration" (I, 1470, 1510, 1305). A good example of men's unholy tendency to pervert everything is the way in which they have handled the great and holy dogma of personal immortality. It seems to call for a host of good and even saintly actions: it has in fact led to countless follies, such as pyramid-building, widow-burning and anthropophagy (I, 1543 *seq.*).

Our soul is thus filled by a general tendency towards evil, much in the way in which the sea is filled by salt. But this evil spirit does not remain in solution: it tends to take shape in various tangible forms such as selfishness, pride, envy and a tendency to lord it over our fellowmen. Selfishness is so great that it can even lead to the paradox of self-destruction. Speaking of the suicide of Brutus and Cassius, this is what Montesquieu

[1] The contrast to Rousseau is especially interesting. It confirms the often made observation that in the measure in which a man improves morally, his estimate of human nature will become harsher and lower, and in the measure in which he becomes morally debased, his estimate of human nature will become higher and milder. Rousseau's *Confessions* show us a scoundrel; yet his philosophical writings call man born good; Montesquieu's *Pensées* show us a man of noble character; yet his books speak to us of the misery, the degradation and the sinfulness of our souls.

writes: "Self-love, the love of our preservation, transforms itself into so many shapes, and acts by such contradictory principles, that it even induces us to sacrifice our existence for the love of our existence; and such is the fuss which we make of ourselves that we agree to put an end to our life by dint of a natural and obscure instinct which makes us love ourselves more than our life itself" (II, 136; cf. also I, 1279). Pride is, rightly understood, only a manifestation of men's basic tendency or drive towards self-assertion. "The desire of glory is by no means different from that instinct which all creatures have for their preservation. It seems to us that we increase our being if we succeed in establishing it in the memory of others: it is a new life which we thus acquire, and which becomes as precious to us as the one which we have received from Heaven" (I, 263). In one context Montesquieu calls vanity "the substance of the soul " (I, 1282); in another he says that "the pride of men is almost the only cause of all moral effects" (I, 122); and in a third (*Lettre Persane* XLIV, I, 191 *seq.*) he insinuates that it is the real root of the class contrast. This general superiority-complex renders men stupid and ridiculous. "The [common] infatuation with astrology is due to pride run riot. We believe that our actions are important enough to deserve to be written in the great book of Heaven. There is nobody, down to the most miserable artisan, who would not believe that the immense and luminous bodies which circle above his head are made only in order to announce to the Universe the hour at which he will step out of his shop" (I, 1570).

Just as pride springs from self-assertion and is, in a manner, identical with it, so envy arises from pride and is its complement. "If people just wanted to be happy, that would be easily done. But they want to be happier than others, and that is almost always difficult because we take the others for happier than they are" (I, 1269).[1] This envious disposition on the part of men must already put a great strain on their mutual relationships; but there is worse. There is a deeply ingrained desire in

---

[1] In *Lettre Persane* CXLV there is a paragraph concerning envy which is of high interest because it strikingly anticipates the basic idea of Max Scheler's celebrated essay *Das Ressentiment im Aufbau der Moralen*: "A man who lacks some talent makes himself amends by despising it; he removes the barrier which he encountered between merit and himself, and thus finds himself on a par with the person whose achievements he resents" (I, 360).

us to lord it over our neighbours, a desire by no means confined to a few particularly masterful personalities. In a dossier of notes prepared for a book *Sur l'Histoire de France*, Montesquieu writes this in the chapter on Louis XIV: "He had an immoderate desire to increase his power over his subjects; but as far as that is concerned, I do not know if I should greatly blame him for a sentiment which is common to almost all men" (I, 1123). The identical idea appears in the *Romains* anent the discussion of the fall of the republic. If Caesar and Pompey had not destroyed it, others would have done so. "One must not blame the ambition of individuals in this; one must accuse man: always the more avid for power, the more he has already, and who craves for all only because he already possesses a lot" (II, 129). The *Esprit des Lois* states tersely that "it is an eternal experience that every man who holds power is inclined to abuse it," and pushes on until he runs into some barrier (II, 395). In this, there is nothing surprising: "The soul tastes so many pleasures when it dominates other souls . . ." We must put the blame for all this on the fall, "a disaster attached to the human condition" (II, 858). As against all this, M. Barckhausen has emphasised[1] that Montesquieu appears to believe in a sympathetic strain in the human make-up, in a kind of inborn neighbourliness. Be it so; but passages supporting this assertion are few and far between. Far more outspoken is Montesquieu when he comes to notice the anti-social tendencies of men, their ever-present itch to attack, to fight, to defy the law. After their exodus to the Mons Sacer, the plebeians were given tribunes to defend them; the tribunate was expressly planned as an institution for the support of social peace. "But, by an eternal malady of men, the plebeians, who had obtained the tribunes for their defence, used them in order to attack; they appropriated by degrees all the prerogatives of the patricians; and that produced continuous strife" (II, 112). In the *Lettres Persanes* Usbek describes men's unwillingness to obey the laws of God and men as "men's shame". The Mohammedan princes are forbidden to drink wine, and they drink to excess; the Christian princes are not forbidden to drink wine, and they do not drink to excess. "The human spirit is contradiction itself: in an excess of licentiousness, man revolts with fury against all precepts, and the Law,

[1] *Montesquieu, Ses Idées et ses Oeuvres*, 1907, 19.

made to render us more just, often only serves to render us more guilty" (I, 178 *seq.*). There is no reason to believe that Montesquieu ever abandoned this position, though he might have expressed himself less pungently in later years when age had mellowed him to some extent.

Naturally, all men's anti-social and wicked tendencies, their pride, their envy, and their lust of domination, are contained or as it were stabilised in well-ordered societies, but they are never eradicated, never truly conquered. They continue to show themselves in a certain corruptibility of men, in a definite moral weakness. Many are the passages in which Montesquieu speaks of the "necessary corruption of all systems of government" (cf. e.g. II, 29). He sees at work a sort of gravitation towards anarchy, and he is particularly bitter against wickedness in high places, for nothing so surely and so quickly corrupts the common run of men as the bad example of an outstanding personality, say a Minister of the Crown.[1]

In view of the fact that Montesquieu lived in the age generally denominated the Age of Reason, it must be asked whether he did not, like Locke and Leibniz, regard man as good simply because he is endowed with rationality. The Baron de la Brède certainly went with his fellow-philosophers in so far as he, too, saw man as an *animal rationale*. But he was not so sure that this reasonableness ought to be regarded as central and decisive. Men are too lazy to use it. "We reflect little: the interest which we have to possess just ideas of things gives way to another interest, which is a certain peace and an agreeable self-forgetfulness" (II, 1037 *seq.*). Sometimes Montesquieu emphasises the irrational element in apparently rational societies; sometimes again he emphasises the rational element in apparently irrational institutions. To the former occasions belongs what he says about the English: "That nation, always agitated, could be more easily guided by its passions than by its reason, which never produces great impressions on the spirit of men; and it would be easy for those who ruled her to make her undertake actions against her true interests" (II,

[1] Cf. *Lettre Persane* CXLVI, I, 360 *seq.*, which discusses in a thinly veiled form the demoralisation of France under and after John Law.—Two of the problems touched in the above paragraph, namely the stabilisation of social relationships (the theory of social control) and their aptness to be spoiled, are discussed in more detail later on. Cf. Chapter V.

577). To the latter we must count the paragraph which introduces the discussion of the legal aspects of judicial combat. "It will perhaps appear surprising to see this monstrous custom of judicial combat reduced to principle and to discover so singular a system of jurisprudence. Men, basically reasonable, put their very prejudices under rules. Nothing was more contrary to common sense than the judicial combat; but this point once conceded, the execution of it was managed with a certain amount of prudence" (II, 823). In a similar context, the power of reason is even more strongly emphasised. "Reason has a natural empire; she even has a tyrannical empire: she comes up against resistance, but that very resistance is her triumph; a little while, and men will be forced to come back to her" (II, 853). Should one, in view of these contradictory passages, accuse Montesquieu of inconsistency? Should one assume that he was given to moods and turned, now to one side, now to the other? By no means. Man is for Montesquieu an intermediate being, half flesh and half fish as it were; for ever suspended between reason and irrationality. Mediocrity is his hall-mark in everything.

Of one thing only Montesquieu seems fairly convinced— that man has the choice between rational and irrational conduct, that he has free will. Of course, free will is not to him a sign of man's high estate, but rather (consistently with what has gone before) an aspect of his mediocrity, his fallen nature. "Freedom is in us an imperfection: we are free and uncertain because we do not know with certainty what is best for us. It is not so with God: as he is supremely perfect, he can never act but in the most perfect manner" (I, 1542). In the *Lettre Persane* which is of all perhaps the philosophically most serious (no. LXIX), there is a discussion of the problem of the coexistence of human freedom and divine foreknowledge, and the emphasis is throughout on the reality of human freedom. "The soul is the worker of its own determination: ... there are occasions when it is so indetermined that it does not even know in which direction to determine itself . . ." Even God cannot then know what will happen. Of course, He can interfere at any time and predetermine the issue; but "ordinarily" He will not interfere. How could we otherwise gain merit or incur demerit? The first truth which Moses has taught us is that God, by a voluntary act of self-restriction, has deigned not to take cognisance of—to look away as it were from—our future decisions; absolute divine prescience is rightly neither a Jewish nor a Moslem dogma (I, 238 *seq.*; cf. also I, 1178 and 1542, fragment 2081). It is because of this fundamental freedom and responsibility that we must educate ourselves into good habits; we can do it if we want to. Montesquieu raises this demand even in an early passage in which he is still under the influence of mechanism and materialism (I, 1126 *seq.*). There was apparently no time in his life when he did not believe that man was free.

This firm belief in the fundamental freedom of man shines particularly brightly in and through the passages which discuss what—by a conscious anachronism—one could call the Malthusian problem. As a rule, the "principle of population" has always been quoted as a proof of man's submission to blind, inescapable, even malignant forces. It is not in this light that Montesquieu sees it. True, there is a tendency on the part of men to marry if they can hope to build up a comfortable home. But Montesquieu is sure that this tendency is not backed up by any kind of necessity. He notes that young women are, for social reasons, keener on marriage than young men: it is marriage that frees them, in the given social circumstances, from sundry irksome restrictions. He also notes that nascent nations (nations, for instance, amid a yet open nature) multiply much more rapidly than nations that are already established. In frontier conditions, as the Americans would say, a family with many hands is a great help in everything; in cramped conditions, it is otherwise (II, 688 *seq.*). We can see from these considerations that, in Montesquieu's opinion, even a physically founded drive operates only through men's conscious endeavour and volitions. But if this is so, then it can also be inhibited by men's plans and wills and caprices. Montesquieu has no doubt that this is so, and he sees in this mastery (or at any rate potential mastery) over a natural tendency a hall-mark of men's humanity. "The females of animals have an almost constant fecundity. But in the human race the manner of thinking character, passions, fancies, caprices, the idea of preserving one's beauty, the inconvenience of pregnancy and that of too large a family interfere with propagation in a thousand ways" (II, 683). In particular, "the principles of religion have had an extremely great influence on the propagation of the human race: sometimes they have encouraged it, as among the Jews, the Mohammedans, the Zoroastrians, the Chinese; sometimes they have checked it as they did with the Romans when they had become converted to Christianity" (II, 706). Even when men breed, they breed in freedom and responsibility.

The foregoing discussion is so particularly instructive because it shows that for Montesquieu free will is not diminished by the existence and the operation of physical drives. In a stray passage which allows us to see rather deeply into his philosophy of man, he distinguishes *raison physique* and *raison morale*. The body draws us one way, morality another. "What is responsible for the greater part of the contradictions of Man is the fact that *raison physique* and *raison morale* are hardly ever in harmony" (I, 1302). To be man is to be caught in conflict; to be man is to choose; in other words, to be man is to be free.

V

MONTESQUIEU'S BASIC DOCTRINE OF SOCIETY

NATURALLY and necessarily, this doctrine of man has decisive implications for Montesquieu's doctrine of society. If society is composed of free men, then it will only flourish—indeed, then it will only hold together—if these men act in such a way as to make social relationships stable and fruitful; if they act, to some extent at any rate, unselfishly. There is little trace in Montesquieu's writings of the doctrine so prominent in Vico and so many other authors looming large in the history of social thought, of the "heterogony of ends"—the doctrine according to which individual selfishness may or even must lead to social advancement, "private vices" may, by dint of a sort of social chemistry in which they are intermixed and mutually neutralised, mean "publick benefits".[1] He comes nearest to this theory so widely current in his own (the Leibnizian) age in the following fragment: "It is the desire to please which gives cohesion to Society, and such has been the good luck of the Human Race that this vanity, which would seem to tend to dissolve Society, in fact fortifies it and makes it unshakeable" (I, 1274). But already a second stray note introduces some sense of distance to the comfortable sociology of Leibniz's disciples: "In the world, Cleland says, there are many people who appear virtuous and are only vain, but this is the same thing for society: vanity represents virtue, as the bank-note represents [true] money" (II, 1381).[2] This

---

[1] It is true that Montesquieu expresses agreement with Mandeville and his famous formula (cf. fragment 1978 in I, 1489), but manifestly only in so far as the *economic* effects of individual selfishness are concerned. His specifically *social* theory is very different from that of Mandeville, Adam Smith, etc.

[2] Cf. also II, 257, penultimate paragraph.

passage is certainly still capable of being construed in an optimistic vein, in the sense that all works out, ultimately, for the best; but who does not notice that Montesquieu implies that a social order that is underpinned, not by a direct moral effort of its members, but only by the oblique consequences of their personal vices, is not the genuine article, but only a regrettable fake? The most that Montesquieu really admits (taking the body of his work as a whole, and disregarding a few stray passages such as those just quoted) is that one vice may at times inhibit another—in favourable circumstances, a minor vice a major—and that society may gain by this internecine warfare among men's immoral propensities. "The world is very corrupt: but there are certain passions which find themselves very cramped; there are favourite ones which forbid the others to appear. Consider the men of the world among themselves; nothing could show more timidity: it is pride which does not dare to reveal its secrets, and which, in the regard which it pays to others, is only put aside in order to be taken up again. Christianity gives us the habit of curbing that pride; the world gives us the habit of hiding it. With the modicum of virtue which we possess, what would become of us if our whole soul were given freedom . . .?" (II, 1163). A rhetorical question this which proves that Montesquieu was far from believing that men's inborn tendencies, if left unchecked, would spontaneously blend themselves into social tendencies, tendencies favourable to the social whole.

No; society can only be a success if men, in a sustained moral effort, will it and consciously work for the promotion of social ends. Rightly does M. Caillois, in his introduction to the *Oeuvres Complètes*, emphasise that for the mature Montesquieu public life (as well as private) appeared inexplicable without the moral effort active in it, and that moral effort is the key to the whole miracle of civilisation (XVIII). Already the fable of the Troglodytes in the *Lettres Persanes* XI–XIV is a moral tale to this effect. In spite of all its *naiveté*, it makes its point very well. At first, the Troglodytes lived in pure selfishness; but the result of this unhappy experiment was their almost complete extermination. Only two survived in the distant hills who, as it happened, "had humanity" and "loved virtue". They restarted the Troglodyte nation and based it on a new foundation, the foundation of moral rectitude, neighbourliness and religion. They took good care to bring up their children in the right spirit; in particular they inculcated into them the conviction that "the interest of the individual is always found in the common interest" (I, 149). And as they succeeded, every bliss and blessing descended on the people thus reborn. It takes nothing from the thesis of this story that its ending is not a happy one, that the Troglodytes find virtue a hard taskmaster and prefer submission to a king who coerces from without to submission to conscience which coerces from within. Montesquieu never claimed that men could live virtuously for very long; all he maintained was that only when they lived virtuously was their social order a success. This truth was confirmed above all, in Montesquieu's opinion, by the glory of Roman history: "Rome was a vessel held fast by two anchors in the storm: religion and morality" (II, 361; cf. also 114 *seq.*).

It is well known that Montesquieu ascribed a high function to the legislator: such as his work is, so will the society be which he founds and orders and organises. But what is the essence of the legislator's task? Not merely, so we must understand our author, the production of technically satisfactory rules and regulations, but rather the exercise of constant constraint upon men to return ever anew to civic virtue. The very first chapter of book I of the *Esprit des Lois* makes this quite clear. Man as a physical being, as body, is indeed subject to natural necessities, we are told there: but man as a moral being, as mind, by no means so. He can err, he can fail, he can sin. It is for the laws to keep him straight, "A being of this kind could, at every moment, forget his creator; God has called him back to himself by the laws of religion. A being of this kind could, at every moment, forget himself; the philosophers have warned him by the laws of morality. Made to live in society, he could [even] in social life forget his neighbours; the legislators have returned him to his duties by their political and civil enactments" (II, 234).

Of course, virtue is not something that Montesquieu wishes to see understood in a strictly ascetic vein. Human nature cannot be turned inside out; it can only be disciplined and ordered. "It is in vain that an austere ethic would [undertake to] efface the features which the greatest of all workmen has impressed on our souls. It is the task of morality, which has to work on man's heart, to regulate his sentiments, and not to destroy them" (I, 993). "To command a being that is ever sensitive not to have sentiments; to wish to banish the passions without allowing that they be rectified; to propose perfection to a century which becomes worse every day; to revolt against weakness amid so much wickedness: I greatly fear that a morality so high would become [purely] speculative and, by showing us so distant a picture of what we ought to be, would leave us what we are" (I, 998). Nevertheless, the compass of morality must always be set in the same direction, even if it would be unreasonable to expect that its most distant goal can ever be reached. "A good citizen will never think of making his private fortune by any other way than by the same methods which also make [for] public felicity. He will consider him who acts differently, as a mean scoundrel who, having a faked key to a common cash-box, filches a part of its contents . . ." (I, 1144). Nor can there be anybody on whom the precepts of ethics cannot be binding. "Heaven has distributed among men different talents and has thereby prescribed to everybody the limitations beyond which he cannot pass; but it has given us an equal right to virtue. We can all acquire it; for virtue is necessary to us, and talents are only useful" (I, 1012). Hence virtue is for Montesquieu the true destiny of man. "If the gods had put me on this earth merely to lead a voluptuous life there, I believe that they would have given me in vain a great and immortal soul. To enjoy the pleasures of the senses is a thing of which all men are easily capable; and if the gods had made us only for that, they would have created a work more perfect than they had intended, and achieved more than they had undertaken" (II, 1237 *seq.*). Indeed, the destiny of man is not simply virtue, but virtue in perfection, however much this may remain unobtained and unobtainable in practice. "Nothing is nearer divine Providence than that general benevolence and that great capacity of loving which embraces all men, and nothing comes nearer to the instinct of the beasts than those limits which the heart imposes upon itself when it is touched by nothing but its own interest or what happens to be near" (I, 1285). These words, read in the twentieth century, have an almost Bergsonian flavour.

The social order, then, must be carried by a moral effort. Now, this is all the more necessary as man is by nature neither social nor a-social, neither gregarious nor solitary. This is one of the points where we can see how great a social philosopher the Baron de Montesquieu really was. The starting-point of his social theory is impeccably sound. He falls neither for the exaggerations of a Hobbes nor for those of a Rousseau; he believes neither in a *homo ferox* nor in a *homo quasi-angelicus*. Man, as he comes from the hands of nature, is poised between contradictory possibilities: a slight push may drive him into the one direction, towards a social culture, or into another, towards an animalistic existence. The clearest passage exposing this opinion is perhaps the following: "I assume that a savage, who has never lived anywhere but in the woods, meets for the first time in his life another man of the same species, and that neither the one nor the other is in a position to flee. Chance, based on the smallest gesture, on demeanour, will [then] determine whether the two men will try to destroy each other or to give each other help. Likewise, the least circumstance will make a people anthropophagous or give it mores" (I, 1419). Primitive man, properly so called, was engaged in a life and death struggle with nature; for this reason alone he did not think of attacking other men (I, 1350 *seq.*). Granting Hobbes that man will always be ready to defend himself against other men, it does not follow that he will necessarily be aggressive towards them. The matter is, at the very least, open.

Seeing man in this way poised, in principle, between sociality and a-sociality, Montesquieu is yet aware that, in practice, the path of association seems always to have been chosen, and he prepares to account for this development. First of all, sex brings human beings together; but sex creates the family which is a form of togetherness in which true sociality can spring up.[1] And then, a solitary life is boring; association means stimulation, spice, enjoyment, "The *ennui* of

---

[1] At first the *patria potestas* will keep a clan of children together. But the father's ageing and death will not necessarily be the end of the social bond among his offspring, as a conventional tie will easily and spontaneously replace the original natural coherence due to the common dependence on the progenitor and bread-winner. Cf. I, 1140 *seq.* and 1466 *seq.* It deserves to be noted that the social order in its developed state is seen here as due to custom and convention, and not to natural tendencies which preside only over its inception.

being alone and the pleasure which all animals feel at the approach of an animal of the same species will induce men to unite themselves . . ." (I, 1140 *seq.*; cf. also I, 269, and II, 235 *seq.*). The latter part of this sentence smacks somewhat of the theory, later elaborated e.g. by Trotter, of inborn gregariousness. It is hardly meant that way, as the first part of the statement can show. But there is no reason to deny that, in Montesquieu's social theory, the scales of human fate swinging uncertainly between solitary and social existence, are yet slightly weighted in favour of sociality. This opinion makes his social philosophy all the more sober and realistic. And it is by no means opposed to his general doctrine of man, to his concept of man as more than animal. What distinguishes Montesquieu from Rousseau, and even more from people like Trotter, is the fact that for him the sociableness of human beings is not an instinct or a quasi-instinct, not a psycho-somatic feature; it is something peculiar to, and distinctive of, man *qua* man. "The beasts," says a passage prepared for *De l'Esprit des Lois*, but not finally included, "who have all separate interests, always harm each other. Men, alone, made to live in society, lose nothing of what they share" (II, 1094). But we see best how far Montesquieu was from all instinct-of-the-herd theory à la Trotter when we consider that it is in his view precisely the social state, precisely the experience of living in a society, which stimulates men's latent anti-social urges and tendencies. Hobbes was not so wrong when he assumed that *homo homini est lupus*; but the state of social war is not characteristic of pre-social existence; it only develops when men are already associated. It is then that they lose their natural sentiment of weakness and its inherent fears and become bold and aggressive; it is then that the individuals as well as the nations begin to measure their means and compare their talents and try to get the better of each other. It is then that individual rivalries, class struggles and international conflicts break out. The desire to dominate is characteristic of the maturity of man, and not of his childhood (II, 236; I, 1140).

It can be seen from all this that Montesquieu's more positive theory of society leads to the same practical end result as his more normative demand for the fostering of civic virtue. "A society", he says, "cannot survive without government".

Government, and the legislation it enacts and implements, is both a call to social integration and a container of socially desintegrative tendencies. Thus a theory of social control is absolutely central to all Montesquieu's sociological thinking. But not only to his general social theory, to his social analysis in the wider sense of the word; it is basic also to his more special and specific sociology of knowledge. Such as the pattern of public order is in a country, such will be its total life, and hence also its mental life: this is one of the root conceptions established in the very subsoil of Montesquieu's mind, and so without a searching study of his theory of social control, the investigation of his doctrine concerning the genesis of ideas would simply remain suspended in mid-air.

Montesquieu is known, and rightly, as a great lover of liberty. But it is characteristic how he defines the concept of liberty. It is, he says, "the right to do all that the laws permit" (II, 395). And he always holds fast to this definition which firmly connects freedom with order and discipline. "It is necessary to be constrained," he writes in one connection. "Man is like a spring which works the better the more it is repressed" (I, 548). The laws ought certainly to be always merciful, but they must never be allowed to become ineffective (II, 331 *seq.*): punishment should be moderate, but the evil-doer should never go scot-free (II, 320 *seq.*).

As for the institutional side of social control, Montesquieu distinguishes substantially three main agencies—mores, law in the proper or narrower sense of the word, and religion. This distinction is theoretically sound and justified; in practice all three influences intermix and work together. The weaker one of them is, the stronger must be either one or both of the others: the total effect of disciplining the members of society must always be achieved. "The less a religion is repressive, the more it is necessary that the civil law should be severe: as the Shinto religion has almost no dogma nor hell, the laws had to make up for these [omissions]. There is indeed no country where the laws are so strict as in Japan, nor so promptly executed" (I, 1472; cf. also II, 724 *seq.*). On the other hand, where the laws are seriously weakened, religion and mores must fill the threatening gap. This is the case "in despotic states where there are no fundamental laws . . . It is due to this that in these countries religion has ordinarily so much strength: it is because she forms a kind of resource and [anchor of] permanence; and if it is not religion, then it is custom that is being revered in lieu of the laws" (II, 249). Indeed, were mores and manners to be shaken in a despotic country, a revolution would be the result. But, Montesquieu implies, this is not too likely to happen, since social life itself will strengthen these elements in the system of social control where the others are less effective: a fine observation of deep sociological significance. "In the countries where everyone, both as superior and as inferior, exercises and suffers arbitrary power, there is less openness in social intercourse than in those where freedom rules among all conditions of men. Hence manners and mores are less [readily] changed. Manners, more fixed as they are, come nearer to [being] laws" (II, 563). Where manners, mores, laws and religion are "the same thing" (as in China), there the social order gains extraordinary coherence: this is the reason why in China the victorious invader had always to adjust himself to the militarily vanquished sitting population and not the other way round (II, 568). From this it also follows that a society's system of social control should always, if possible, be well co-ordinated: this co-ordination is particularly essential, and comparatively easy to achieve, in the narrow field of law—a subject dealt with in a more practical spirit in book XXVI of the *Esprit des Lois*.

M. Dedieu has justly emphasised that Montesquieu, in his discussion of the mores, has come very near indeed to the position taken up by Plato.[1] Granted that both positive enactments and freely grown and educationally inculcated manners can ensure social peace and co-ordination, the latter method and means of social control is preferable as far as it will go, because it works spontaneously and from within man, through habit, reason and conscience: the laws are imposed, Montesquieu says, whereas the mores are inspired (II, 563); and inasmuch as that is so, "the mores contribute still more to the happiness of a nation than the laws" (I, 1431). But Montesquieu is clearly unwilling to make the dividing line between mores and the law too sharp: on the one hand, even the rules of politeness and civility are "a sort of unwritten legal code"; on the other, the laws of a nation are also its customs, and that is

[1] *Montesquieu*, 1913, 42 *seq.*

why they are loved (I, 1145 and 1460. Cf. also II, 385, and 564 *seq.*). Nor is there much difference as to their binding character between mores and enactments: "the mores rule as imperatively as the laws" (II, 193). Sometimes they rule even more imperiously, for "when the mores and the genius of a nation have become fixed to a certain extent, a revolution is needed to change them, and not laws" (I, 1071). However, they are less effective, comparatively speaking, in large scale societies than in small ones such as the Greek city state. Because the mores are inculcated into rising generations by example and education, they operate best "where it is possible to give a general training [to all citizens alike] and to bring up a [whole] people like a family". Montesquieu shows at this point real sociological penetration. Analysing the influence of the mores further, he sees that their relative strength in small societies and their relative weakness in large ones is due to a difference in the working of the social pressures behind them. Only when the citizens constantly supervise and check each other, will a social order based predominantly on custom be really effective. This cannot be expected among the confusion, superficiality and manifoldness of social relationships such as are characteristic of a large nation (II, 270).

A large nation, then, will have to rely mainly on law for the ordering of its communal life. Now, the law is different from the mores in that it is legislation, the will of the legislator rather than that of the community, something made rather than something grown. It is different also because the sanction behind it—the strong hand of the ruler—is more in evidence and more to be apprehended. Indeed, it is necessary to some extent that the law be feared (II, 752). If this accounts for the strength of the laws, their weakness lies in the fact that they can only control external acts and never attain internal thoughts or motives. The legislator must remember this; and he must also remember that only the socially important sector of conduct need and, indeed, should be legally controlled. A legal code going beyond what is reasonable and necessary in this respect, and a system of sanctions inflicting inhumanly cruel punishments, would only thwart its own work by causing resistances and ultimately revolt and revolution. "What I am saying is— and it seems to me that I have written this book [*De l'Esprit des*

Lois] only in order to prove it—that the spirit of the legislator ought to be the spirit of moderation" (II, 865; cf. also 320 *seq.*). The lawgiver ought to bark rather than to bite. " 'God lets the thunder roll,' says Seneca, *'paucorum periculo et multorum metu'*. The legislator ought to do the same thing in the institution of penalties" (I, 1472). But Montesquieu means by moderation not only mildness and self-restriction on the part of the law-giver; he also means—and that is sociologically more interesting —that he should, when formulating his laws, aim at normal man, at average man as it were, at the man who is half-way between human perfection and moral corruption, at typical man who constitutes the bulk as well as the core of the society for which he is to legislate. "Solon was asked if the laws which he had given the Athenians were the best: 'I have given them', he answered, 'the best of those which they could bear' " (II, 571). The legislator ought to bear in mind the limitations of human nature which are nowhere more stringent than in moral conduct, and only if he does so can legislation be realistic as well as effective, especially in a mass society.

The law appears in this way to Montesquieu in a somewhat more sombre light than mores and religion. It is in its very nature a repressor of evil rather than a creator of good. He notes that the code grows as soon as the land is divided up, hence as soon as private property and with it private selfishness have got a foothold; among people who are still "tenants in common", it is the mores rather than the laws which are the prime and decisive institution (II, 538). The same basic conception is behind the following passage: "The simple nations, and those who devote themselves [personally] to labour, have usually more kindness for their slaves than those who have given up labouring. The first Romans lived, worked and ate with their slaves; they treated them with consideration and justice . . . The mores sufficed for maintaining the fidelity of the slaves; laws were not needed. But when the Romans had aggrandised themselves so that their slaves were no longer the companions of their labour but rather the instruments of their luxury and of their pride; as there were then no mores, laws were necessary" (II, 502). If we remember the general attitude of Montesquieu towards the whole institution of slavery, especially inhuman slavery, his contempt of the slave-holder and his sympathy for the slave, and his sadness at the fact that human nature should allow the existence of such an arrangement, we understand that this passage contains in its depth almost a moral condemnation of "the law". The law—positive law—has about it something of a necessary evil. This, of course, makes the office of the legislator not one whit less exalted, perhaps the opposite. But it explains why Montesquieu could write, in his *General Maxims of Politics*: "One should never do by means of laws what one can do by means of mores" (I, 1150).

In contrast to the law, religion, the third link in the chain of social control, aims more at creating good than at forestalling evil. It is more concerned with the individual than with the masses—a fact not unconnected with its higher ambitions and aspirations. It also tends to penetrate more deeply, in favourable cases right into the heart, whereas the law remains superficial in that its action is restricted to the control of external behaviour. "The laws of perfection, drawn from religion, have for their object more the goodness of the man who observes them than that of the society in which they are observed: the civil laws on the other hand have for their object more the moral goodness of men in general than that of individuals" (II, 759; cf. also 720, 723 and 1318 *seq.*). In putting forward these ideas, Montesquieu shows himself both as the heir of an old tradition and the forebear of a new. He repeats the Christian distinction between council of perfection and general precept;[1] and he anticipates much of what sociologists like, e.g., E. A. Ross, had to teach later on. There is only one point which he presses, in this context, more than anyone else: the fact that religion, where it is alive, is a limit even to the power of those whose power is unlimited: the tyrant, the despot, the dictator. "There is one thing which one can sometimes oppose to the will of the prince: it is religion. A man will abandon his father and even kill him if the prince commands it: but he will not drink wine [even] if he wishes and commands it. The laws of religion are of a higher power because they are given over the head of the prince as over that of the subjects" (II, 260). Here again we must remember, in order to appreciate the bearing of these

[1] Cf. II, 719: "The human laws, made in order to speak to the mind, should give precepts and not counsels; religion, made in order to speak to the heart, should give many counsels and few precepts."

words, the basic opinions of our philosopher: his love of liberty; his hatred of absolutism; his deep conviction that no man should ever be allowed to give free rein to all his desires and inborn drives.

Looking at his tripartite theory of social control as a whole, we find as its theoretical core the thesis that the social order rests in the last analysis on social pressure—on those pressures towards law-abidingness which associated men in their mutuality are for ever exercising upon each other. There are only a few passages in which this fundamental persuasion comes out quite clearly, but there is at any rate one which leaves little to be desired in clarity. "Aristotle says that vengeance is a just thing founded on the principle that one must render to everyone what is his due. And this is the only method which Nature has given us to arrest the evil inclination of our neighbours; this is the only coercing power which we have in the state of nature; everyone has under it a magistrature which he exercises by means of vengeance. Hence Aristotle would have reasoned correctly if he had not spoken of the civil state in which ... [certain] people have been established [in power] who have taken over [as it were] all the passions of the others and exercise their rights in coolness ... When the Christian religion forbade the practice of vengeance, what it did was [simply] to support the power of the tribunals" (I, 1471). All this is certainly spoken in the jargon of the age; but the substance of it is a basic sociological conception which had adherents in every age, and always will have—the basic sociological conviction of those who regard the social order as the outgrowth, not of natural and instinctual forces, but of a semi-moral effort of mutual control and civilisation, as a cultural achievement. At the root of all social life is for Montesquieu not a fact, such as a social or gregarious instinct, but a will, the will of the associated individuals to stick and to stay together. "A society cannot be based on anything but the will of those who have associated" (I, 1593; cf. also I, 246). A sentence like this is, of course, reminiscent of the contractual theory which was so widely accepted and entertained at the time; perhaps it was even inspired by it; but Montesquieu saw deeper than the contractualists around him. M. Barckhausen has rightly emphasised that the term *contrat social* is not to be found in the works of Montesquieu.[1] He thought of society as underlaid by a pattern of mutuality, a *do-ut-des* principle, perhaps by a quasi-contract, secured in its permanence by pressures and sanctions. This is sound and respectable sociology, or at any rate one kind of it. From Montesquieu there seem to go some threads, however thin, however invisible, to such authors as Alfred Fouillée, William Graham Sumner, or Georg Simmel.

That the social order was conceived by Montesquieu as a pattern of mutuality, the coherence of which is guaranteed by mutual supervision and mutually coercive sanctions, can also be seen from his idea of good and perfect society. If *do-ut-des* is the basic principle of the common life, then, ideally, there must be a proportion between what I give to others and what others give to me; in other words, there must be justice. "If association is to bind us, it must be just" (I, 272; cf. also I, 256 *seq.*). A good society is simply a just society. A perfect society must go beyond this because justice in and for itself is apt to be cold. But it is interesting to see how Montesquieu derives, in a stray passage, even the image of social perfection from justice, and thus, indirectly, from mutuality. If men know, as they ought, that they will have to pay their fellows in equal coin and may expect to be so paid by them, then it will be expedient and, indeed, right and meet, if they will not wait with their contribution until the others have made theirs; then they will make their return for the services of their neighbours by anticipation as it were; then they will "oblige" as we say, *zuvorkommend sein*, as the Germans have it. "For this purpose we must endeavour to be, with our attentions, ahead of the people with whom we live . . . From this [conduct] there springs in a society that sweetness and ease of manners which renders it happy and brings about that everybody in it lives contented both with himself and with the others" (I, 1144 *seq.*).

The social theory which we have now pieced together from scattered passages was, it must be confessed, more in the background of Montesquieu's mind than in the forefront. And yet he was essentially a social theorist, for all his interest in legal form (an interest natural, and naturally uppermost, in a *Président à Mortier* of the *Parlement de Bordeaux*). Rarely does he

---

[1] *Montesquieu, Ses Idées et ses Oeuvres*, 1907, 28.

speak of legal form without giving us good proof that he sees the social reality that is hidden behind it. Durkheim has pointed out that what Montesquieu calls despotism and what he calls monarchy are, formally, both incarnations of the monarchical principle—not only because in both cases one man is at the helm, but also because even in the monarchies as defined in the *Esprit des Lois* the monarch has the right to modify the laws.[1] What is really different is the social structure: simple under a despotic régime, it is complex under monarchies in the specific sense of the word, in that it shows a multiplicity of ranks and orders and distinctions. Montesquieu's definition of the republican state is equally sociological. He is not satisfied with saying that a republic is a government so constituted as to make the people the sovereign power in the land. He emphasises that behind this formal front there must be certain social arrangements, which fall in with, and underpin, the basic principle of democracy. One possible social basis for a democratic régime is an equal distribution of landed property, as exemplified here and there in antiquity (cf. *Esprit des Lois*, book V, chap. 5). Montesquieu calls this "real equality" the "soul of the state" (II, 278). Another is commerce, what one could call the capitalist spirit. Here republicanism and democracy can co-exist with a large measure of economic inequality because "the spirit of commerce brings with it that of frugality, economy, moderation, labour, prudence, calmness, order and regularity" (II, 280). On the other hand, commerce cannot very well co-exist with political inequality, i.e. with an aristocratic set-up in the state: noblemen, once they descended into the arena of trade, would soon abuse their political privileges and become monopolists, thus throttling free enterprise. "Commerce is the profession of equal men" (II, 286). A fine recognition this, before history herself revealed the truth, of the fact that a formal democracy is the socially appropriate political frame for certain phases in the development of "liberal capitalism". But Montesquieu saw even deeper. He realised that, if democracy is to last, even a *république commerçante* must keep fairly near the principle of economic equality. The accumulation of wealth must be counterbalanced by its constant redistribution, otherwise the political order will be

[1] *Montesquieu et Rousseau*, 1953, 71.

deeply affected and perhaps upset. Montesquieu recommends, by another amazing anticipation, the very remedy which the Code Napoléon was to try later on—the division of inheritances.

But it is not only republican government that needs a broad social basis in order to function and to survive. Even despotism cannot do without it. In principle giving the plenitude of power to one individual, this power is yet in practice dependent on the will of the community. We have here another deep insight of Montesquieu the sociologist. "It is an error to believe," he writes, "that there is in the world a human authority that is despotic in every respect; such a one has never existed and never will exist . . . There is in every nation a general spirit on which power itself is founded; if [despotic] power offends that spirit, it harms itself and necessarily renders itself impotent" (II, 202 *seq.*). Things are not in reality what they seem to be on a purely formal view.[1] We also see this cleft between a formal view of the situation and its real social implications when we consider a state that has fallen into the calamity of a civil war. For the formalist, the lawlessness, the misery, the chaos of a civil war means a weakening of the community; he cannot see how it could possibly be a source of strength. Montesquieu, being more than a formalist, being, in fact, a true sociologist, recognises that, paradoxically, a great social upheaval such as a bloody civil war, brings an accession of strength, especially military strength, to a country. It releases forces which were tied before; in particular, it so liquifies the class structure that able individuals from the lower orders can more freely ascend into leading positions, thus bringing the actual and factual hierarchy more into conformity with the hierarchy of merit—with that hierarchy of merit which, in more quiet times, remains unrecognised and unrecognisable, covered as it is by the inherited, largely ossified class distinctions (II, 129; cf. also I, 1356). Montesquieu gives a string of historical examples in order to prove his point; history has since added many more.

These samples of Montesquieu's sociological analyses are

[1] Cf. also II, 162 where Montesquieu points out that the later Roman empire for all the apparent power of the emperors, was yet in point of fact an aristocracy—indeed, a *république irrégulière*—rather than a one-man rule. The harangues of the emperors to their soldiers were not so very different from the addresses of the consuls and the tribunes to the people in the days of the republic.

adduced here in order to give the reader an idea of the true depth of his penetration. Often hidden beneath surface material, it is yet everywhere in evidence. Perhaps it may be permissible to give yet one more proof of it. His explanation of the origin and of the meaning of the incest-taboo so widely distributed in the world is a masterpiece and anticipates a much later phase of sociological thinking both in method and in outcome. Montesquieu sees clearly that the incest-taboo is not based on a natural or instinctual revulsion from intercourse between father and daughter or brother and sister. There is no such revulsion in nature, prior to social education. After all, unlike sodomy or masturbation, incest is not "against nature". Yet though not natural, the prohibition of sex contacts between near blood relatives is nearly universal. Hence we must seek for a cause of it which roots in the common human condition as it were, in the total human situation such as it will everywhere assert itself, however different different societies may be. Montesquieu finds the key to the problem in a clash of sentiments. The father-daughter relationship is one based on authority, hence on distance; and the further we go back in history, the more do we see the stature of the father increase, until we come to such overpowering father-figures as the Roman *pater familias* who was "progenitor, magistrate, monarch" all in one. But the husband-and-wife relationship is one that demands intimacy and hence abhors distance. Indeed, in it a certain minimum of equality is in the nature of things indispensable. Now, a human relationship cannot be one of distance and nearness at the same time and so a father-daughter marriage becomes in the minds of men something "impossible" —not indeed in the sense of unnatural, but in the sense of disgusting, monstrous, illicit, impious. "How should a daughter have married herself to her father? As daughter, she would have owed him unlimited respect; as wife, there would have been equality between them. These two qualities would have been incompatible" (I, 1463 *seq.*; cf. also fragment 1931 on p. 1465). The clash between these irreconcilable feelings is so strong that the condemnation and taboo arising from it overspills and overflows into the brother-and-sister nexus which is also put under a sexual ban; but this ban is secondary and derived according to Montesquieu, and he hints that it is (for this reason) weaker. This whole theory, however problematic it may be, is not the sort of rationalistic speculation characteristic of the eighteenth century; it is already modern sociology almost in the technical sense of the word.

This excursion into Montesquieu's general sociology was well worth the effort if it has shown how able a social theorist he was. But we must edge nearer to our central subject, his sociology of knowledge, and we can do this best at this juncture by bringing his doctrine of the types of society into the discussion. We have already touched upon this subject when, a few pages above, we showed that his formal or legal distinction between democracy, monarchy and despotism implied a deeper real or social distinction between social democracy, a complex class structure and a state which M. Alengry has called equality in fear,[1] a state, that is, where divisions like those between rich and poor or landowners and capitalists do not seem to matter, but where the dominating trait of social life is the contrast between the power-holding one and his minions on the one hand and the subject many on the other. Here we want to speak of a few further ideas which are even more specifically sociological. Disjointed *aperçus*, they are yet of the highest interest because they foreshadow, however faintly, the distinction later so prominent in sociological thinking between organical and mechanical social coherence. In one fragment Montesquieu points out that landed property and moveable property tend, where they are respectively prevalent, to give rise to different types of society: landed property, where it is the basis of a society, makes that society a closed whole rooted in the soil (a community, as Tönnies would have said later on); moveable property on the other hand, such as "money, notes, bills and shares", tends to establish an international society, a world-order (an associational integration, in Tönnies' terminology; I, 1488). In another context Montesquieu makes another pertinent remark which aims in the same direction, although the distinction is historical there rather than economic. In Rome, many ties connected man and man (community): "today, all [that] is abolished, down to the parental power: each man is isolated" (association; I, 1130). But our author comes nearest to the contrast community-

[1] *Essai Historique et Critique sur la Sociologie chez Auguste Comte*, 1900, 339, footnote.

association, *Gemeinschaft-Gesellschaft*, in a passage of his *Romains*. "What is called union in a body politic, is a very equivocal matter: the true union is a union of harmony which brings it about that all the parts, however much they may appear to us to be opposed to each other, co-operate for the general good of society; as dissonances, in music, combine to form an all-embracing accord." But there may also be societies in which this "true union" is not achieved; in which, on the contrary, "there exists permanently a real division" among men, and co-existence is the side-by-side of "dead" bodies rather than the co-operation of live citizens. It is the curse of "asiatic" despotism that it prevents the formation of the former (organic) type of cohesion in the society over which it is set and keeps it for ever in the latter, lower (purely mechanical) form of integration (II, 119).

If Montesquieu had thus an inkling of the contrast between organical and mechanical social coherence, he also realised that distinctions of this kind are distinctions between clear-cut, artificially constructed types rather than distinctions between actual historical societies. A. Sorel, in his book on Montesquieu[1] has remarked (88), somewhat disdainfully, that the thumb-nail-sketches of monarchy, republic and despotism which the Baron de la Brède presents, remind one of Molière's Miser and Misanthropist: they are *outré*, not so much portraits of real people as caricatures which bring out one set of characteristics only by neglecting others. No doubt he is right; but he is far from understanding that this criticism can be turned in Montesquieu's favour as easily as it can be used to attack him. We have just looked back upon Montesquieu with the eyes of Tönnies; we can do so now with the eyes of Max Weber. It would be an illicit exaggeration to say that M. de la Brède has anticipated Weber's concept of ideal type; he did not theorise about the nature of his generalisations, and that is to some extent a weakness on his part; but in what he does, however semi-consciously, he comes very near to the conceptualisation of complex reality later demanded by the German sociologist. He was very far from believing that all concrete countries or constitutions can be pushed, as it were, into three or four neatly labelled pigeon-holes or drawers: republic is different from

[1] 1887.

republic, monarchy from monarchy, despotism from despotism; sometimes an aristocracy (the fourth type defined by Montesquieu) may be to all intents and purposes a republican, sometimes again a monarchical system; and a despotism may be so mild in its practical operation as to arouse the envy of the citizens of "moderate" governments. Furthermore, reality often intermixes features of these theoretically distinguishable types and forms them into flawless wholes. Indeed, this is even desirable. The "gothic" government which France had in the fourteenth century was as good as any before or since, and it had in itself monarchical, aristocratical and even democratic elements.[1] The same can be said of the English constitution, another political system for which our author had the highest possible admiration. But perhaps we can best see how he thought of his "types" from an incident in his life. Why did he go to Hungary? Because there was forming in his mind the concept of feudalism as exemplified in French history. Over and done with in France, something like it still existed along the Danube's shores. "Something like it": Montesquieu was not so childish as to expect that he would find in the Hungarian *comitats* exactly what had once upon a time flourished in the French *comtés*: what he expected to find, and what he did find, was what M. Dedieu has, with a happy phrase, described as *un reflet de la féodalité française*.[2] But perhaps it would be even better to say that he found, and was conscious of finding, another reflection or incarnation of that ideal typical feudalism of which French feudalism, too, had been, in its individual way, a concrete example, a mirroring, and an embodiment.

Those who have seen in Montesquieu no more than a geographical determinist, have asserted (not altogether without reason) that he distinguishes social types according to the size of the area in which a society may be established. The *locus classicus* is book VIII of *De l'Esprit des Lois*, chapters XVI–XX (II, 362 *seq.*). "It is of the nature of a republic that it has only a small territory." "A monarchical state should be of medium extent". "A large empire presupposes a despotic authority on the part of the man who rules it". Sentences of unmistakeable

---

[1] All this is best seen and understood by Barckhausen. Cf. *loc. cit.* 54 *seq.* and 66 *seq.*

[2] *Montesquieu, L'Homme et l'Oeuvre*, 1943, 65.

import these, but yet sentences which demand careful interpretation out of the totality of Montesquieu's thought. Those
who look more closely will soon see that even here social types
are not classified according to an external principle of specification but according to their own internal characteristics, even
though these are, in the last analysis and by remote reference,
linked to the extraneous fact of geographical extent. In a small
republic, Montesquieu writes, "the public good is better felt,
better known, nearer to each citizen; abuses are less extensive
and consequently less dissembled." "In a great republic," on
the other hand, "there exist great fortunes, and in consequence
little moderation of minds: too great trusts[1] must be placed in
the hands of one citizen; interests fall apart; a man feels at first
that he may be [personally] happy, great, glorious without
[regard to] his fatherland; [but] soon [he begins to see] that he
may achieve solitary greatness on the ruins of his fatherland"
(II, 362). It is moral corruption that will destroy a republic
which, unlike Lacedaemon, widens her territory until it is too
large to admit of that homely neighbourliness, that close social
control of equals by equals, which was the making of Rome at
her best, and which will for ever be the making of flourishing
democracies. It is not the number of square miles that distinguishes social types, but the nature of the social and moral
tone that prevails in them. We can see that this is Montesquieu's
true opinion equally clearly when we read what he says about
the appropriate size of a (constitutional or limited) monarchy
in comparison with a despotic government. If a monarchy is
too large, the king at the centre will be unable to control the
counts palatine at the periphery; there will be not one court,
but many; not one nodal point of power, but many; and hence
coherence will be constantly in jeopardy. But again, it is the
human element that is decisive, not the bare fact of physical
distance, important though that obviously is. Montesquieu
implies that if and as long as a king finds paladins that are truly
faithful to him, the ideal monarchy may and will subsist, the
number of leagues between capital and frontier notwithstanding; just as the classical republic could and would survive
in spite of an undue widening of her area, if only the human
relationships characteristic of the small neighbourhood unit

"*depôts*".

could be preserved and adjusted to the new conditions without losing their essential human content.[1] This cannot, normally, be expected, and that is why the lover of democracy should strive to keep her geographically small, and why the upholder of monarchy should see to it that she does not outgrow medium size. But the essential consideration is always social control, the problem of social coherence. If Montesquieu asserts that a "State will change in spirit in the measure in which its frontiers are narrowed or widened" (II, 365), he does not mean to propose a direct geographical determinism, but only to elaborate his theory of social control and social coherence. This result of our study of Montesquieu's ideas concerning the types of social life should not pass from our mind as we approach the core of his sociology of knowledge.

[1] That geographical size and physical distance are not, to Montesquieu, ultimate determinants can also be gathered from the fact that he was well aware that both are relative to the means of communication which, in turn, depend upon human inventiveness, ingenuity and power of organisation. In two fragments he emphasises that the introduction of the postal system has deeply influenced, nay in a manner created, *"la politique, telle qu'elle est aujourd'hui"* (I, 1421).

VI

MONTESQUIEU'S FINAL SOCIOLOGY OF KNOWLEDGE : PRELIMINARY OBSERVATIONS

THIS sociology of knowledge is rooted, in the case of Montesquieu (as it indeed always is and must be), in the double conviction that all cultural phenomena in one and the same society are closely akin, and that all cultural phenomena in one society are also akin to the non-cultural, sub-cultural phenomena characteristic of that same society. Durkheim has rightly emphasised that the realisation of the oneness of all elements of a social system, of its integral character, is basic to all Montesquieu's thought.[1] But it is, once again, a realisation which, however fundamental and ubiquitous it may be, is seen behind his texts rather than in them, in action and application rather than in pure theoretical formulation. It comes out, for instance, in one of Montesquieu's *bon mots* which he noted down, with obvious pride, in his *Pensées*. "I said: Rameau is Corneille, and Lulli, Racine" (I, 1258). "Often a particular taste is an indication of a general taste: the Muses are sisters, touch each other and live in company" (I, 1234). "All is extremely mixed in the world. The individual wickednesses in a state where the basic order[2] is sound, are always affected to some extent by the public virtue and the virtues which one sees in a corrupt republic are in the same way infected by its corruption" (II, 214; cf. also 357 and 359). Sometimes Montesquieu formulates this idea in a way which is not too different from later formulations. In one fragment, for instance, he notes that in his own century, martial glory and vainglory seem somehow out of place; and he moves on, from

[1] *Montesquieu et Rousseau*, French translation, 1953, 103.
[2] *"l'institution"*.

this statement, to a semi-theoretical consideration. "Each century has its own particular genius: a spirit of disorder and independence grew up in Europe with the gothic form of government; the monastic spirit infected the time of Charlemagne's successors; thereafter reigned the spirit of chivalry; with standing armies appeared that of conquest; and it is the spirit of commerce which rules today. This spirit of commerce makes everything subject to calculation. But glory, taken for itself, enters into nobody's calculations but those of fools" (I, 130 *seq.*).

In the *Esprit des Lois* the same conviction of the unity of cultural life makes its appearance in a somewhat different shape. "There are principal laws and accessory laws," a preliminary note runs, "and there arises, in each country, a kind of generation of laws. The nations, like each individual, have a succession of ideas, and their total way of thinking, like that of each private person, has a beginning, a middle, and an end" (II, 1102). All the laws and enactments in a state flow from its fundamental principle: they draw their vitality from it and, in their turn, by a sort of reaction, impart vitality to it (II, 273). But the laws are not, by any means, alone in this dependence upon the constitutive principle at the root of the community. It can also be traced in sundry other aspects of social life, some central, others more peripheral. To the former belongs education. As the "laws of education . . . prepare us for the role of citizen, each particular family should be governed on the plan of the great family which comprises them all. If a people in general possesses a principle, the parties who comprise it, that is to say the families, will have it also. Hence the laws of education will be different in each kind of government. In monarchies, they will have honour for their object; in republics, virtue; in despotic countries, fear" (II, 261 *seq.*). Perhaps less central to the social order, but certainly no less dependent on its fundamental principle, is the regimen to which women are subjected. "The change in the mores of the women will, without a doubt, have great influence on the government of Muscovy. All is extremely interconnected: the despotism of the prince is naturally united with the servitude of women; the freedom of women, with the spirit of monarchy." "At all times in Asia domestic servitude and despotic government have been seen marching in step . . . In a republic," on the other hand, "all reflects public liberty. A strict control over women could not so well be exercised" there (II, 565 and 514 *seq.*).

A third facet of Montesquieu's mind which also shows up his conviction that all contemporary and contiguous social phenomena are vitally connected, is his conservatism. If he is so doggedly conservative, this is not least due to the opinion that every change, however minor in itself, will reverberate through the whole socio-political organism and force adjustments even in its most distant parts—adjustments whose end result nobody can foretell and which might, conceivably, be disastrous. "It is with a government as with a number composed of several figures. Take away or add a single figure and you change the value of all the others. But as one knows in arithmetic the value of each figure and its place, one is not deceived. It is not the same in politics: one can never know what will be the result of the change which one has made" (I, 1461). "A State which, with one stroke, increases its strength is subject to all the inconveniences of a change of fortune which demands an infinity of other changes; these different new changes demand new principles. But as wisdom is the adherence to principles which experience has successfully applied, it is more difficult for a State which increases its fortune rapidly to conduct itself with wisdom, than for a State which augments its fortune by insensible increments" (I, 1508).

This all-connectedness of cultural phenomena, and consequently of mind-contents, is by no means incompatible with a very real mental independence on the part of individuals, because the relation between collective and individual thought is that between theme and variation. Montesquieu saw that, too. "Our thoughts all revolve around the ideas which are common to us," he writes in a brief note. "Yet, by their circumstances, their turn, and their particular application, they may have something original, even to infinity, just like faces" (II, 1281 *seq.*). This is indeed a happy phrase. There may be a study of individual physiognomies; and there may also be a discipline of the human countenance as such, of which individual features and faces are variations. The latter is a social science—and this social science, dropping the metaphor, is, in the realm of ideas, the sociology of knowledge.

Many observers, if not indeed all, have found in Montesquieu a persistent preoccupation with the exceptional and the monstrous, with the *cas tératologiques* as the French usually say. This preoccupation, which was one of the motives and motors that propelled his mind towards the elaboration of a sociology of knowledge, was in the last analysis due to the conviction just emphasised, that even the exceptional, the puzzling, the outrageous is part and parcel of the culture-complex within which it occurs and hence, in principle, understandable in terms of it. "What is real, that is reasonable," Hegel was to preach later on; Montesquieu had this feeling a hundred years earlier. What is real must have a sufficient reason that will explain it. This reason lies according to Montesquieu's way of thinking, in the *ratio rei publicae* rather than in the *ratio* of the individual. As Durkheim has happily summed up his opinion: laws "arise, according to him, not from the nature of man, but from that of society."[1] This is the salient point at which, as with seven-league-boots, he steps beyond Cartesianism and the whole Cartesian and rationalist century. If society is a whole, then the individual himself is to be interpreted as part and parcel of it; then concrete society and not abstract reason gives the key to the understanding of mental structures. Those before him had always seen the timeless individual apart from society, and ideas as his proper product; Montesquieu began to see the time-bound individual *in* society, and his ideas as special variations of a general theme. To grasp the meaning of any law, and indeed any idea, out of the concrete situation from which it had sprung was one of his overruling ambitions, perhaps the controlling ambition of his life. "The laws" he writes, "may have an origin . . .[2] which one ought to know. How can one apply a law if one does not know the country for which is has been made, and the circumstances in which it has been made? Most of those who study the science of jurisprudence follow the course of the Nile, overflow with it, but do not know its source" (II, 1076). What is really needed is a genetic approach, a theory of the social genesis of legal ideas, and of ideas in general. "I should prefer to teach [my readers] to consider the laws in their origin, than to write a book on the origin of the laws" (II, 1116).

[1] *Montesquieu et Rousseau*, French translation. 1953, 50.
[2] ". . . *une origine de conformité* . . ."

But if Montesquieu had searched only for the explanation of strange and outlandish phenomena, phenomena that shock our minds, he would not have been the great social philosopher which we see him as. M. Caillois has rightly said[1] that he brought about a *révolution sociologique*, and this revolution consisted in the radical turn-about of thought—so indispensable a preliminary to all true social analysis—after which we manage to see our own society, that is to say, social phenomena to which we are fully adjusted and which we take for granted like day and night, with new eyes, with the eyes of wondering and surprised outsiders. In this connection even the naughty work of the master's frivolous youth, the *Lettres Persanes*, has its important and honourable place. Usbek, Rhédi and Rica are, after all, the Monsieur de la Brède himself who, by dint of the sociological revolution in his mind, has learned to see many familiar and contemporary customs as *cas tératologiques*. Although he had not, in 1721, been on a long journey, he could truly say of himself what he makes Rhédi say to Usbek: "I am stepping out of the clouds which covered my eyes in the land of my birth" (I, 177).

Montesquieu was very much aware of the great mental and moral difficulty involved in a sociological study of one's own society and its customs and ideologies—more aware than many later sociologists. As soon as Usbek is out of Persia, he develops doubts concerning the sacred traditions in which he had been brought up. He lays them before the Mollak Mehemet-Hali, but Mehemet-Hali's answer (letter XVIII) is nothing but a tissue of the most crying absurdities. What Montesquieu here finely intimates is this, that in Persia these absurdities are not absurdities but convincing arguments, indeed "truths", whose weaknesses are not recognisable by those who have continually lived in their atmosphere. It is the same Usbek who doubts out of Persia who believed in Persia. But the Persians only free themselves of their original prejudices in order to fall into new ones. The longer they are in Europe, the less odd do the mores of Europe appear to them (I, 129, 222). It seems that we are for ever condemned to be slaves to some particular point of view (unless indeed we have achieved the "sociological revolution"). "It seems to me, Usbek," Rica writes to his friend,

[1] *Oeuvres Complètes*, I, 1949, V.

"that we never judge of things any otherwise than by a secret reference to ourselves. I am not surprised that the Negroes paint the Devil in shining white colour and their Gods as black as coal; that the Venus of certain nations has breasts which hang down to her very thighs; and, in short, that all idol-worshippers have represented their Gods under a human form and have made them partake in all their inclinations. It has been well said that if the triangles made themselves a God, they would give him three sides" (I, 217 *seq.*).

With such ideas, Montesquieu is already moving in an atmosphere which is apt to condense itself into a proper theoretical sociology of knowledge. Letter LXXXIX is the first definite step in the direction of such a theoretical formulation. All men desire esteem, reputation, glory: this desire grows out of, or rather is identical with, the instinct of self-preservation. But though this instinct and its concomitant drives are everywhere in evidence, they do not always show themselves in the same shapes. A good deal will depend on the general tenor of life, which in its turn is vitally connected with the nature of the political set-up. The greater freedom, the keener will be the desire of glory: the weaker freedom, the less ardent the desire of glory: where servitude exists, glory will not be found. In France, where men are free, they have developed *honour* as their main principle of action. It is regard for honour that makes them conduct themselves as a good citizen should, it is regard for honour which induces them even to go to war and to sacrifice their lives. Among the slaves of a despot, no such sentiment of honour can possibly be found. The slave will fulfil his duties only under the pressure of the knout. *Fear* will be the social bond in a despotic state, not honour. Esteem grows slowly because it is a collective judgment; but under despotism it is the caprice of the ruler that decides, and it is today this, tomorrow that. "A man who has gained public esteem, is never sure of not being dishonoured tomorrow: today he is the general of an army; perhaps the Prince will [presently] make him his cook, and leave him no other hope of praise than that of having made a good ragout" (I, 265).

Anybody who knows the *Esprit des Lois* will recognise in this early *Lettre Persane* the first sketch of Montesquieu's later theory concerning the social genesis of ideas. As yet he distinguishes only two types of social action and social thoughts: freedom and despotism are neatly confronted as two contrasting roots of two contrasting moral and mental structures. Letter LXXXIX expressly says that honour may flourish in republics like Rome, Athens and Sparta, as well as in monarchies like France. In later years this dichotomous division is replaced by a tripartite one: honour is split into honour properly so called (which is characteristic of monarchies) and civic virtue (characteristic of republics). This is an important refinement, though only a refinement. In a sense, the confrontation of free constitutions and despotic ones remains basic to Montesquieu's thought: the former are desirable types, the latter despicable. As can be seen the specific sociology of knowledge of our author reaches back into his earliest years.[1]

But not only the clear kernel of Montesquieu's maturer sociology of knowledge is traceable in the *Lettres Persanes*, the main difficulty that, as we shall see, besets it, is also present already in this early work. The influence of the political constitution on the mental culture of a country, which we have just studied in letter LXXXIX, Montesquieu called the moral factor; unfortunately he acknowledged a physical factor as well, without knowing how to co-ordinate the two, and this physical factor likewise makes its appearance, along with the moral, in the epistles of Usbek, Rhédi, Rica and company. Both crop up together in the discussion of a very special, almost marginal problem: the supposed depopulation of Europe. "Independently of its physical causes, there are moral causes which have produced this effect", Montesquieu writes in letter CXIII (I, 299) and thereby raises a difficulty which was destined to dog his steps for many a year—the problem of the relationship between the two types of causal factor. For the rest, neither the physical causes nor the moral ones are here studied with any profundity. To the former belong such things as pests and diseases, to the latter such things as polygamy, the

[1] Another striking formulation of a persistent idea of Montesquieu's occurs at the end of letter XCIX: "It is with manners and the mode of living as with fashions; the French change their mores according to the period of their king. The Monarch could even manage to make the Nation grave, if he should undertake to do so. The Prince impresses the character of his spirit on the Court; the Court on Town; the Town on the provinces. The soul of the Sovereign is a mould which gives its form to all the others" (I, 278).

indissolubility of the marriage bond, and celibacy. Religious conceptions are also seen as important. But as the most important cause emerges even here, even in spite of the acknowledgement of a purely physical element in the complex of causes, the political constitution, the nature of the state. Under a free government, the population is always buoyant; under a despotic one, sluggish and dwindling. Freedom is life, slavery death. It deserves to be noted that already in the *Lettres Persanes*—as in more mature discussions afterwards—the moral factor is regarded as the ultimately decisive one. Montesquieu does not, indeed, say so directly in 1721: this was reserved for later, for the *Essai sur les Causes qui peuvent affecter les Esprits et les Caractères*. But the most vital of all decisions which Montesquieu had to make in his efforts to build up a closed and consistent sociology of knowledge, is already implicit in the first paragraph of *Lettre Persane* number CXXII: "The mildness of government contributes marvellously to the propagation of the Species. All the republics are a constant proof of this, and, more than all [others], Switzerland and Holland, which are the two worst countries of Europe, if one considers [them from the point of view of] the nature of the territory, and which are yet the most populous ones" (I, 313). The political factor here triumphs over the geographical, the moral element over the physical.

As will emerge later on, these passages of the *Lettres Persanes* are, to a considerable extent, a striking anticipation of the sociology of knowledge of the older Montesquieu. Yet, as a whole, the *Lettres Persanes* are still immature, still too far removed from the basic attitude essential to any and every sociology of knowledge, to count as more than just an anticipation. This becomes quite clear when one considers the picture of Usbek's wives—Roxane, Zachi, Zélis—as it is sketched by Montesquieu's pen. These ladies are not seen as Persians, as Orientals; they are much rather little *Parisiennes* who happen to find themselves in an eastern seraglio, and have all the spirit and the foibles of Frenchwomen, of Europeans. Montesquieu himself was to criticise this shallowness later on when, in his last years, he noted: "To judge of the beauties of Homer, one must place oneself in the camp of the Greeks not in a French army" (I, 1023). But this was said by the aged author of the posthumously published *Essai sur le Goût* of 1756/7, not by the young author of the *Lettres Persanes* of 1721. In 1721, M. de la Brède had not yet begun to look beyond the confines of his native France.

It was his grand tour which gave to his sociology of knowledge depth and provided it with that basis in experience without which it would have for ever remained shallow and pale. We have already noted his ability to enter deeply into the life of the foreign societies which he visited. "When I travelled in other countries," he says in an autobiographical fragment, "I attached myself to them as to my own: I took part in their vicissitudes and wished that they were in a flourishing state" (I, 976). This was no empty boast. Montesquieu truly understood, once living experience had opened his eyes, what he himself habitually described as the *"différence des esprits"*. "An Englishman, a Frenchman, an Italian: three minds," he noted (I, 1327). And he learned to see that human conduct was altogether different in the one culture area from what it was in another. "Had I been born in England, I should have been inconsolable for not making money. I am not at all grieved at not having done so [here] in France" (I, 984). His best observations were made in Holland and in England: then two countries were to him a laboratory, so to speak, in which his theory of ideas was matured. Let us admit, as we must, that his remarks on the Netherlanders which follow show his prejudices—the aristocratic prejudices of a nobleman of the *ancien régime*. Nevertheless, they recognise and reflect the drift at any rate of a commercialised culture. "In commercial towns, like ... those of Holland, the general habit is to put a price on every-thing; all actions are for hire; moral virtues are an object of traffic; and the things which are demanded by humanity are sold for money" (I, 1288 *seq.*; cf. also 1338). He found a similar spirit in Britain, but yet was keen-sighted enough to realise that it was not quite the same: "The English are calculators; this is because there are among them two extremes who envelop the middle: the merchants and the philosophers" (I, 1292 *seq.*). Also, the influence of the women, so prominent in France, is absent there. Yet, though the English are calculators and respect wealth, they also respect personal merit where it does not transpose itself into wealth. "If I were to be asked what prejudices they have, I would, truth to tell, be at a loss what to say: neither war, nor birth, nor dignity, nor the men who have succeeded in life nor a mad preoccupation with ministerial favour. They wish men to be men" (I, 1334). The Duke of Marlborough, the Duke of Argyle and Lord Cobham have made their mark simply because they were strong personalities. Has Montesquieu not, with these observations, come fairly close to a sound understanding of British individualism, one of the hallmarks of classical British society? However that may be, his travels also changed his attitude to, and understanding of, history; they taught him, by a kind of reflex action, to appreciate the *différence des esprits* between age and age in the same way in which they taught him to see it between country and country. Men always have been vain, just as they are vain everywhere, and yet the vanity of one century is not that of another. "There are astonishing examples of Roman vanity. Nothing could be so ridiculous as Trebonius, who writes to Cicero that, if he should give some account of Caesar's assassination, he hopes he will not have the least place in it. Nothing is so ridiculous as Cicero himself, who asks that he be put into Roman history, and even that one should lie for his sake. That vanity was entirely different from the vanity which some nations have today. The latter concerns only the present moment; the former was always bound up with the idea of posterity. A stylish dress for a certain day suffices for the one; a name engraved on a stone was necessary to flatter the other. These things are the effect of the education of that century and of ours, and hang together with the institutions of the two peoples" (I, 1328). It is interesting to see how in this last passage observation and penetration press forward, by their own impetus, towards an appropriate theory which would explain the phenomena concerned.

This theory Montesquieu endeavoured to provide in the *Essai sur les Causes qui peuvent affecter les Esprits et les Caractères*, a project which, characteristically, he took up and tried to tackle as soon as he returned home from his sojourn abroad. As far as we can tell, it was drafted in or around 1732. Unfortunately it was never finished and lacks, in the form in which we have it, the balance and the polish of Montesquieu's other works. But it is, for all its shortcomings, an invaluable source for the understanding of the master's sociology of knowledge and even for the correct appreciation of his *magnum opus* of the Spirit of Laws, of which it constitutes one of the most essential, indeed, perhaps the most essential preparation. It will, together with the appropriate sections of the larger work, provide the basis for the systematic exposition of Montesquieu's theory of the genesis of ideas which is now to follow.

There remains only one preliminary question to be cleared away before this systematic exposition is at long last attempted. Was the mature Montesquieu's sociology of knowledge of the "debunking" or of the "preserving" type? The *Lettres Persanes*, needless to say, belonged, like the *Dissertation sur la Politique des Romains dans la Religion*, still to the destructive category.[1] In letter C Rica-Montesquieu uses his knowledge of the history of French law only in order to show that it is really alien and imported, Roman and papal in origin, rather than autochthonous and Gallic, and winds up by calling it, with its undue formalism, "the disgrace of human reason" (I, 279 *seq.*). And even later on he can still, at times, write with a fairly caustic pen.[2] He inflicts some severe handling upon two contemporary historians, the Comte de Boulainvilliers and the Abbé Dubos,

[1] The following letters show this particularly clearly: XXIX, XXXV, CI, and CXLIII.

[2] There are certain passages in which Montesquieu seems to criticise the concept of liberty in a manner curiously near to the one in which Pareto "debunked" it in the twentieth century. This is *prima facie* somewhat surprising in view of his avowed and consistently advocated political ideal. "This word *liberty* does not in its policital signification come anywhere near the meaning that orators and poets have given to it. This word expresses, properly speaking, no more than a relation and cannot serve to distinguish different kinds of government: for the popular state is the liberty of the poor and weak and the servitude of the rich and powerful; and monarchy is the liberty of the great and the servitude of the small ... When, during a civil war, it is said that the struggle is for liberty, this is not true: the People strive for domination over the Great, and the Great strive for domination over the People." Cf. the whole fragment 631 in I, 1151 *seq.*; also fragment 1674 in I, 1402; also II, 394 *seq.* "Everyone has called liberty the government which was in harmony with his customs or his inclinations" (394). Montesquieu did not mean, however, to lower liberty, to deflate it as an ideal, as Pareto intended to do. His aim was only to show that it can flourish in a monarchy as much as in a republic. "As, in a corrupt monarchy, the passions of the Prince may become fatal to individuals, so in a corrupt republic, the dominating faction may be as furious as a prince in his rage ... From this it must be inferred that [the term] political liberty may apply to moderate monarchies as well as to republics; [freedom] is no more removed from a throne than from a senate; and every man is free who has reason to believe that the fury of one or of some will not rob him of his life or the possession of his goods" (I, 1152 *seq.*).

both of whom seem to him to have misconstrued the early history of France, the one by making it more aristocratic, the other by making it more democratic than it really was, and in either case his most wounding argument is the stock argument of the "debunkers" among the sociologists of knowledge: the assertion that the writers concerned have, knowingly or unknowingly, allowed contemporary class prejudices to enter into their would-be scholarly historical researches. "M. le comte de Boulainvilliers and M. l'abbé Dubos have each made a system, of which the one seems to be a conspiracy against the third estate, and the other a conspiracy against the nobility. When the Sun gave to Phæton his chariot to drive, he said to him: 'If you climb too high, you will burn up the heavenly mansion; if you come down too low, you will reduce the earth to ashes. Don't go too far to the right, (or) you will fall into the constellation of the Serpent; don't go too far to the left, (or) you will get into that of the Altar: keep in between the two.' " (II, 891 *seq.*). However, this attack on two rival authors is definitely something of a special case in the *Esprit des Lois*, and understandably so. Boulainvilliers and Dubos are to him adversaries he wishes to combat, not phenomena he wishes to understand. He meets them on the level of contemporary discussion, *quâ* critic, not on the level of sociological exploration, *quâ* observer or analyser. But in the rest of the book, where Montesquieu is the student, the scholar, the sociologist, and not the debater, where a subject-and-object relationship obtains, and not as here the subject-versus-subject attitude, the approach is throughout that of the detached philosopher who endeavours to comprehend, to explain, and to justify. M. Dedieu has very well summed up the general spirit in which everything in the *Esprit des Lois* is conceived: "Montesquieu was . . . so profoundly traditionalistic that, far from rejecting some parts of the heritage of the past, he accepted it in its entirety, and even the inherited prejudices assumed in his eyes a profound meaning. He saw on them the imprint of reason. What we call error was, at a certain time and in a certain place, a beneficial truth. The moral usages established in all countries, were thus postulated by a kind of necessity . . . They have entered into indissoluble links with the political institutions. They are in fact the result of a long accumulation of experiences, of a multitude of gropings and experiments, by means of which the nations have finally arrived at the way of life which alone is adjusted to their political constitution and in conformity with their deep[est] tendencies."[1] Montesquieu himself tried to express this attitude and made it clear that it was specifically his own: "I do not write," he says in the Preface to the *Esprit des Lois*, "to censure what is established in whatever country it may be. Each nation will find in this book the reasons of its maxims . . . If I could achieve [through my work] that all the world had new cause to love their duties, their prince, their homeland, their laws; that men could better feel their happiness in each country, under each form of government, in each place in which they find themselves, I should deem myself the happiest of mortals" (II, 230). Montesquieu has striven hard to carry out this programme, so much so that he has managed to see the relative justification, the local and temporal *raison d'être* even of institutions which he abhorred, such as certain forms of slavery and even certain forms of despotism. This shows both his human greatness and his scholarly consistency, and the deep conservatism which informed his mind once he had freed himself from the youthful radicalism of his early years.

[1] *Montesquieu*, 1913, 180 *seq.* For Montesquieu's general conservatism cf. I, 1153 (fragment 632), 1461 (fragments 1920 and 1921), 1485 (fragment 1969), II, 168 and 558 *seq.*

VII

THE GENESIS OF IDEAS : SOME SECONDARY FACTORS

THE most important passage in the whole *Esprit des Lois*, so far as the sociology of knowledge is concerned, is chapter 4 of book XIX which bears the promising title: "What the general spirit [of a society] is". "Several things," Montesquieu writes "govern men: climate, religion, laws; the maxims of government, the example of things past, mores, manners; from which there forms a general spirit which is their product". They always act jointly, yet not everywhere with the same relative strength, a fact which explains the variations observed between different societies in space and different stages in the development of the same society in time. "To the degree that, in each nation, one of these causes acts with more force, the others give way to it correspondingly. Nature and climate rule almost alone over the savages; manners govern the Chinese; laws tyrannise over Japan; once upon a time mores set the tone at Sparta; the maxims of government and the ancient mores did so in Rome" (II, 558). Two other passages—fragments 1903 and 645—seem to be earlier drafts of this same chapter (I, 1458 and 1156 *seq.*). The former mentions five factors—climate, manners, mores, religion and the laws; the latter also speaks of five, but they are not identical and appear in a different order—religion, the general maxims of government, the particular laws of the state, mores and manners. Though substantially the same, if we disregard for the moment the absence of the geographical factor in fragment 645, which may well be due to a simple slip of the pen, the three formulations yet show by their detailed differences that

Montesquieu was not altogether sure of his ground, and it is characteristic that he abandoned the more definite assumption of five [or six] causes for the less definite assertion of several co-effective factors. In fact, we have before us, in chapter 4 of book XIX and the preparatory material of it, both the gist of Montesquieu's sociology of knowledge and an indication of its basic problem. If the mental structure of a society has more than one root, how is their relative influence to be assessed; and—more important still—is the multiplicity of causal elements to be the last word, is it irreducible to final unity? Montesquieu was to struggle hard with these problems; in the depth of his mind he wanted, as we all do, a one-factor-theory. He never properly achieved it. The disorder of the *Esprit des Lois*, so often emphasised by critics from Voltaire down to the present day, is in the last analysis due to Montesquieu's persistent uncertainty about the inner enchainment of the factors which he had discovered jointly at work.

A lesser spirit than Montesquieu might, in view of this intractable difficulty, have decided to abandon the whole problem of the genesis of ideas, and declared the "spirit of the age", the "genius of the century" (I, 125), as unamenable to further analysis. In fact, there is half a move in that direction in the early essay *De la Politique*. "In all societies, which are but a union of mind, there arises a common character. This universal soul accepts a manner of thinking which is the effect of an infinite chain of causes which multiply and combine from century to century. Once the tone is given and received, it alone rules supreme, and all that sovereigns, magistrates and peoples can do or imagine, whether they appear to conflict with this tone or to follow it, has always reference to it, and it holds sway until total destruction . . . If a given tone is lost or destroyed, it is always through means that are unique and cannot be foreseen. They derive from causes so distant that any other might seem as potent as they themselves, or else they are due to a petty effect, which is hidden under a great cause, which produces other great effects which impress all the world, while it [the decisive factor] remains covered up in order to become effective sometimes as much as three centuries later" (I, 114 *seq.*). These sentences breathe a spirit of defeatism; mental structures are due to causes so remote and minute that they simply cannot be tracked down. If this attitude had prevailed, Montesquieu would not have built up a sociology of knowledge at all, or would have moved along the line of least resistance towards an "idealistic" theory, i.e. would have declared "culture mentalities" to be absolutes and ultimates. But he was both too bold and too analytic a spirit to do that. He pressed on.

There are several undeveloped, some semi-developed and two fully developed germs of a sociology of knowledge in Montesquieu's voluminous works. The sympherontic approach[1] which explains the mental world of men as an outgrowth of their interests, appears only once in the nearly 3,300 pages of his *Oeuvres Complètes*. The passage in question is contained in the *Romains* and occurs in connection with the Byzantine practice and problem of image-worship. "What rendered the quarrel about the Images so lively and brought it about that later on sensible people could not propose a moderate cult," Montesquieu writes, "was that it was tied up with rather delicate things: the question of power was involved, and as the monks had usurped it, they could only increase or maintain it by adding incessantly to the external cult of which they themselves formed an integral part. This is why the wars against the Images were always wars against them; and why, once they had gained their point, their power became boundless. At that time there developed the situation which came to a head some centuries later in the quarrel which Barlaam and Akindynos had with the monks, and which troubled the empire to its very end. It became a matter of disputation whether the light which appeared around Jesus Christ on [Mount] Tabor was create or increate. In truth, the monks did not care whether it was the one or the other; but as Barlaam attacked them directly, it became a necessity that that light be increate" (II, 198). This passage, which traces a theological idea back to an underlying power interest, is not only the lone representative of the sympherontic approach in Montesquieu, but it is also out of keeping with his whole mature thought which, as we have

---

[1] For the definition of this technical term, cf. Stark, *The Sociology of Knowledge* (1958) 221. It is derived from the Greek word for profit or advantage and is meant to describe theories which assert that it is a man's self-interest which determines his mode of thinking.

seen, turned its back to the flat rationalism which had dominated him in his earlier years. It is a link in the chain from Machiavelli to the Encyclopædists into which Montesquieu had at one time thought of inserting himself. But as he did not, ultimately, join in this tradition, the passage we have quoted and the spirit which informed it remained undeveloped.

Another possible root-idea for a sociology of knowledge—the idea that class is behind thought—also crops up in Montesquieu, but also remains an alien body in the corpus of his work. In the late *Essai sur le Goût*, the differences in taste between the "people" and the "high born" are emphasised, but only in a vague and fleeting manner: two sentences are all we get (cf. II, 1258). There is only an aside as it were in which the assertion that class affiliation may determine (and falsify) ideas is seriously pressed, and that is Montesquieu's polemic, already mentioned, against his two fellow-historians, Boulainvilliers and Dubos. As we have seen, however, we are confronted here with an attempt, not to understand a set of ideas, but only to discredit them. Boulainvilliers and Dubos are simply rivals to Montesquieu, and an argument he brings forward against them can have no claim to be regarded as an indication of his deeper philosophical convictions. For the rest, the class factor as such is not brought into the picture in any other discussion of the genesis of ideas. It only appears as an undertone or implication in connection with the analysis of the culture-forming power of the political constitution, as we shall see later on.

It is necessary, however, as well as amusing, to note here a curious anticipation of Veblen's theory of the genesis of ideas. "There are several parts of the earth," Montesquieu writes, "where people let their finger-nails grow in order to demonstrate that they do not work. The women of India believe that it is shameful for them to learn how to read: this, they say, is the job of the slaves who sing hymns in the pagodas. In one caste, they do not spin; in another they make nothing except baskets and mats, they must not even pound rice; in others it is forbidden that they go to fetch water . . . The people of Achim [on Sumatra] are proud and lazy: those who have no slaves hire one, even if it is only to take a hundred steps and to carry two quarts of rice; they would regard themselves as dishonoured if they were to carry it themselves" (II, 561). This is again a stray passage, a seed of thought lying on the surface and not taking root in Montesquieu's mind.

Not quite the same can be said of the idea developed in this century by Max Weber that occupation has a determining influence on mental processes. Montesquieu gives it a few hundred words in his *Essai sur les Causes qui peuvent affecter les Esprits et les Caractères.* "The different professions may affect our mind a good deal. For instance, a man who teaches may easily become opiniated, because he plays the part of a man who is never wrong. A philosopher may easily lose the charm of his spirit because he becomes accustomed to seeing and judging everything with much precision and exactitude" (II, 64). And so on, and so forth. Montesquieu gives a string of examples, but what he discusses is men's character rather than their mode of thinking. Judges become vain, army men vainglorious, scholars and courtiers talkative (II, 65). The only more interesting insight which appears on this page is this, that "generally all professions destroy the harmony of ideas. We are inclined to regard the things which make up our own merit, and which people like ourselves do every day, as very important" (*ib*). This is, no doubt, true, but in this context hardly more than a platitude. We see here Montesquieu once more on the brink of an ocean which he does not plumb and care to chart.

One of the avenues which he explored much more fully and carefully was the possibility of an explanation of the genesis of ideas along cœnonic-holistic lines,[1] the explanation of a total world-view through the total social set-up within which it occurred. Certain ideas are seen here as outgrowths of a certain way of life. An example of this is his account of the rise of the ancient fable of the golden age. It was due to a transition from one way of life to another, the latter preserving a somewhat nostalgic memory of the former. "The Greek idea of the age of gold, of which it is said that it corresponds to the state of innocence with the Hebrews and Christians, does not come from the same origin: it came to the Greeks only from the pastoral life which was innocent and tranquil, and which men abandoned in order to live in cities; this [change-over] was followed by trade, industry, the arts, business and consequently crimes

---

[1] Cf. *The Sociology of Knowledge*, 224. A "coenonic-holistic" theory explains mental modes with reference to the *total* social matrix within which they arise.

which engendered the iron age" (I, 1348). Another series of chapters which tries to derive ideas and ideals from a basic way of life occurs in book XVIII where the mental habitus of the primitives is investigated. ("Way of life" is defined there, a little more narrowly than in the passage quoted immediately above, as "the fashion in which various peoples procure their subsistence"; cf. II, 536). Tribes that do not cultivate the land will be warlike; as their field of operation and that of their neighbours will be territorially undefined or badly defined, be it an area devoted to the chase, to fishing, to grazing or to the recruitment of slaves, there will be constant clashes and conflicts and warlikeness will arise as a matter of course. The generally unorganised state of things will bring it about that the social order will be based on custom rather than on law; but where custom prevails, the carriers of tradition will be the most important people, that is to say, the old. Gerontocracy will engender an appropriate ideology. Where nomadism is habitual, the marriage-bond will be brittle, not having a centre of coherence in a stable home, and men will think and feel accordingly. But where nomadism is specifically pastoral, some tendency towards marital stability will appear because the cattle-breeder must keep to his herds and he needs his wife as his helpmate. "All this must march together" (II, 538). The transition from a wandering life to a settled agricultural one, and especially the building of permanent houses, will also produce a change in religious ideas. With the appearance of houses will appear houses devoted to the cult of the deity, and with them, in turn, a certain strengthening of religious fervour, a certain all-round development of religious life. Genghis Khan could not understand the Mohammedan duty and desire to go to Mecca; why should one worship God in one place rather than another? With this fluid state of religious sentiment goes a definite sense of toleration. It is a toleration due, not to virtue, but rather to comparative indifference. This indifference to the traditional religion is the reason why nomads, like the barbarian invaders of the Roman Empire and the savages of North America, were so easily converted. Once primitives are used to permanent places of worship, as in Paraguay under the Jesuits, they become as zealous for their faith as other people (II, 737 *seq.*).

If the transition from a nomadic to an agricultural mode of existence induces these mental adjustments, the transition from a social life without money to one with money will have similar repercussions. Before the introduction of money, crime will always take the form of force; after the introduction of money, crime may also appear in the guise of fraud. Furthermore, where money is unknown, theft and robbery will always be the appropriation of concrete goods which are easily identified; whereas where money is known, an *abstractum* will be the object of many if not most felonies, and an *abstractum* is not easily tracked down and shown up. If this must impart a certain contrasting character, moral and mental, to the societies concerned, the differences between the two types will be further increased by the fact that moneyless communities, where wealth cannot easily be accumulated, will tend to be egalitarian, whereas societies where money is established and hoarding can take place, will tend to be class societies (II, 540). In all these passages, there is some slight emphasis on the economic aspect of the total culture-complex, but it is the total complex rather than any particular feature of it which is held responsible for the resulting mental outlook; the theory is, in our terminology, cœnonic-holistic and not cœnonic-monogenetic.

A similar idea is behind the comparison sometimes drawn by Montesquieu between town life and country life, and the contrasting mental attitudes to which they respectively give rise. The happiness which seems to lie over the whole realm of fable is due to the rural existence which our remote forefathers led, a mixture of passion and tranquillity, it inspired the graceful pantheon of the Greeks: Diana, Pan, Apollo, the Nymphs and all the other smiling sprites and spirits of wood, meadow and springs. "If the first men had lived, as we do, in cities, the poets could not have described for us anything but what we see every day with disquiet or what we feel with disgust. All would breathe avarice, ambition and tormenting passion" (I, 1016 *seq.*). Town life, Montesquieu teaches, induces men to live, think and feel on a superficial level. "In Paris, one is stunned by the crowds; all people know are manners, and there is not the time to learn to know the vices and the virtues" (I, 1333). In general, town dwellers are cowardly. In the war of

1741, the French proved themselves bad soldiers for three years and developed a martial spirit only in the fourth, that is, after a long spell of camp life. They had forgotten the art of war "It is Paris and the small[er] towns which lead them to forget it . . . The Italians [are] bad soldiers because they all live in towns" (I, 1397). Quite in general, "it was necessary that large scale societies should form in order that certain prejudices could become general and give the tone to all the rest" (I, 1074). Had man remained in the lap of village life, his mind and morals would have been different. He would not, for instance, have developed a taste for luxuries. In the anonymity of the town, everybody can try to impress those who do not know him by dressing above his station; but as all are up to the same game, nobody really succeeds in his design, and sheer waste is the result. Luxury, in fact, is in proportion to the size of a town. "People have more desires, more needs, more fancies when they are together" (II, 333 *seq.*). But in spite of this unfavourable estimate of Montesquieu's of the influence of the urban atmosphere on men, he sees clearly that a capital city at any rate is needed in a country of some size in order to act as a unifier of the national outlook, as a focus of the national mind. "It is above all a great capital which creates the general spirit of a nation; it is Paris which makes the French; without Paris, Normandy, Picardy, Artois would be German like Germany; without Paris, the Bourgogne and the Franche-Comté would be Swiss like the Swiss; without Paris, Guyenne, Béarn, Languedoc would be Spanish like the Spaniards" (II, 1076).

These passages on town and country mentality are still more clearly cœnonic-holistic than even those quoted before concerning pastoral and settled life, natural and money economy. But there is yet another fragment, originally destined for, but ultimately excluded from, *De l'Esprit des Lois* where things assume a somewhat different hue. In it, Montesquieu discusses the connection between the political constitution on the one hand and capital cities on the other, and although he clearly implies that there is mutual influence between the two, he is yet inclined to see in the political constitution the stronger factor, the determining rather than the determined element. In other words, he is moving, in this passage, towards a cœnonic-monogenetic theory, singling out the state constitution as the one root of mental life—a theory[1] on which, as we shall see, he finally tended to settle. "In despotic states, the capital must, of necessity, grow. Despotism, which presses and weighs more strongly on the provinces, drives all towards the capital city. This city is, in a fashion, the only place of refuge against the tyranny of the rulers which exists. The Prince is, in these conditions, a peculiar kind of star: it warms those who are near and burns those who are far" (II, 1073). All the evils which an excessive concentration of the population is apt to engender, are thus due to the vicious form of government. In a limited monarchy, wealth may attract and poverty may direct many towards the main town, the monarch's seat, but if he is wise he will and can establish and preserve an equilibrium between the capital and the provinces by an appropriate policy of taxation, by fostering the local courts of law, by enforcing the residence duties of magistrates and nobles, etc. Hence "a monarchy which has rules and laws is not ruined by its capital. It may even derive from it its splendour" (II, 1074). Such considerations show Montesquieu, perhaps unconsciously, abandoning the idea that a way of life is the primary cause of certain appropriate mental structures and substituting for it something more definite, namely the political and constitutional order as the definite groundwork of cultural life.

But there is yet another aspect of the *Esprit des Lois* in which the way-of-life theory can be seen at work; we must investigate it before we move on. It is the study of commerce and its mental concomitants. Commerce calls forth on the one hand a pacific attitude, a spirit of internationalism: he with whom we traffic is no enemy. But it also engenders on the other hand a certain human estrangement noticeable in one's own country: he with whom we traffic is no friend, even if he belongs to the same community. "The spirit of trade produces in men a certain sentiment of exact justice"—the justice of the scales as it were, correct but cold; and that sentiment is "opposed on the one side to brigandage, and on the other to those moral virtues"—like hospitality and generosity—"which ensure that men do not always discuss their interests with rigidity, and that

[1] Cf. *The Sociology of Knowledge*, 222. Unlike the "coenonic-holistic" theories, the "coenonic-monogenetic" ones explain modes of thought with reference to some particular social fact or feature, e.g. the political constitution or the distribution of property, rather than with reference to the social system in general or as a whole.

they may [even] neglect them for the sake of those of others" (II, 585 *seq.*).[1] Trading is here clearly seen as a way of life which expresses itself in a definite mental and moral habitus. But, as in the case of urbanism, an inclination makes itself felt in Montesquieu which tends to depose commerce from the position of a determining to that of a determined phenomenon. Commerce itself, we are told, is dependent upon and shaped by such factors as climate and the constitution. "Although trade is subject to great revolutions, it may happen," Montesquieu cautiously writes, "that certain physical causes, the quality of the terrain or of the climate, fix for ever its nature" (II, 601). Trade between the West and India, for example, has always been an exchange of Western precious metals for Indian commodities. The Indian climate does not inspire a desire for Western articles, for instance of dress; nor does the religion of India permit the consumption of Western foods.[2] While commerce *may* thus have a connection with the climate, it *does* have a connection—one may even interpret Montesquieu by saying: it *must* have a connection—with the constitution. There is a difference between the *commerce de luxe* and the *commerce d'économie*. "Under the government of one, [trade] is ordinarily based on luxury, and although it is also based on real needs, its principal object is to procure for the nation who carries it on all that may pander to its pride, its voluptuousness and its fancies. Under the government of several it is more often founded on economy" (II, 587). Republics tend to have the principle: large turnover, small profit per unit. However, these are only tendencies; occasional deviations from the norm are quite possible. Rome, for instance, unlike Tyre, Carthage, Athens, Marseilles, Florence, Venice and Holland, although she was for long a republic, was not strongly inclined towards an active commercialism. "In the town, people were only preoccupied with wars, elections, intrigues and lawsuits; in the country, with agriculture; and in the provinces a hard and

---

[1] Part of this chapter 2 of book XX is taken almost *verbatim* from fragment 1120 in I, 1288 *seq.*, quoted above, which deals more particularly with Holland. We can see very clearly at this point how the experiences and observations of the years of travelling underlie Montesquieu's mature thought.

[2] This cropping up of the religious factor in a chapter devoted to the discussion of the influence of the geographical element is highly significant, as will presently appear.

tyrannical government was incompatible with trade." Thus, as far as the Romans were concerned, "their genius, their glory, their military education, the form of their government turned them away from commerce" (II, 632). It cannot be said that in this latter context Montesquieu has made it clear why a democratic constitution should not have led in Rome, as it is said to have done in other republics, to a *commerce d'économie*. He touches only very lightly, and without being aware of it, on the real reason why Rome was not as active a trading centre as, say, Marseilles. Speaking of the law of Constantine, he notes (*loc. cit.*) that females who kept shops were thrown together with slaves, theatre women and daughters of brothel-keepers. "This was derived and descended from the ancient institutions of the Romans." In this anti-commercial attitude there still survived the one-time spirit of the Roman peasant-warrior who had founded the city, and who—like all of his kind—understood fighting and ploughing but disliked higgling and haggling. Such an explanation would have fitted in perfectly with Montesquieu's semi-developed cœnonic-holistic theory; but as he was obviously pushing beyond it towards a cœnonic-monogenetic-constitutional theory, he did not bother to explore this possibility, even though it is clearly suggested by his own remarks; indeed, he probably did not even see it.

It is clear from all that has gone before that the cœnonic-holistic theory, the explanation of a system of ideas by the underlying contemporary system of human relationships, by the underlying total configuration of social reality, had only a precarious hold on Montesquieu's mind. He certainly toyed with it, but he as certainly had a desire to abandon it and to go over to some other sociology of knowledge. And yet, if we read the important *Essai sur les Causes qui peuvent affecter les Esprits*, we find that he not only applied this particular theory at times when he wanted to elucidate some puzzling historical problem, but also tried to provide a theoretical formulation and elaboration of it.

This theoretical formulation starts from the Baconian-Lockean concept of the mind as a *tabula rasa*, as an empty cabinet. Being as yet without content, "the first ideas are always received", and they lodge themselves very firmly in our thought. There is nothing to keep them out, nor yet to criticise or modify them. On the contrary, they become the standard by which later incoming ideas are judged, and these new arrivals must needs accommodate themselves to the conceptions and configurations which they find established in the field. Thus the initial, basic bias becomes a kind of selecting agency which ensures that the original bent remains, on the whole, in possession. "The first things which have struck home . . . seem to be, in a manner, indestructible" (II, 55). But they are not alone in our developed mind. "After the impressions which we have received in childhood, our soul receives little by little a great number of others which arrange themselves with the first, but in an order which may have formed in a thousand [different] ways." Suggestions which come from people congenial and sympathetic to us will be accepted more readily and assume a higher place in our hierarchy of ideas than others (*ib*).

If there is a strain of consistency running through our individual minds because later impressions and ideas must accommodate themselves to earlier, and, in the last analysis, to the earliest ones, there is also a strain of consistency running through a whole culture. Spanish society has, for a variety of reasons, developed a norm of grave deportment, French society of lightheartedness and vivacity. Individuals will fall in with this pattern. "A Spaniard, born lively, would be able to slow down the movement of his machine, and a ponderous Frenchman to liven up his" (II, 60). The fact of the matter is that "our mental habitus (*génie*) forms itself largely upon that of the people with whom we live. The intercourse with men of spirit gives us a perpetual education . . . [and] we likewise impart character to each other. The human machines are invisibly linked with each other; the springs which make one of them go also set the others going. People of moderation shape us towards mildness; impetuous people, towards vivacity" (II, 62). Books, too, are a kind of society in which we move and which makes our mind, only that we are here better able to choose the atmosphere in which we wish to live. Travelling is important in widening the reach of our spirit. There is, in brief, a constant give and take between the self and others, in the course of which our whole thinking is developed in a certain direction (II, 62 *seq.*).

The end result of this may very well be, and, indeed, often is, the emergence of a type to which the individuals will conform. "Of this, the religious orders are a great proof. Each has its particular philosophy which is embraced in all its extent by all the members. If you see the habit of [such] a man, you see right into his soul. If the habit is grey you may reckon that the man who wears it has plenty of entities in his head"—i.e. if he is a Franciscan, he will be a dyed-in-the-wool scholastic. "You must not imagine that you will find the same [sort of] brain when the habit is white and black. But it would be quite different if the habit were all black" (II, 64).

This unity of minds in well-integrated societies has deep roots. "It is not the spirit which makes opinions," Montesquieu writes in introducing the last passage, "it is the heart". Perhaps this is a somewhat enigmatical sentence, but what other meaning can it have than this, that the outlook of a man who really belongs, root and branch, to his group, is bound to the collectivity not only by mental ties which are always comparatively superficial, but also by vital ties which grip even the centre of being?

This account of the "furnishing of the empty cabinet", as Locke would have said, explains well enough why in different societies[1] different systems of ideas seem to prevail: the original

[1] In view of the widespread, not to say universal opinion that the ideas of progress and development played no part in Montesquieu's philosophy, that he was, in fact, an entirely unhistorical thinker, it is important to draw attention to one passage in the *Essai sur les Causes qui peuvent affecter les Esprits* where the concept of intellectual progress is at least foreshadowed (II, 53–54). In this passage a distinction is drawn between a *peuple barbare* and a *peuple policé*. Those who learn to use their reason amidst a barbarous nation will be mentally different from those who grow up in the lap of a refined society (an insight this which contains the rudiments of an evolutionary sociology of knowledge). Among barbarians, the drive of self-preservation will dominate thought to the exclusion of everything else; individual differences, so far as the mind is concerned, will be small, if they exist at all. Indeed, Montesquieu surmises that the very brain fibres of savages will become stiff for lack of exercise so that they are in the end even physically incapable of complex thought. In a developed society, this will never happen. Education will instil many ideas into growing minds, and where there are many ideas about, their individual differences will be great. "Those who bring us up are, so to speak, producers of ideas: they multiply them; they teach us to join them up, to make abstractions; they give us at every moment new ways of being and of seeing . . . Education [furthermore] does not multiply our ideas without multiplying also our ways of feeling. It increases the senses of the soul, refines its faculties, [and] leads us to find those subtle and delicate differences which are imperceptible to lowly born or poorly educated people." But the difference between the mind

impressions being different, all the rest follows. There is, in Montesquieu's view, something haphazard in the fashion in which our mental outfit is got together. "It is rare that men should receive the impressions of objects in a manner proportionate to their value" (II, 55). That is where education must come in. "Good education consists in putting our ideas in proportion" (II, 57). But "proportion" can mean two things: it can mean giving to facts their due intrinsic value (*valeur intrinsèque*) or giving them their due conventional value (*valeur d'opinion*). If we know the former, we can judge correctly; if we know the latter, we can "please", i.e. be a success on the social stage. Hence there must be two kinds of education both of which we ought to receive: education from our masters, who should teach us to see the intrinsic values, the values-in-themselves, and education from men of the world, who should introduce us to the valuations current round about us (II, 56 *seq.*). These are most important speculations from the point of view of the basic problem which in my book "The Sociology of Knowledge" I have called problem D: the relation of socially determined to absolute knowledge. Both, Montesquieu implies, are kinds of knowledge, the one knowledge of eternal validity, the other knowledge for the day, for the set, for the salon. One could be tempted to call the one scientific, the other socially conditioned. Montesquieu himself distinguishes them, from another point of view, as analytic and synthetic. "*Esprit*, according to the men of the world, consists in bringing together the most remote ideas; according to the philosophers, in distinguishing them" (II, 58). This is a very shrewd observation, for scientifically functioning knowledge has indeed the tendency to be analytical (just because it is scientific), whereas socially functioning knowledge is rather configurational and synthetic. Montesquieu, by another deep insight, emphasises that one man will only very rarely have both kinds of *esprit*, or knowledge in full measure, because they

formed in a primitive and in an elevated society consists not only in the greater variety and sensitivity of the latter. Progress is also a progress towards truth—an opinion which is particularly noteworthy from the historical point of view and shows Montesquieu clearly as forerunner of Turgot, Condorcet, and Comte. "The men who have few ideas must be mistaken in almost all their judgments. Ideas are inter-connected. The principal faculty of the soul is that of comparison, and it cannot exercise it in such poverty."

are so different in nature—"almost physically incompatible," as he finely says. "There is in truth as much difference between what is called an *homme d'esprit* in the world and *homme d'esprit* among philosophers, as there is between an *homme d'esprit* and a fool" (II, 58).

Montesquieu skirts this same problem—problem D—once again later in the essay when he speaks of the influence of habits on mental processes. Just as engravers see on the wall before them, and believe to be real, pictures which are not there at all but which are constantly reproduced by their brains because they were deeply imprinted on them in the effort of engraving, just so professional mathematicians see everywhere, often wrongly, measurable and calculable relationships, and just so metaphysicians come in the end to take their conceptions for solid, for as solid as physical phenomena, and lovers of antiquity fabulous Greek stories for as reliable as modern history. By developing such commanding habits, "we make for ourselves the spirit which pleases us, and we are its true artisans" (II, 64). This consideration does perhaps no more than to raise, in its way, the problem of the objective validity of habitually (and therewith socially) conditioned knowledge; or perhaps it just hints that it is apt to be delusionary; but it is interesting that it occurs at all.

It is fairly plain that these considerations of Montesquieu's do not amount to a complete and completely satisfactory sociology of knowledge of the cœnonic-holistic (or, indeed, of any other) kind. Apart from everything else, there is too little emphasis on the connection between the modes of thought established in a society and the modes of action of that same society, on the connection between superstructure and sub-structure. Nevertheless, several important elements of the cœnonic-holistic type of theory are present, notably the *ab initio* different bias of the mind in different societies due to the variation in primary impressions, the adaptation even of potentially or spontaneously non-conforming individuals to the prevailing norm, the emergence of typical attitudes characteristic of large numbers of associated persons, and the rooting of the unity and uniformity of a total world-view in a sub-rational stratum of being, in the "heart".

At any rate, Montesquieu had in these speculations a stock

of ideas which he could have—and probably would have—
worked up into a more rounded theory of the genesis of ideas,
if he had continued to think along these lines. But, as already
indicated, his mind did not, in the end, cast anchor in the
cœnonic-holistic mode of analysis. Nor yet did it find its final
rest in another possibility which he also explored—the explanation of a total world-view out of a basic religious attitude and
inspiration. Several moves in the direction of such a theory (in
our terminology: of a cœnonic-monogenetic theory with
religion as the root-phenomenon) are traceable in Montesquieu's writings, especially those of early date. The fragmentary
essay *De la Manière Gothique*, penned sometime between 1728
and 1731, perhaps in 1729, ascribes to the religious factor a key
position and sees, in particular, art-forms conditioned by it.
The gaiety and joyousness of Græco-Roman life is elsewhere
attributed to ancient heathenism. "Religion was sweet and
always in harmony with Nature . . . Plays, dances, feasts,
theatres, all that can stir the emotions, all that causes men to
feel, belonged to the religious cult . . . Today, Mohammedanism and Christianity, made solely for the life to come, annihilate
all that" (I, 1080 *seq.*). The tenor of a culture is here obviously
assumed to flow from the character of religion, or even of the
cult. The drift of Judaism, particularly as a creator of emotion
and emotional art, is similarly explained by reference to its
religious centre: "There is, in the system of the Jews, much
aptitude for the sublime, because they were accustomed to
attribute all their thoughts and all their actions to specific
inspirations of the Deity: and this gave them a very great
inspirer (*agent*). But, although God appears to act, in the
Jewish system as well as in the heathen, as a corporal being,
yet he appears to be moved by certain passions only, and this
not only robs [the Jewish culture] of what is gracious, but also
of variety in the sublime. And, furthermore, a single agent
cannot give variety: he leaves for imagination an astounding
void, in place of that fullness which was provided by the
innumerable number of heathen deities. The Christian system
. . . in giving us saner ideas of the Divinity, seems to give us an
[even] greater inspirer (*agent*). But, as this agent neither permits nor experiences passion, the sublime necessarily falls
down. Furthermore, mysteries [like those of Christianity] are

sublime for reason rather than for the senses, and it is the senses and the imagination which are important in works of the spirit" (I, 1018 *seq.*). Here again, a total culture-habitus is genetically linked to religion. But the best example, for Montesquieu, of the all-pervading influence of religion is the case of Mohammedanism. Wherever it went, prison-houses sprang up and gratings and bolts came into evidence. The dogma of predestination, of the *fatum mohammedanum*, made men passive and fatalistic. On the other hand, "the Mohammedans became speculative by habit; they pray five times a day, and each time it is necessary for them to make an act by which they throw all that belongs to this world behind their back: this drives them towards speculation" (II, 722). This indifference to worldly things is not unconnected with the triumph of despotism in Moslem lands.

In the *Essai sur les Causes qui peuvent affecter les Esprits* the importance of religion for the formation of ideas and ideal systems is also stressed, but not to the same extent. In it, religion only takes its place as one factor alongside others of equal influence. And the matter is not lifted to the level of theory. All Montesquieu gives is a string of examples: "The laws which prescribe ignorance to the Mohammedans, the customs which prevent them from communicating with each other, leave their spirits in a state of torpor. The books of Confucius, which mix a great many details of civil ceremonial with the precepts of morality, thus making the most childish things go hand in hand with the most essential, strongly influence the spirit of the Chinese. The logic of the Schools modifies by its extreme influence the spirit of the nations who cultivate it. The great freedom of saying anything and writing anything which exists in certain countries produces there an infinite number of individual spirits. The extraordinary in little things which constitutes the character of the Talmud, as the extraordinary in great things constitutes that of the Sacred Books, has greatly narrowed the minds of the Jewish doctors" (II, 58 *seq.*). This passage is remarkable for its consistent use of superlatives, but it does not really convince because a string of examples, however long, can never match, for convincingness, theoretical argument and analysis in the abstract.

Something of this belief in the power of religion to determine culture-content remained with Montesquieu to the end of his days. The passage concerning Judaism quoted above (I, 1018 *seq.*) is taken from notes prepared for the *Essai sur le Goût* and thus belongs to his very last active period. In the *Esprit des Lois*, too, there is ample evidence of the survival of this same opinion. The third chapter of book XXIV is an important proof of this. Christianity, where it is well established, will keep out despotism. The mildness so strongly recommended in the Gospel and thereby introduced into the national character of Christian peoples, does not allow the development of a government of sadistic techniques. Montesquieu quotes as his prime example the case of Abyssinia. "It is the Christian religion which, in spite of the largeness of the empire and the viciousness of the climate, has prevented despotism from establishing itself in Ethiopia and has transported to the centre of Africa the *mores* of Europe and her laws" (II, 717). Not far from that country, the evil effects of the Mohammedan faith can be seen: in Sennar (in Nubia) cruelty is rampant. "Admirable thing! The Christian religion, which seems to have for its aim nothing but the happiness of the life to come, yet makes our happiness [even] in this!" (II, 716).

Thus the essential assertion of chapter 3 of book XXIV is still as can be seen from this sample, that religion is a determining rather than a determined factor, and that it determines in particular the form of government. But we need only turn over a single page, and we are face to face with the contrary assertion, with the doctrine that government is the determining and religion the determined phenomenon. Indeed, this conviction is expressed with the greatest clarity in chapter 5 of the same book. "When a religion comes to birth and forms itself in a State, it usually follows the plan of the government where it is established: for the people who receive it and those who propagate it have rarely other ideas of order[1] than the ones of the State in which they were born. When the Christian religion suffered, two centuries ago, that unfortunate split which divided it into Catholic and Protestant, the nations of the north embraced Protestantism and those of the south preserved Catholicism . . . Even in the countries where the Protestant religion became established, the revolutions [which took place]

[1] *"de police"*

were modelled on the plan of the political State. Luther, having great princes on his side, could hardly have made palatable to them an ecclesiastical authority which did not imply external privilege; and Calvin, having on his side nations which lived in republics or burghers oppressed by monarchies, could well avoid introducing privileges and dignities" (II, 718 *seq.*). "The magnificence of the public cult" too, "has a close connection with the constitution of the State." Many "good" republics have enforced "laws of economy" in religion, in agreement with their general policy and with their whole essential nature; monarchies, on the other hand, are given to splendour in church as well as to splendour at Court (II, 742). The religious life, in other words, follows the pattern of the political; it is the fruit rather than the root, the effect rather than the cause.

But the constitution is, even in this chapter 5 of book XXIV, not regarded as the only root cause of religious thought and sentiment. Another influential factor makes its appearance here, and it is geography. Why did northern Europe embrace Protestantism, while the south remained faithful to Rome? In the same breath in which he speaks of the political background of the Reformation, Montesquieu remarks: "This happened because the peoples of the north have, and always will have, a spirit of independence and freedom which the peoples of the south have not, and because a religion which has no visible head is more in keeping with the independence of the climate[1] than the one which has such a head" (II, 718). Some details of the two religious and ecclesiastical systems are also due to the geographical factor. The north, less favoured by nature, demands of men hard and uninterrupted labour; hence Protestantism is a religion with few feasts; Catholicism, at home in the warm and fertile south, a religion with many holidays. Music and dancing (comparative luxuries as it were) will also, for the same reason, flourish towards the south rather than towards the north. Hence Montezuma was talking sense when he said that the religion of the Spaniards was all right for Spain, that of the Mexicans for Mexico. Montesquieu applies this geographical determinism most consistently to India and Indian religion. "The theory of the transmigration of souls is made

[1] "*l'indépendance du climat*".

for the climate of India" (II, 732). The excessive heat of those latitudes burns the meadows; hence only few cattle can be kept, and there is constant danger that their number be too small to suffice for the purposes of ploughing; hence, again, "a law of religion which preserves them is appropriate to the police of the country". On the other hand, rice and vegetables grow freely because there is water available which can make them grow. "Hence a law of religion which permits no nourishment but this is very useful to men in those climes" (II, 733). The special protection afforded by Hinduism to the cow has a similar explanation. Milk and butter are important foodstuffs whereas the meat has no taste under so hot a sun. Montesquieu drives this ecological theory furthest where he claims that climate is responsible for the mutual delimitation of Christianity and Mohammedanism. "Whenever a religion, founded on [one] climate, has clashed too violently with the climate of another country, it has not been able to establish itself there, and if it has been introduced into it, it has been driven out again. It seems, humanly speaking, that it is the climate which has prescribed limitations to the Christian religion and to Mohammedanism" (II, 734). In other words, should Christianity ever penetrate into the hot countries which Mohammedanism holds at the moment, this would be *praeter rerum ordinem*, a miracle in fact. Not unnaturally, the Theological Faculty of the Sorbonne, the appointed defender of orthodoxy, took exception to this paragraph, and Montesquieu, *"pour finir tout"*, decided to omit it in later editions (II, 1174). But this change of the text can hardly be said to have betokened a change of heart.

Indeed, the belief in the mind-determining and thought-producing power of the physical environment became one of the main strands in the texture of Montesquieu's sociology of knowledge, a strand second in importance only to the belief in the ideogenetic influence of the political order of the state. Looking at this texture as a whole, we can say that the minor tendencies he saw at work are altogether overshadowed by the two major ones which we have discovered in his discussion of religious thought—climate and the constitution. Nowhere do we find a more balanced statement of his final opinion concerning the genesis and determination of ideas than in the following sentences from the first book of *De l'Esprit des Lois*. Though more specifically referring to legal ideas, they also express his views on the origination of all other thought-contents. "They must be *en rapport* with the nature and principle of the government which is established, or which it is desired to establish . . . They must be in relation to the *physique* of the country; to the icy, burning or temperate climate; to the quality of the territory, its situation, its size; to the way of life of the peoples, be they tillers of the soil, hunters or cattle-breeders; they must be adjusted to the degree of freedom which the constitution may allow; to the religion of the inhabitants, their inclinations, their wealth, their number, their trade, their mores, their manners. Finally, they have connections among themselves, as also with their origin, with the aim of the legislator, with the order of things on the basis of which they are established. It is from all these points of view that they must be considered" (II, 237 *seq.*). In a way, this important passage shows up the essential weakness of Montesquieu's sociology of knowledge: he sees thought-contents influenced and determined from many sides, not to say from all sides, without being able clearly to apportion weights to the individual factors, without wholly penetrating to the manner and to the mode of their interaction and co-efficiency. Yet, this passage also indicates in which direction his mind was travelling, what order and relative importance he was inclined to attribute to the various tendencies which he saw conjointly at work. It is no accident that he mentions government first, and geography second. These two are the main lines of interest which he follows up; the others are allowed, comparatively speaking, to fall into the background. From a multiplicity of causes he moves on to a duality. To that extent, he masters the chaos of his mind. But, of course, the difficulty remains: if there are two causes of thought-contents, what is their relationship? How do they interact, how do they co-determine what goes on in men's brains? If there are two main strands in the texture, how can they be tied up with each other? Montesquieu did not find it easy to answer these questions which, half-formulated at any rate, were present in the background of his mind.

VIII

THE PRIMARY FACTORS :

(*a*) THE PHYSICAL ENVIRONMENT

THIS dichotomy of moral causes and physical causes of mental phenomena, this parallel of governmental and geographical determination of thought-processes and thought-contents, runs through all Montesquieu's writings. Sometimes it is on the surface, sometimes it is subterranean and must be dug out as it were by the student of his works. In the *Essai sur les Causes qui peuvent affecter les Esprits* it is quite obvious, because the text falls into two chapters of which the first deals with the physical and the second with the moral factor. The latter, in discussing education, contains the following remarkabe statement: "There exists, in every nation, a general character which is imposed, to a greater or lesser degree, on the character of each individual. It is produced in two ways: by physical causes which depend upon the climate ... and by moral causes which are the combination of the [existing] laws, religion, mores and manners, and that kind of emanation of the way of thinking, the atmosphere and the follies of the Court and Capital which spread far and wide" (II, 58). In a fragment which belongs to the same kind of material, this dichotomy is frankly declared irreducible to unity. "When medical men and moral authors discuss the passions, they never speak the same language: the moralists put too much to the account of the soul; the others too much to that of the body; the one regards man more as a spirit; the others more like the machine of an artisan. But man is equally composed of two substances which each, as by a flux, exert dominion and are subject to it" (I, 1015). In the *Considérations sur les Causes de la Grandeur des*

Romains et de leur Décadence the duality is not expressly stated or declared irresolvable, but both its existence and its irreducible character is assumed and can be seen at the very core of the book's argument. When Rome was small and the Romans virtuous republicans, she was great; when Rome became a world-wide empire and the Romans corrupt underlings of despots, she decayed. Was it the physical extension of the territory that destroyed virtue and republicanism, or was it the loss of virtue and the right republican spirit that led the Romans to become conquerors and push out their border lines *ad ultimas fines terrae?* Who can tell? Government and geography are to Montesquieu the two blades of a pair of scissors: though distinct, they can only be effective when they work together, and it is senseless to ask which has done the cutting—the nether blade or the upper. In *De l'Esprit des Lois* the basic dichotomy is visible in the very table of contents in the contrast between books II to VIII on the one hand, and books XIV to XVIII on the other: the former deal with the influence of government, the latter with that of geographical conditions. Sometimes also the complex co-operation of the two factors comes out quite clearly, as for instance in the crucial chapters on slavery. Where there is despotic government, slavery will spring up because men will naturally be in need of, and on the look-out for, protectors; where there is a tropical climate, slavery will spring up because men will naturally be disinclined to work and will have to be put to it, and pushed into it, by overseers and taskmasters. Slavery seems to be associated both with despotism and with heat. Can analysis penetrate more deeply into the maze of things than to this double root of phenomena, to this double fountain-head of causation?

M. Barckhausen has expressed the opinion that, for Montesquieu, geography and government form a unitary physico-political environment which cannot be further analysed and broken down, simply because, as an atmosphere and setting, it works and acts as a unity,[1] and M. Caillois is inclined to take the same view.[2] This is certainly an ingenious and seductive interpretation and would save Montesquieu's face, but the fact of the matter is that he gives nowhere any positive proof that

[1] *Montesquieu, ses Idées et ses Oeuvres,* 1907, 260.
[2] *Oeuvres Complètes,* I, 1949, XIV.

this is indeed his basic conception of the nature of the co-operation of the two basic ideogenetic factors. On the contrary; reading his texts without prejudice, we are reluctantly driven to the conclusion that he is simply experimenting with two different and irreconcilable theories, and, indeed, that he would have been glad to discard the one for the sake of the other if it could have been done, but that he could not, or dared not, embrace so radical a solution of the problem which was presented to him by the duality of the causative influences.

In the circumstances, all we can do is to study the two theories separately and then seek, as diligently as we can, for indications of a final preference on Montesquieu's part. The one doctrine looks on the surface like a pure ecological sociology of knowledge and has generally been interpreted as such. Chardin, whose *Voyages* Montesquieu knew inside out, has given as clear a formulation of it as our author ever did. "I always find the cause or the origin of the mores and habitudes of the Orientals in the nature of their climate;" he wrote,[1] "having observed in my travels that, as the mores follow the temperament of the body, so the temperament of the body follows the nature of the climate, so that the customs and habitudes of the nations are by no means the effect of pure caprice but of some causes or natural necessities." In this spirit Montesquieu ventures both some generalisations and some concrete analyses. The former are by far the best known part of Montesquieu's doctrine. A hot climate makes men sluggish in body and mind, a cold climate active. A hot climate makes them conservative, over-conservative even, because "a certain laziness of the spirit [is] naturally associated with that of the body" (II, 479) a cold climate makes them progressive. On the other hand, a hot climate makes them sensitive and excitable, a cold climate indifferent and phlegmatic. The same operas are put on the stage in England and Italy. But how calmly do the English take the music, and how enthusiastic are the Italians! (II, 476). A hot climate also makes men cowardly and a cold brave. "This is not only observable between nation *and* nation, but also in the same country between one part and another. The people of the north of China are more courageous than those of the south, the people of the south of Corea are not

[1] Ed. 1723, V, 219 seq.

as courageous as those of the north. One must not, therefore, be surprised that the cowardice of the people of the warm climates has almost aways made them into slaves, and that the courage of the people of the cold climates has preserved their freedom. This is an effect which springs from its natural cause" (II, 523). "In America, the peoples subject to despotic kings, like those of Mexico and Peru, have been found towards the south, and the free nations towards the north" (I, 1412).[1] Even such deeds of valour as we meet among southern nations, as for instance the bravery with which Indian women mount the funeral pyres of their husbands, are, paradoxically, due to fear. "Nature, which has given to these peoples a weakness which renders them timid, has also given them so vivid an imagination that everything strikes them to excess. That same organic delicacy which makes them fear death, also serves to make them dread a thousand things more than death. It is the same sensibility which makes them flee all perils, and which makes them face up to them" (II, 478).

The poverty and richness of the soil have similar consequences as the warmth or coldness of the air. Where the soil is fertile, a slave-mentality will appear; this is often the case in plains. Where the soil is hard and infertile, an independent, aggressive type of man will form; this is often the case in mountainous regions. The poverty of the soil of Attica led to Athenian democracy; the comparative fertility of that of Lacedæmon to Spartan submissiveness to an oligarchy. Even in Attica itself, the influence of the environment could be observed. The hill-dwellers were bent upon a popular government, the plains-people demanded an aristocratic constitution, and those at the sea-shore preferred a mixed state (II, 531 *seq.*). A maritime situation, especially an island in isolation, will tend to produce that courageousness and self-reliance which is also characteristic of northern lands and poorer soils; a continental, land-locked place tends to the opposite mental characteristics in its inhabitants. "The people of the isles are more inclined towards liberty than the people of the mainland" (II, 534). "The Dutch broke the yoke of Spain. This was the effect of their maritime forces. The land has been given to monarchies;

---

[1] Cf. also the very well formulated chapter 3 of book XXI of *De l'Esprit des Lois*, too long to be quoted here, and II, 94, *re* Macedonia.

the sea to free peoples" (I, 1108). "The dominion of the seas has always given to the nations who have held it a natural pride; because, feeling able to inflict insults on all sides, they believe that their power has no more limitations than the Ocean" (II, 579).

If such passages bespeak an almost extreme geographical determinism and have indeed been grist to the mill of such schools as that of Le Play, others give the theory a more sociological—one might even say, a more human—twist. "The more the nations are in contact, the more easily they change their manners, because each is more of an example to the other. ... The climate which brings it about that a nation is glad to establish contacts, also evokes in it a love of change; and whatever makes a nation love change, also causes it to refine its taste" (II, 560). Characteristically, this passage is headed: "*Effets de l'Humeur Sociable*"; geography is, comparatively speaking, in the background.

Montesquieu's tendency to build up a sociology of knowledge from the geographical and geopolitical angle, can also be seen in some less generalising and more concrete investigations. Sometimes he advances from geographical facts to mental phenomena said to be arising from them; sometimes he travels in the opposite direction, takes certain mental phenomena and follows up their supposed filiation until he arrives at some geographical fact. To the former efforts belongs what he has to say about Asia, especially China and Japan, about England and Germany; to the latter, his explanation, or attempted explanation, of the subjection of women, of jealousy, and of a few religious forms such as Buddhism.

The mentality of the Asiatics, Montesquieu tells us, is one of servitude; the mentality of the Europeans, one of freedom. He sees two geographical reasons for this. Asia has no temperate zone: the war-like northerners are directly confronted with the effeminate southerners, strong and weak stare at each other across a very thin border-line. Hence conquest is of frequent occurrence and it habituates men to a spirit of submissiveness and subjection. In Europe, on the other hand, the temperate zone is broad, transition from the valour-producing north to the cowardice-producing south very gradual. Hence neighbours are generally of more or less equal strength, and conquest is correspondingly rare. In addition, Asia is a territory of few internal divisions; large empires consequently form in response to the geographical lay-out, and large empires are regularly dominated by despots: where a far-flung country had to be defended, a strong central power is needed to ensure quick and efficient action. Europe falls naturally into smaller sub-divisions, she consists, for geographic reasons, of many medium and petty states, and in these democracy is possible because only a small territory need be defended and every attack is an attack on all. This confrontation of Asia and Europe looks at first sight like an abandonment of Montesquieu's basic contrastation of north and south. But he is careful to bring his concrete explanation into line with his abstract principles. If there is despotism even in the north of Asia, this is due to the geographic influence of the south. The Tartars, for instance, fell under the yoke of a cruel master because they lost their love of freedom when they experienced—and, as it were, contracted—the slavishness of the Chinese whom they themselves had conquered. In Europe, on the other hand, all freedom has one outstanding cradle, and that is Scandinavia. "I do not know," Montesquieu writes, "if the famous Rudbeck who in his *Atlantica* has so much praised Scandinavia, has spoken of that great prerogative which should place the nations who live there above all peoples of the world; it is that they have been the source of the liberty of Europe, that is to say, of almost all liberty which exists today among men" (II, 528). At this point Montesquieu moves very near to the idea later so lavishly developed by the Le Playans, according to which modern democracy was born on the hard and ice-bound ledges along the Norwegian fjords.[1]

The traditional liberties of the British nation are also growths from geographical roots. The nation has "received from the climate a certain character of impatience which does not allow it to suffer the same things for long," Montesquieu writes. But this restlessness is a good guarantee against the encroachments of a would-be despotical government. "Servitude always begins with sleepiness. But a people which finds no rest in any situation, which is incessantly irritated and finds every spot painful could hardly fall asleep" (II, 486 *seq.*).

[1] For all this, cf. II, 23 *seq.*, and 524–530, as well as I, 1211 *seq.*, and 1354.

Indeed, the control of the climate over the British mind is so great that it even induces a certain state of positive disease. As the body cannot work properly, although it feels no concrete and concentrated pain anywhere in particular, a general lassitude and tiredness develops in the mind which sometimes thickens into *taedium vitae* and leads the afflicted individuals to blow their brains out. The Romans, when they committed suicide, did so because of certain moral conceptions and philosophical convictions; the English take their lives because they are ill—ill with an illness due to their abominable climate.

The physical environment can also serve to explain a characteristic of the ancient (and presumably the modern) Germans, their lack of imagination. They "lived in a climate where the passions were very quiet" (II, 487). Montesquieu sees certain consequences of this climate-born trait of the Germanic character in the Germanic laws, for instance in their treatment of offences against women. When the Western Goths left the north and settled in the south, in Spain, their laws changed in this respect. The imagination of the people was awakened, that of the lawgivers fired, and a new legal tradition began to take shape. Thus does the mind of man respond to his climatic environment.

It is hardly necessary to emphasise wherein lies the great problem raised by these generalisations. We have seen that Montesquieu's mind settled down to the conviction that thought-contents are in the last analysis due to two root-causes —geography and government, but here there is a tendency (to put it no higher) to push government out of the picture by showing that it is itself dominated by geography. But this does not mean that Montesquieu abandons the conviction that government is an ultimate and ultimately independent determinant. In discussing his theory of social control, we have already pointed out that the sheer fact of extent means little to our author; that what matters to him is the social content filling a territory rather than its square mileage. Here we must go further and emphasise that even the extent of the area covered by a society is not for him univocally and unilaterally determined by its physical configuration but also by certain political actions, among which conquest is the most important. True, a broken territory seems to favour democracy (as in

Europe), whereas vast open spaces seem to call for despotism (as in Asia)—a point made with special insistence in chapter VIII of the *Réflexions sur la Monarchie Universelle* (Cf. II, 23 *seq.*). "In Asia, there have always been found large empires; in Europe, they have never been able to survive. This is because the Asia which we know has greater plains . . ." But a society may, if it sets its mind to it, push out its frontier beyond the "reasonable" or appropriate limit. It will do so, or at any rate try to do so, when and where the political forces active in it press for such a territorial adjustment. Thus the political geography of the world is dependent as much on the human forces in it as on underlying physical conditions. "We have seen above", Montesquieu writes in an interesting fragment, "that the large extent of the State determined it to despotism. The conquests which caused that aggrandisement lead in this way by a natural development to that form of government" (II, 1059). Thus conquest is described as the root-fact here, and conquest is not a physical fact but a political activity. Conquest may be easier where the neighbours' territory lies open to invasion and technically is difficult to defend; but it can and will climb over mountains and cross over streams where a strong enough government decides to grab more land, and so government may be the ultimate determinant, not geography. In spite of the many passages which we have quoted, and in spite of the many more which we have not quoted, the general key problem of Montesquieu's sociology of knowledge—geography versus government—remains open.

Of the more specific social phenomena and mental attitudes explained by our author with the help of the geographic factor, the subjection of women is treated at the greatest length. Under burning skies, women develop very quickly; they become mature in body before they are mature in mind; and when their reason has reached its acmé, their beauty has already started to fade. This puts the female sex under a great and lasting disability. When their physique would seem to give them a strong position vis-à-vis men, their lack of intellectual maturity spoils things for them; when their intellectual endowments come into play, their physical attractiveness has decayed or departed, and they are again precluded from asserting themselves. Unhappy fate that has divided their advantages and never allows them to use them all to the full at the same time. No wonder the East is a realm where women are weak and little thought of. In the northern countries, the body matures at the same speed, or rather at the same slow rate, as the mind. Hence the women are not under a handicap there, and there will be a tendency towards equality in estimation for the sexes. Montesquieu also assumes that in different climates different numerical ratios obtain between the sexes: too many baby girls are born in the tropics and semi-tropics so that the law of supply and demand works against them and polygamy becomes a practical necessity (especially as the women are so rapidly worn out where the climate is hot). In the north, the birth-rates are more nearly in balance, there is even a preponderance of male births, the health of women is more robust and more easily preserved, and hence all is different. Monogamy will become the legal norm. But the influence of the climate does not end with the determination of the laws of matrimony; it extends further into family life; polygamy in turn leads to the seclusion of women. If a man has many families, the danger is that they may drift apart, that divergent interests may develop and make his life very difficult. Where all wives of a man are safely behind the same harem walls, their unity is assured. Furthermore, in a hot climate, the women's sexual passions are also hot, like all the rest. Hence they must be severely disciplined and repressed, and the purdah is again the means to this end. "It is the climate which must decide in these things" (II, 517). Nowhere does Montesquieu drive his geographical determinism further forward than here. In particular, religion seems to him very secondary in these matters, climate almost all-powerful. But it is worthy of notice that he develops doubts. Speaking of the disproportion of male and female births, he writes in or around 1740: "I find it difficult to believe that there are many countries where the disproportion is so great as to make it necessary to introduce a law concerning the multiplicity of wives or a law concerning the multiplicity of husbands." The words "I find it difficult to believe" are replaced in 1750 by the more definite phrase "I do not believe ..." (II, 511; cf. Dedieu, *Montesquieu*, 1913, 230). A straw in the wind this, certainly no more, but yet a straw in the wind![1]

[1] Cf. I, 1282 *seq.*; II, 187, 509–511, and 515–517.

But perhaps there is more in these passages than meets the eye at first sight. We have to remember that the phenomena which Montesquieu here explains are institutions which he thoroughly abhors: nothing went so much against the grain with him as the despotic and dehumanising harem-régime which all the travel-books he had read had taught him to despise. "In all this" he writes, with obvious emphasis, at the end of the discussion of polygamy, "I do not justify the usages [concerned], but [only] give their reasons" (II, 511). More characteristically still, he speaks of *"vices du climat"*, a vicious climate, as if it were admissible morally to condemn a certain set of geographic facts (II, 479 and 516). But most revealing is chapter 5 of book XIV which is well worth quoting in full: "The inhabitants of India believe that rest and nothingness are the foundation of all things and the end to which they lead. Thus they regard total inaction as the most perfect state and the object of all their strivings. They give to the supreme being the name 'the immovable one' . . . In those lands where the excessive heat enervates and overwhelms, rest is so sweet and movement so painful that this system of metaphysics appears natural; and Foë [i.e. the Buddha], the legislator of India, has [only] followed out what he felt when he placed men into an extremely passive state; but his doctrine, born of the inertia of the climate, and supporting it on its part, has caused a thousand evils. The legislators of China were more sensible when, considering men, not in the peaceful state in which they will be some day, but in the active state appropriate to the fulfilment of their duties of life, they gave their religion, their philosophy and their law an altogether practical turn. The more the physical causes incline men to inactivity, the more the moral causes should lead them away from it." Thus Montesquieu is convinced "that the bad legislators are those who have supported the vices of the climate, and the good those who have opposed them" (II, 479 *seq.*).

A passage such as this—and it is a most important one, one which expresses Montesquieu's inmost, if not uppermost thoughts—puts a complexion on his "geographical determinism" which shows that he was by no means a geographical determinist in the common meaning of the term. For the typical geographical determinist, nature is the seal, society but wax under the seal, forced to accept the configurations pressed upon it. For the Baron de la Brède, on the other hand, the influence of the environment is something preliminary, something which indeed presses towards and upon man but need not and, what is more, should not, determine him and his thinking. Where man is weak, where man is passive, there his mind will fall into a pattern which is of nature's making, not of his own; in certain latitudes, the same nature inclines man to passivity, lulls him to sleep as it were; but he never need give in, he never should give in; if he does, he resigns his humanity, he becomes smaller than the human stature, and he forfeits the right to regard himself as the crown of creation. However "natural" institutions like polygamy and slavery and their associated ideas and ideologies may be in the tropics, however appropriate to the local circumstances, however excusable in their setting, they will never be worthy of man as a rational creature because, as a rational creature, man ought to assert his independence of nature, and, where the need arises, against nature. It follows from all this that geographical determinism is not regarded, by Montesquieu, in his heart of hearts, as a sociology of knowledge that can be applied to a fully developed and matured culture-complex, because cultural maturity means independence of, nay domination over, the physical forces of the environment. It is only applicable to those unfortunate societies which, like the lower creation, are still in leading strings and have not yet reached man's proper level, man's estate.[1]

For the rest, Montesquieu is well aware that the geographical setting of human life is not fixed but modifiable and often modified by man. He speaks more than once of the Netherlands, Holland and Frisia. Those countries, he says with

---

[1] Cf. chapter 4 of book XIX (already quoted) where Montesquieu adduces all the mind-determining factors, rational and cultural, and remarks: "Nature and climate rule almost alone over the savages" (II, 558). Even on a low level of development, there may, however, be instances of a departure from the laws of geographical determination. The Tartars are a case in point. They are "politically enslaved", i.e. under despots, even though other nomadic peoples are, for geographical reasons, free. "In a country where the various hordes make continuous war upon each other and incessantly defeat each other; in a country where, by the death of a chief, the body politic of each vanquished horde is always destroyed, the nation in general can hardly be free: because there is no part of it which will not have been subjugated a great many times" (II, 542).

admiration, have been "formed in our modern times by the industry of their inhabitants and have emerged, so to speak, from beneath the reeds" (II, 223; also II, 195). Here man was not only mentally but even physically the maker, the master, the determiner.

The attentive reader may have noticed that in the foregoing discussion Montesquieu's doctrine has been referred to throughout as a kind of geographical determinism and not (in our own terminology) as an ecological sociology of knowledge. The reason for this is that his theory appears as a purely ecological one only so long as the mode of connection between the geographical substructure and the intellectual superstructure is left out of the account. When it is taken into account, it becomes clear that Montesquieu develops a mixed ecological and materialistic doctrine rather than a purely ecological one. The environment does not shape thought directly, but only indirectly, through its influence on the body and the bodily organs, especially the organs of thought. There are two links between physical setting and mental phenomena, and the brain, the physical brain, with its co-ordinated bodily structures, stands at the nodal point between the two.

The *Essai sur les Causes qui peuvent affecter les Esprits* is full of a far-reaching philosophical materialism, especially its first part, *Des Causes Physiques*. Northern nations need coarse nourishment; their "fibres" will in consequence be stout; southern nations need refined fare; their fibres will naturally be fine as well. These physical characteristics at once express themselves in mental endowments and weaknesses. "From this physical constitution"—Montesquieu speaks, a little later, even more clearly, of "the different structure of the machine"—"certain effects must follow. The peoples of the North will not have that rapid penetration, the vivacity of comprehension, that facility of receiving and communicating all sorts of impressions which are present in other climates. But if they do not have the advantage of quickness, they will have that of cold-bloodedness; they will have more constancy in their resolutions and will make fewer mistakes in their execution. The Dutch are famous for the slowness with which they receive their ideas. It is to this that they owe that consistency in the principles of their policy and that perseverence in their passions which have made them do so great things. Thus the imagination will be more tranquil with the nations of the North; they will be less capable of producing what are called works of *esprit* than works of compilation; and, for the same reason, they will be better fitted than the other peoples to make, in the arts, those discoveries which demand assiduous labours and protracted researches" (II, 39 *seq.*).

It is hardly necessary to go into the detailed physiology with which Montesquieu tries to underpin this doctrine. What he has to say about nervous vibrations and body juices is in keeping with the primitive biology of the age,[1] and can philosophically be characterised as a development of Locke's sensationalism on the physiological side. Suffice it to say that he sees several physical differences, caused by the climate, behind the mental differences between different societies. Northerners have in their brains a "superfluous humidity" and their nerves, being always in a bath as it were, relax and become incapable of quick and lively vibrations, whereas the comparative dryness in the skull, and in the body generally, of southerners, gives them a much greater mental vivacity. Montesquieu surmises that the contrast between Dutchmen and, say, inhabitants of the Pyrenees, could be experimentally shown to be due to this cause.[2] Breathing, too, has a definite influence on the mind. Where the air has *beaucoup de ressort* (whatever that may mean), there it is more likely to produce *une abondante sécrétion d'esprit*. "To the subtlety of the air of Athens has been attributed that of the spirit of the Athenians, and there is much evidence that it was [indeed] one of its most important causes" (II, 44). "If the air of each country acts on the spirit, the winds, which are movements of air, affect it no less. There are very remarkable proofs of this all over the world." Those who dwell on the northern slopes of the Pyrenees are mentally different from those who dwell on the southern slopes; those who dwell on the eastern slopes of the Apennines are mentally different from those on the western slopes. The winds bring from abroad thicker or subtler, drier or moister air, and generally air impregnated with a foreign climate, and

---

[1] Cf. II, 39–52, *passim*, and 67 *seq.*

[2] Cf. also fragment 1952 in I, 1473, about the "thickness of the blood" of the Muscovites which influences all their customs.

so, for physiological reasons, they must modify the mind. "The Sirocco is the intelligence which lords it over all heads in Italy" (II, 45), and the English are much affected by their east winds. Finally, the physical environment gets into our system through the food we eat. If the soil is full of iron, for instance, water and vegetation will be full of iron also, and through them iron will enter our stomach, our blood, and ultimately our mind as well. "Behold here spirit and character truly subject to the difference of the soils!" (II, 44).

In *De l'Esprit des Lois* the very same theory is set forth as in the *Essai sur les Causes*, and the only difference that is noticeable is the fact that somewhat greater emphasis is laid on the favourable effects of the northern climates. "The cold air contracts the ends of the exterior fibres of our body; this increases their elasticity and helps the return of the blood from the extremeties to the heart. It reduces the length of these same fibres; hence it increases their strength even more. The warm air, on the other hand, relaxes the end-pieces of the fibres and extends them; hence it diminishes their strength and their elasticity. For this reason, people have more vigour in cold climates. The action of the heart and the reaction of the ends of the fibres function better there, the body-fluids are better balanced, the blood is better directed towards the heart and, in return, the heart has more power. This greater strength must produce many effects [in the mind]: for instance, more self-confidence, that is to say, more courage; more awareness of one's superiority, that is to say, less desire for vengeance; more feeling of safety, that is to say, more frankness, less suspiciousness, craftiness and ruses . . . At the time of the Romans the peoples of the north of Europe lived without arts, without education, almost without laws; and yet, exclusively by the good sense attached to the coarse fibres of these climes, they maintained themselves with admirable wisdom against the Roman power, until the moment when they came out of their forests to destroy it . . . You will find in the climates of the north people who have few vices, plenty of virtues, much sincerity and straightforwardness. Approach the lands of the south, and you would believe yourself to move away from morality itself: more vivid passions will multiply crimes; everyone will try to gain over his neighbours all the advantages which may help [in the indulgence of] these same passions" (II, 474 *seq.*). Here again, Montesquieu impresses his modern reader as a fore-runner of the Le Play school, above all, it must be feared, of its most objectional character—of its *mystique*. Just as writers like Demolins saw in the tropical forest some obscure evil-generating powers at work which kept man low in body and mind, so Montesquieu sees in the northern atmosphere some value-evoking influence in activity which lifts the head and the heart of man high. The argument is substantially obscure. In spite of the physiological link between physical environment and moral and mental mettle, the dependence of the latter on the former cannot be said to be entirely explained in Montes-quieu's argument.

This mixed ecologico-materialistic doctrine gives way, on occasions, to a purely materialistic theory. For instance, differences in outlook and character between man and man within the same geographical environment are explained by Montesquieu by a reference to "the physical constitution of our machine". "Ideas which will do no more than touch the brain of one man will pierce that of another" (II, 56, but cf. especially 45–52). It all depends on the contents of our skulls and skins rather than on the contents of our minds. However, appearances of this purely materialistic opinion are comparatively rare. The doctrine as a whole is and remains a mixed ecologico-material-istic one, with a definite over-all predominance of the ecological factor.

The materialistic bias remained with Montesquieu to the end of his days. The *Essai sur le Goût* still shows some traces of it (cf. II, 1249). Nor does he seem to have had serious doubts about it. Only once does he bring up a decisive argument against it. "The ends of the fibres of our brain receive a small shock which produces a stimulation or sensation in us. That suffices to explain everything ... But," Montesquieu writes, a little uneasily, "if what I have just said is really true, why do the beasts not reason in the same way as men?" (I, 1537 *seq.*). Surely, a highly sensible and entirely legitimate question. But Montesquieu only raises it; he does not even try to give an answer.

IX

THE PRIMARY FACTORS :

(b) THE POLITICAL CONSTITUTION

To the ecologico-materialistic doctrine which we have just reviewed there is opposed, in Montesquieu's thought, a cœnonic-monogenetic theory which singles out the political constitution as the first cause of all mental life. The two conceptions and convictions face each other across a crevice in his mind, like two armies entrenched on different sides of a frontier, ready to do battle and yet loath really to come to grips. Its earliest or germinal form can be found in *Lettres Persanes* LXXXIX and XC, of which the former discusses liberty and servitude as political principles, or rather principles of political and social organisation, while the latter shows the overriding influence of the *point d'honneur* in certain countries such as France. Out of this there was to develop Montesquieu's all-pervading distinction of three types of state and society (the forms of government are to him the forms of society: social organisation is consequent upon, and carried by, the political constitution): democracy, monarchy, despotism, associated with, vitally connected to, made possible by, three types of sentiment or mentality: civic virtue, honour, and fear. In so far as men are free to choose for themselves, by a collective decision, the kind of constitution under which they want to live, they set, unbeknown to themselves, certain influences to work, which will tinge, permeate and shape their thoughts down to considerable detail and depth. And men are, in principle, free to pick one type of political organisation rather than another. For are they not reasonable and responsible for their actions? True, geography pushes them in one direction rather than in another. But need they follow the push as if they were inert masses? By no means. The push is strongest in the tropics; so much so that a despotic state is "natural" there; but though natural, it is not necessary. Montesquieu, for all his inclination towards an ecologico-materialistic doctrine, does not accept the proposition that man is fated to be dominated by physical necessities. Like polygamy and slavery, despotism is abominable and unacceptable wherever it is found. Indeed, it is to be resisted wherever it is found, even if it seems to fit in with the climatic conditions—with the "vices of the climate", as he so eloquently says. "The more the physical causes incline men towards an evil way of life," we may say, slightly modifying one of our author's most important sayings, yet remaining fully within his spirit (II, 480), "the more their moral efforts should lead them away from it." Indeed, resistance to an unfortunate push on the part of the physical forces of the environment in political matters is imperative and vital precisely because the basic decision concerning the constitution of the state sets up a new independent causality, a new independent chain of connections and concatenations, which determine, on their part and without reference to the geography in the background, the general character of social life, including its mental drift and cultural detail.

That this cœnonic-monogenetic theory was the rival rather than the complement of the ecologico-materialistic theory which lived cheek by jowl with it in Montesquieu's mind, can already be seen in the *Lettres Persanes*. The cowardliness of Oriental troops is contrasted there with the dash and daring of the French armies, but there is no reference to the relaxing quality of the Persian climate or the astringent quality of the Western European air. No; the reason given for the difference in valour is connected with the constitutional life of the two territories. The Persian armies are "composed of slaves who are naturally cowardly" and "overcome the fear of death only by the fear of punishment, which produces in the soul a new kind of terror which reduces them to something like stupidity" (I, 264), while those who enlist under the French colours are free men with all the qualities which independence can give, and who gladly expose themselves to danger and death because they are actuated by the hope of, and sensibility to, honour (freedom and honour, in other words democracy and monarchism, are as yet not distinguished by Montesquieu): "One can put it forward as a maxim that in each state the desire of glory increases with the liberty of the subjects and decreases with it: glory is never a companion of servitude" (*ib*). If the geographical element is here prominent by its absence, the same can be said of a definition of "national character" which seems to have been drafted by Montesquieu on the threshold of his maturity: "I call *genius of a nation* the *mores* and the mental character of the different peoples which are directed by the influence of the same court and of the same capital" (I, 1327). One would have thought that in a definition of this kind the environmental factor could not have been left out; but the fact of the matter is that it was.

The power of the cœnonic-monogenetic theory, the sway which it had over Montesquieu's mind, can best be seen from the fact that, in its progressive application, it forms the backbone of *De l'Esprit des Lois*. With remarkable consistency it is shown how the totality of the life-manifestations of a society flows from the political principle which is at the basis of its organisation. A society can only survive—indeed, can only come into being and be—if it is organised, ordered, pacified: hence the central power which guarantees the coherence of the social whole is studied first (books II and III). Once the die is cast and a specific form of organisation and ordering is selected the practices of education must accommodate themselves to it if the state and society so created are to continue and to survive—book IV. But if a specific education creates a specific type of man in response to the fundamental principle of socio-political organisation, then the detailed laws which are to control the doings of that kind of man must also fall into line;[1] and so book V is devoted to legislation other than constitutional.

[1] Speaking, in a fragment, of the unwisdom of changing established laws, Montesquieu adds: "I would not, however, blame the Romans for the great changes which occurred in their jurisprudence: they changed the government, and it was necessary that their civil laws should follow their political laws" (II, 1111). Cf. also II, 788 *seq.*, where the same idea is applied to the development of the Roman law of succession from a purely agnatic system (appropriate to a republican constitution) to the later cognatic system of Justinian (fitting in with the changed political situation). Cf. furthermore the interesting chapter I of book VI where Montesquieu explains why in a monarchy law will grow and legal thought will flourish, whereas both will languish in despotically ruled countries.

Now, where there is established an educational and a legal norm, there can also be deviations from that norm, there can be lawbreaking in the widest sense of the word, which will threaten the preservation of the order and organisation at the root of state and society. Books VI–VIII deal with these corrupting influences and the ways in which each particular menace can be held at bay. It is clear that both attack and defence will be determined by the social order already defined —by what is to be attacked and what is to be defended. As the menace can come from outside as well as from within, two books (IX and X) are then devoted to alliances and armies. Even the military field is closely tied to the general nature of the socio-political whole: both what can be done and what should be done by the armed power of a state depends upon that state, i.e. in the last analysis on its political nature. Finally, the existence and importance of a central power raises the problem of individual liberty. The citizen must be defended against arbitrariness on the part of those in power (book XI), against the harshness and possible injustice of the penal laws (book XII), and against oppression in the matter of taxation (book XIII). Thus one impetus travels through all departments of the social life, and it is imparted by what is behind and prior to them all, the principle of political organisation, which appears in this way as a truly active influence, as a source of energy almost, which, like a power plant, sends its shocks and waves and radiations into every nook and cranny of the structure, determining without exception all phenomena within its confines.

A discussion in which the *modus operandi* of Montesquieu's mind can be well observed is that of the penal law. Other writers see the legal system determined by such principles as retribution, deterrence, or reformation, in other words, principles resting in themselves and independent of the political set-up. Not so Montesquieu. What the nature and the measure of punishment will be like in a state or society will depend on the character of the constitution. "It would be easy to prove that, in all or almost all the States of Europe, punishments have diminished or increased in the measure in which they have drawn near to, or moved away from, liberty ... Severity suits despotic government, whose principle is terror, better than monarchy and republic which have for their basis honour and virtue" (II, 318). A despot who is isolated from his subjects can only keep his state together by striking fear into his subjects' hearts; a monarch who stands near to his people and has many distinctions to bestow, can play upon their sense of honour; a republic which rests on the shoulders of all can be controlled by a moral censorship exerted by citizen over citizen. Plainly, the three situations with their respective needs are altogether different, and this forces the penal law into three distinct forms. There is, in Montesquieu's opinion, no point in seeing the criminal or the crime or the penalty inflicted in isolation. The student of legislation, and more particularly the student of the mental genesis of legal enactments, must see them in the concrete framework of state and society, for only then will he comprehend why they are what they are.

Another point at which we can see that, for Montesquieu, everything is determined once the form of the state is fixed, is the chapter of taxation. Where there is liberty, there man is active, and there is wealth; where there is despotism, there the springs of economic action are paralysed, and industry will languish. Hence in a despotic state it would do no good to tax commodities; there will be too few of them; poll taxes will be more appropriate. But in free countries, taxation can be based on merchandise; and this both fits in with the existing freedom and augments it, while the poll taxes of despotic countries make slavery doubly slavish. The rate of taxation is similarly determined, by remote action as it were, by the constitution: "It is possible to raise higher taxes in proportion to the liberty of the subjects; and it is necessary to reduce them in the measure in which servitude increases. This has always been so and will always be so. This is a rule drawn from nature which does not vary; it can be found [confirmed] throughout all countries . . ." (II, 466). There are, then, no all-embracing truths concerning public finance; what is true, as what is appropriate, will depend upon the political order in which the system of public finance is to operate.

But not only taxation and material production—the production of goods—depend upon the political framework of society, even population—the production of men—is determined from that side. "Colonies are more convenient for republican States," Montesquieu writes. "As they abound in men, their loss does not make itself felt . . . Because the countries governed by one man are as a rule less populated than others,[1] colonies lead to [their] depopulation" (II, 1007). A passage such as this is particularly interesting because it shows how far, in Montesquieu's opinion, the chain of causation which starts with the constitution as *causa causans* extends: it not only runs through the whole of society, but it also stretches beyond it into the semi-biotic field of the birth-rate and survival-rate.

From the point of view of the sociology of knowledge, population, penal legislation and public finance are, of course, no more than marginal phenomena. But Montesquieu also applies the very same method of derivation, analysis and interpretation in connection with purely abstract, philosophical ideas. Why do we find in the Orient the belief in absolute predestination which forms one of the chief articles of the Moslem creed? Because, Montesquieu answers, we find there the political system of tyranny: "The Mohammedans," he writes, "have every day before their eyes examples of events so unexpected, of facts so extraordinary, effects of arbitrary power, that they must naturally be inclined to believe in the doctrine of a rigid Destiny which directs all. In our climes, where power is moderate, our actions are ordinarily subject to the rules of prudence, and our good or our bad fortune is ordinarily the consequence of our wisdom. For this reason we have not got the idea of a blind fatality. In the romances of the East, you see men incessantly led by that blind fatality and rigid destiny" (I, 1568).

In all this long chain of causal connection, it is the first link which seems to Montesquieu the firmest. The constitution is the substructure; a certain mentality—civic virtue in republics, honour in monarchies, fear in tyrannical states—is the superstructure; why? Because we cannot imagine that the substructural principles of social and state organisation would ever work, unless they were supplemented by the appropriate ideologies. How could a democratic state function, unless the *demos* were patriotic (i.e. "virtuous") and imbued with that love

---

[1] Cf. II, 689 where the reasons why despotism leads to a low birth-rate are given.

of universal equality which sees in every man a co-partner in the basic political rights and duties, unless it were aware of its heavy responsibilities and felt in accordance with them? How could a limited, law-obeying monarchy function, unless men fell in with the hierarchical principle constitutive of it, unless everyone in the social pyramid stretching, with many intermediate stations, from serf to king, took a pride in his particular place and upheld its duties, i.e. its honour? And how, finally, could a despotic order ever survive, unless the victims of it were afraid to break the chain that holds them down, unless a sentiment of fear were at the bottom of their minds? Montesquieu here appeals to our intuition. We must see, with the help of our imagination, indeed, with the help of a certain "logic of life",[1] how things are hanging together, and, indeed, have to hang together. A republic that was pervaded by strong upward- and downward-looking sentiments, by sentiments of aristocratic superiority and popular inferiority, or that was filled with suspicion and hatred of the men at the controls, would simply cease to be a proper republic: just so would a monarchy with a universal feeling of absolute equality or with an isolated, law-defying, capriciously commanding ruler cease to be a proper monarchy: and a despotic state in which the despot was just a citizen, or at any rate, like a good king, near the citizens and bound by a traditional hierarchical order, would not, by any stretch of the imagination, be describable as truly despotic. "Here are principles," Montesquieu writes in connection with a brief summary of these ideas, "of so great a fertility that they make up almost the whole of my book" (II, 1181).

Around virtue, honour and fear there gather, in Montesquieu's opinion, three total world-views which fill men's minds as long as the three political systems respectively connected with these three basic sentiments continue to function as they should. The picture which our author sketches out of these three total world-views shows the deeply realistic nature of his mind. Quite obviously, the system of ideas appropriate to virtue and hence to republicanism is, for him, best exemplified by republican Rome, by the Rome of Cato the Censor. There is a love of equality which, in turn, is bound up with a love of frugality.

[1] Cf. Stark, *The Sociology of Knowledge*, 1958, 287.

(It is only by virtue of universal frugality that general equality can survive.) Luxury is abhorred as effeminating and demoralising. Women are severely kept in their place. A certain rude and hard honesty prevails and citizen watches over citizen in a general anxiety to keep the civic life clean. Individualism will be strong in so far as every man will be a highly disciplined, sternly self-responsible person; but there will be little difference between neighbour and neighbour as far as the style of life is concerned. All, having more or less the same means, will also have, and wish to have, the same pleasures and joys and hopes as all the others. Likewise, there will be a great deal of uniformity in the basic breadwinning activities. All will have, and be content to have, more or less the same amount of land to till and to harvest, the same kind of herd and the same number of beasts to tend and to breed, etc. etc. All this will sum up to a way of life and mode of thought and feeling in which private interests will fall into the background and public concerns rise to the pinnacle of importance. This is precisely what Montesquieu means by civic virtue: a preoccupation with the welfare of the community rather than with personal advancement, and he sees it growing out of the spirit of frugality which is the logical and necessary complement of that fundamental equality which in turn is the very substance of all democracy, of all republicanism. Such, he fancies, was Rome, such were the Romans in their happy halcyon days of rustic simplicity, when they embodied one of the fundamental principles of political and social organisation and showed forth its inherent glories to all the world and to all centuries.

The description of the monarchy and its associated habits of life, thought and feeling is even more realistic. If Montesquieu relied for his sketch of republicanism on certain historical researches, more particularly on his reading of the Roman historians, he based his picture of the monarchic system on direct observation, the observation of contemporary conditions. No doubt, it is inspired by the French society to which he himself belonged, or at any rate by the idea which he entertained of what French society could be like, should be like, and would be like, if only certain alien and illegitimate surface phenomena were lopped off, such as the excrescences which absolutism had brought forth under Richelieu's nefarious influence. If equality is the hall-mark of democracy, inequality is of the very essence of true monarchy: the king occupying the centre of the stage, all other inhabitants must of necessity be relatively near to him or relatively far away from him, and thereby they fall into status-groups each with its own appropriate position and radius. The public function will, naturally and necessarily, also be broken up in the same hierarchical fashion, and with public office will be associated a parallel style of life, the more brilliant the nearer an office bearer is to the central sun, to the *roi soleil*, and the greyer and drabber, the further away from him. "If the monarchical state is to maintain itself, luxury must increase by degrees from the labourer to the artisan, to the business man, to the nobles, to the magistrates, to the *grand seigneurs* . . . to the princes; without this, all would be lost" (II, 336). In contrast to the despotic constitution, it is this gradated pattern which determines the life of the monarchy, and not the will of the ruler, however much he may be at the apex of the social pyramid, however much this pyramid may fall away from him on all sides. Durkheim, his eyes sharpened by a particular sympathy with these sections of Montesquieu's work, saw quite clearly that Montesquieu was thinking here in terms of the organological simile.[1] The king is the head of the body social, other functionaries are its organs, each at its appropriate place. Now, an organ is by definition a part, not the whole. It will be—it ought to be even—absorbed in its proper task. Hence the ideologies springing up in a monarchy will be partial, status- and function-bound, not a global patriotism as under a republic. The good man will be proud of his specific duties: he will, in other words, be filled with a sentiment of honour in accordance with the vital function which it has fallen to his lot to fulfil. Characteristically, Montesquieu defines honour in one context as "the prejudice of each person and each condition of life" (II, 256). Man will here, as it were, turn inward upon himself, upon his work—not outward towards the *polis* as under the democratic dispensation. For this reason, the degree of moralisation, of self-denial, will be lower in a monarchy than in a democracy. Absorption in a narrowly-circumscribed office, which tends to cover up the vital concerns of the whole *quâ* whole, leads to a certain amount of self-preference:

[1] *Montesquieu et Rousseau, Précurseurs de la Sociologie*, ed. 1953, 63.

all division of labour contains a centrifugal element. "It is the nature of honour to demand preferences and distinctions" (II, 257). Ambitiousness will belong to the mental habitus of man as bred under a monarchical order. The habit of looking upward will be universal and will give rise to invidious comparisons. "The virtues which come to the surface here are always less [concerned with] what one owes to others than [with] what one owes to oneself: they are not so much what directs us towards our fellow-citizens as what distinguishes us from them" (II, 262). However, this very diversity of functions and interests and preoccupations is the guarantee of ultimate harmony. At this crucial point Montesquieu comes very near to that Leibnizian doctrine of pre-established harmony which later on was to be carried into almost every brain by Adam Smith's *Wealth of Nations*. The natural way in which ambition will work itself out will be by inspiring every one with the desire to fulfil his function particularly well. Montesquieu says it is one of the "supreme rules" of "honour" "when we have once been placed in a [certain] rank, not to do or allow anything that may make it appear that we hold ourselves inferior to that same rank" (II, 264 *seq.*). The sentiment which dominates the type of man born and bred in and for the monarchy, and whose main ingredients are restriction, partiality, ambition and pride, will above all induce him to live up to his station in life, and that means, of necessity, also its specific and inherent duties; hence it will strengthen the body social and political, not weaken or destroy it: all division of labour contains a centripetal element which will keep the centrifugal tendencies well in check. "Ambition is pernicious in a republic. It has good effects in a monarchy; it gives life to that government . . . One might say that it is as with the system of the universe where there is a force which, without ceasing, drives all bodies away from the centre, and a gravitational force which brings them back. Honour sets all the parts of the body politic in motion; it binds them together by its very action; and it will be found that everybody works towards the common good in the belief that he is working for his particular interests" (II, 257). It is because of this spontaneous, even automatic identification of discordant interests that the monarchy is admirable as a socio-political system. Whereas the republic will produce in men's minds more virtuousness, the monarchy will be able to do without that constant (and ever precarious) ethical effort—a fact which will give it as much superiority over the other system as inferiority. "In the monarchical states, the political constitution [*la politique*] induces men to undertake great things with the absolute minimum of virtue; as, in the most admirable machines, art employs as few movements, forces and wheels as possible. The state subsists independently of love for the fatherland, desire for true glory, self-renunciation, sacrifice of one's dearest interests, and all those heroic virtues which we find in the ancients, and which we know only from hearsay" (II, 255). Here, then, is a type of society, of life, of thought, of feeling, which is different from, though as distinctive as, the republican displayed in Catonian and pre-Catonian Rome—the type traditional, *par excellence*, to France.

Montesquieu meant his estimate of the despotic government to be just as realistic as his discussions of the other two basic forms. If he did not succeed—and it must be admitted that the chapters of *De l'Esprit des Lois* concerned read more like a piece of caricature than like a piece of pure description—the reason was that he trusted too much to his sources, that he took the brass farthings of the travel books too readily for gold coin. However, his analysis remains interesting, even if it is to some extent hypothetical. For the rest, it is comparatively crude and brief. The characteristic feature of despotism is the subjection of all to the caprice of one: as in republics, all are equal in despotic states, but they are equal not because they are all in and for public life, but because they are nothing; as in monarchies, all are subject, but they are not subject to a law-abiding king who is merely the steward of the common weal, but to a law-less tyrant who pleases nobody but himself. Men are here cut off from the intellectually vivifying conduct of public affairs. "As for the enchainment of events, they cannot follow it, or foresee it, or even conceive of it" (II, 293). Their minds will become sluggish because their wills have nothing to exercise themselves upon. *Dolce far niente* will be the slogan of thought and action. Conservatism will be rampant. The large-scale tyranny of the head of state will breed petty tyranny on the part of the heads of families. Women will be treated like slaves, locked away in seraglios and harems and will become correspondingly denaturalised and stultified. If the state holds together, if the family holds together, this will be due to the couldn't-care less attitude of all subjects and to the fear of the tyrant's vengeance which will be the backcloth of all political life (if indeed we can speak of a political life at all here). Such a social system will not achieve much in the realm of thought and artistic creation, and what it will achieve will be tainted by the faults of the constitution. The mind will, as it were, be obscured by the shadow of the tyrant and of tyranny. "Extreme obedience presupposes ignorance in him who obeys; it presupposes it even in him who commands; he need hardly deliberate, doubt, or reason; all he needs is to exert his will . . . Knowledge would here be dangerous, [mental] effort unfortunate" (II, 265). An active intellect can only be a source of evil both for the individual and the state. "All must turn here upon two or three ideas; new ones must not come in. When you train a beast, you take good care not to change its trainer, its lesson and its tricks; you knock into its brain two or three movements, and no more" (II, 292). But under a despot's heel, men are apt to sink down in spirit to the level of the beast.

This, in sum and substance, is Montesquieu's cœnonic-monogenetic sociology of knowledge. The best proof that it dominated his mind like no other theory is the fact that he applied it on a large scale and used it as a key to the analysis of the two phenomena which interested him most—Roman history and British politics. He sees the abolition of the regal office and the introduction of the republican magistrature of the consuls as the beginning of Rome's ascent in the world as well as of the specific Roman republican character. Kings, he says, certainly have spells of military ambition, but, being human, they also have other passions, and they also have spells of laziness; so, under kings, war will not be continuous and the martial virtues will not always be stirred. But the consuls held office only for a year, and had to make their mark within that year, especially if they wanted to be re-elected. So they were supremely ambitious while in office, and were replaced by equally ambitious men when they went out. Constant war-plans were the result. But the other power-holders in the city according to the republican constitution were only too ready to fall in with these plans. The Senate, always irritated by the groaning and grumbling of the people, was only too pleased to see their energies deflected from domestic issues to foreign enterprises, and the people themselves were keen on war because war meant booty for those who joined the expedition and lots of land for the poor, even for those who stayed at home. Thus the impetus towards war and warlikeness, due ultimately to a constitutional detail, the annuality of the consular office, spread through all the limbs of the body politic and produced the specifically Roman bellicose character both of mind and action which we know from the annals of history. It also produced the very glory of Rome, Roman patriotism. This patriotism was engendered not only by the elation of victory, but also by the fear of defeat which must have haunted the Romans; the luck of arms being what it is. "Always exposed to the most frightful vengeance, constancy and valour became necessary for them; and these virtues could not be distinguished with them from the love of self, of their family, of their fatherland, and of all that is held most dear among men" (II, 73). Here then we have a consistent explanation of the Roman mentality on the basis of Montesquieu's cœnonic-monogenetic theory.

But not only the rise of that mentality, even its decay can be made understandable with the help of these same analytical conceptions. The fact that Rome was a proper republic meant that it had at its basis a more or less egalitarian distribution of the land. This universality and equality of possessions made for a spirit of unity, or rather gave to the spirit of unity forged in the fires of war a solid, one could almost say, territorial basis. But this basis was unstable. Inequality is always apt to creep in, and it did. Once a rich class was established—established by "the greed of some individuals, and the prodigality of others"[1]—corruption began to set in. Luxury appeared; a class of artisans pandering to that luxury formed in consequence. Artisans, unlike landholders, Montesquieu says, have no fatherland. Their skill is mobile and can be put to use anywhere, whereas land is bound for better and for worse to the state where it is placed. Thus a measure of impure blood was beginning to flow through the veins of Rome's body politic. Worse still: the bulk of Roman wealth was no longer in the

[1] Notice here the moral emphasis of the argument!

hands of her soldiers, but in the hands of a lot of effeminates and idlers. The warriors no longer felt that, in fighting, they fought for themselves. An ominous crack had appeared in the edifice of the Roman constitution (II, 81).

Montesquieu supports this argument by a brief application of the comparative method. The Spartan kings Agis and Cleomenes noticed that the land-less inhabitants of their city (a considerable proportion of the population) were cowardly, and restored the situation by leading the polity back to the old egalitarianism in land distribution; and this was why "Lacedæmon resumed her pristine power, and again became formidable for all the Greeks" (II, 82). Sparta, then, was wiser than Rome; but Carthage was even more foolish. She fell so soon, because she allowed her social and political constitution to disintegrate. "Ancient mores, a certain practice of poverty, made fortunes more or less equal in Rome: but at Carthage individuals had the wealth of kings" (II, 84). So Carthage became a place of dissensions, of factions, of class struggles; and her humiliation and annihilation was fated to follow her moral corruption—that moral, social and political corruption which, in the end, overtook the Roman republic also.

But the political democracy of Rome perished not only because the social democracy underneath it decayed and disappeared. It also degenerated because the Roman, characteristically republican, system of social control could no longer effectively operate once the limits of the Roman state had been pushed out beyond the mountains and the Mediterranean. "When the legions passed the Alps and the sea, the military, who had to be left during several campaigns in the countries which had been subdued, lost little by little the spirit of citizenship; and the generals who disposed of armies and kingdoms felt their power and could no longer obey" (II, 117). The soldiers were no longer the city's soldiers—they were the soldiers of Sulla, of Marius, of Pompey, of Cæsar. The Senate no longer knew whether the men to whom they had entrusted their armies, were their servants or their enemies. The extension of Roman citizenship to other Italic towns had the same effect. All disintegrated when Rome was no longer Rome but a multitude of cities, each with a different character, a different magistrature, a different set of deities. The republic was lost, and with it liberty and the old Roman mentality. "*Les sentiments romains ne furent plus*" (II, 118).

Superficially, this second cause of Rome's decay and of the replacement of the old proud and powerful citizen spirit by the corrupt spirit and semi-slave mentality of the imperial age, is the sheer growth of the area controlled by Rome, her sheer spacial extension. But in the last analysis even this surface cause is in the depth linked with that constitutional subsoil in which all developments, substructural and superstructural, are, in Montesquieu's firm conviction, rooted. Why did Rome grow? Why did her eagles cross mountains and seas? Why did her very heart become dilated and diseased by the association of other Italian tribes with the Roman master race proper? Only because she was constantly at war and successful in war. And she was that because of her republican constitution. Paradoxically, but unavoidably, Rome's downfall was the remote effect of her rise. "She lost her liberty, because she achieved her purpose all too soon" (II, 120). All too soon, we may add, and all too well. In the end, the cause of causes was throughout the constitution of the state[1] and its inner dynamic.

In all this discussion and analysis of the Roman culture mentality, there is hardly any reference to the climatic factor. It is different with the chapter (it is 27 of book XIX) in which Montesquieu tries to explain the character of the British culture from the British constitution which is its fostering soil. Not only is there, right at the beginning, a formal acknowledgment of the fact that "the climate has produced, in great part the laws, the mores and the manners of that nation" (II, 574 *seq.*), but the geographical element keeps breaking into the text even later on. Nevertheless, Montesquieu states it to be his prime concern to find out the effects which must have followed, the character which must have formed, and the manners which must have grown up in this nation under the influence of "the principles of her constitution", and he is convinced that, all the

---

[1] Montesquieu hints—though he does no more than hint—that the rot might have been stopped and the republic preserved by a timely halt to the policy of constant extension. "A wise republic," he says in the chapter discussing the causes of Rome's decay, "should not hazard anything that exposes her to good or bad fortune: the only good which she should pursue is the perpetuation of her constitution [*son etat*] (II, 117). In other words, if Rome fell, she fell because she followed too mechanically and too long the impetus coming from her original and basic socio-political organisation.

environmental pressures notwithstanding, "the mores and manners of that people must have a close connection with its [fundamental] laws" (*ib*).

England is a free country: every citizen can follow his own sweet will. The first consequence of this will be that all the passions will proliferate, especially "hate, envy, jealousy, [and] the greed for enrichment and distinction". This is even necessary because "if this were otherwise, the State would be like a man laid low by sickness who has no passions because he has no strength" (II, 575). As there are two organised political powers, the executive and the legislative, a certain factiousness must appear: the English will be either royalistic in their inclinations or parliamentarian. But freedom, or rather capriciousness, will often induce people to change over from the one party to the other, and these changes, being an accepted thing, will weaken the sense of loyalty to one's friends. The masses, being neither in the confidence of the Crown nor effectually in control of the Commons, will tend to be suspicious and always agitated. But their disquiet will have no hard and fast object, and so it will have no bad effect; on the contrary, it will keep the politicians on their toes. The popular disquiet will, in truth, be so innocuous and so weak that it will give way to a burst of loyalty and patriotism as soon as a foreign power should threaten the realm. The love of liberty, being justified, will be very real; it will be so great that the taxpayer will cheerfully bear a considerable burden and that that burden will appear smaller in peoples' minds than it really is.

A curious trait of the British social system which seems to have struck Montesquieu with particular force (as it has other foreign observers since his day) is the fact that in some respects the class contrast is more definite in Britain than in other countries, whereas in other respects it is far less so. Montesquieu's explanation is characteristic of his cœnonic-monogenetic constitutional theory: "The dignities, forming part and parcel of the fundamental constitution, will be more fixed than elsewhere; but the great will, in this land of liberty, approach closer to the people; hence the ranks [as such] will be more separated, and the individuals [as individuals] more intermixed" (II, 581).

Indeed, in a state so democratically constituted as Britain

is, a strong individualism will come to birth. People will be judged less by inherited position than by individual achievement. The "real qualities" which, Montesquieu says, will count, will be the making of money and personal merit (II, 581). Human relations will be characterised by the same basic individualism. If we may, anachronistically, express Montesquieu's pertinent idea with the help of a terminology developed much later, we could say that he regards Britain as a "society" in Tœnnies' sense rather than as a community. "As the laws are here no more made for one person than for another, everyone will consider himself a monarch; and men will in this nation be confederates rather than fellow-citizens"—held together by a contractual tie rather than by an organic one (II, 582). Men will live side by side rather than together, and they will even show each other a certain measure of haughtiness and disdain. "As no citizen will fear any other citizen, this nation will be proud; the pride of kings is [after all] only founded on their independence" (II, 582 *seq.*). But individualism, independence, self-reliance, pride—all the salient features of democratic man—will bring something uneasy, something strained into human relations. "These men who are so proud, as they live a good deal in isolation, will find themselves often in the midst of strangers; they will be shy, and they will show, most of the time, a curious mixture of bashfulness and haughtiness" (II, 583). There are many foreign observers who have noted the same fact. Montesquieu's personal merit is to have tried to understand it, to have linked it up with the British constitution.

The basic British freedom will (together with the geographical fact of the country's insular situation) have another effect of very great consequence for the mental life of the British— it will give them economic prosperity and thereby turn them towards commerce. There will spring up a certain xenophobia. "A trading nation has a prodigious number of petty individual interests; hence she can offend and be offended in an infinity of ways. She will become supremely jealous; and she will be more grieved by the prosperity of others than cheered by her own" (II, 578). Her commercial policy will be hard and sharp. On the other hand, she will be pacific. Colonies, for instance— which the colonists, filled by the love of British institutions, will make into new overseas Britains—will be established for the sake of profit rather than for that of domination. Her navy, though strong, will be a tool of defence, not of aggression. Her sea-power will, however, give her citizens a feeling of superiority over other nations and thus breed a certain national pride. In diplomatic negotiations, Britain will be a shade more honest than the other powers; as the ministers are constitutionally forced to justify their conduct before Parliament and are held responsible for it, secret diplomacy will be somewhat less secret here than elsewhere, and a salutary check to dishonesty will thus come into operation.

However, the democratic way of life produces some dubious effects on the mental and moral tone of the nation, as well as some favourable ones. It will, for instance, induce people to argue about politics without necessarily arguing and reasoning well; though this, Montesquieu assures us, is not likely to lead to any untoward consequences in a free nation. Satirical writings will tend to be ferocious—*sanglants*. This will be due to the individualism and to the retiringness of the British. "Society teaches us to see the ridiculous; isolation renders us more apt to notice vices." There will be many Juvenals among the British and hardly a Horace. The historians will not be over-careful of the truth, and though this may not be a direct consequence of the democratic constitution, it is an indirect consequence of it, in so far as liberty produces politics and political parties, and these in turn prejudice and propaganda. "In extremely absolute monarchies, the historians betray the truth because they are not free to express it: in extremely liberal states they betray the truth because of their liberty itself, which, always producing divisions, makes everyone as much the slave of the ideology of his faction as he would be of a despot" (II, 583). Montesquieu acknowledges, however, that, on the highest level, British individualism will have a favourable effect on the work of the spirit. The best British philosophers will be men of concentration who will be thinking for themselves (*ib*).

One of the finest observations of Montesquieu's is the awareness that the British have managed to express their democratic way of life in essentially undemocratic (e.g. monarchical) forms. This, too, is the effect of constitutional law, of constitutional developments. "It may be that this nation, having in the past been subject to arbitrary power, has in several respects preserved its style; so that the form of absolute government will often be seen above the real basis of free government" (II, 580).

It is also due to the memory of one-time absolutism that the British hate and persecute Roman Catholicism. The old religion is, by an association of ideas, connected in the British mind with the old constitution and must share its fate, that of banishment. If this attitude is the negative side, as it were, of the working out of British constitutional freedom in the religious field, its positive side is twofold. Free men will follow their lights or their fancies even in religious matters. Hence they will either become indifferent, and that will often mean in practice that they will, by sheer inertia, remain in the Church of England, or they will become fired by religious sentiment, and then they will found all manner of sects. It is remarkable, however, how jealously even the religiously indifferent will defend religious freedom. Religious freedom will be for them the first line of defence of all freedom; it will be upheld, not for its own sake, but for its importance to the constitution. In the generally democratic atmosphere of Britain the clergy will be less of a closed estate than abroad; they will tend to merge with the generality of citizens. Hence they can only assert their dignity by exemplary conduct. And they can only gain the people for religion by means of argument and persuasion. For this reason "there will be seen to come from their pen very fine works in proof of the revelation and the providence of the Great Being" (II, 580 *seq.*).

With this analysis of religious attitudes, Montesquieu has entered the higher reaches of the superstructure, of the realm of the spirit. But he presses further forward towards the comprehension of even more intangible traits, and here a certain tendency to compare Britain and France, i.e. democracy and monarchy, makes itself felt. In Britain, the political power of those who rule must be renewed, regained, every day; for that reason the upper classes will be more interested in those who can be useful to them than in those who can amuse them. In France, the nobles are secure in their position; they are not preoccupied with politics; they have plenty of time on hand; and so there will grow up around them a group of courtiers, flatterers and toadies who will help them to while away their idle hours. The British, constantly taken up with the pursuit of their interests, will not develop refined forms and manners; the French, on the other hand, in their idleness and emptiness, will develop the canon of politeness and bring it to high perfection. This is characteristic of an undemocratic mode of life. "The period of the [rule of] politeness among the Romans is the same as that of the establishment of arbitrary power. Absolute government produces idleness, and idleness calls forth politeness" (II, 582). Another factor leading in Britain in the same direction, towards a life without social graces, is the comparative absence of women from public life, which Montesquieu also thinks natural in a democratic country. Where all men bear the burden of political rule, the frivolities of *galanterie* will not be able to unfold, and the pursuit of sex will be apt to take place in cruder forms, in the forms of debauchery. Both Britain and France will, in the upper reaches of the social pyramid, develop luxury, but democratic luxury will be different from monarchical-aristocratic luxury. The democratic society will develop habits of "solid" luxury— luxury "founded not on the refinements of vanity, but on that of real needs"; the monarchical society will, so Montesquieu implies, breed a form of luxury which will be less "solid", more ostentatious, more showy, more extrovert. Montesquieu, it seems, is thinking here of the difference between Scottish homespuns and Lyons silks, Staffordshire mugs and Sèvres cups, English barons of beef and French *hors d'oeuvres*. English civilisation will, in a word, be civilisation without frivolity. Those who have more money to play with than they can reasonably use will become splenetic rather than effeminate and corrupt. The riding of odd hobby horses is in line with a democratic culture, but voluptuousness is not.

England, as one can see, emerges fairly unscathed from Montesquieu's critical analysis. Yet he says—a typical French judgment—that "in that nation there will be more cleverness than taste" (II, 581). And he carries this opinion ultimately into the very citadel of culture—into the highest reaches of art, into poetry. "There poets," he says of the British, winding up this whole discussion, and thinking particularly, so we are told,[1]

---

[1] Cf. II, 1514, M. Caillois' notes.

of Milton—"their poets will have more often an original rudeness of invention than a certain delicacy such as taste can give: what one will find in them will come closer to the power of Michelangelo than to the grace of Raphael" (II, 582). For democracy the virtues of naturalness and honesty; for the monarchy, the glories of *raffinement* and *finesse*.

X

THE PROBLEM OF THE ULTIMATE
DETERMINANT

THE two thought-determining influences, geography and government, sometimes work together, pressing the mental life of the men subject to them in the same direction. It is both the heat and despotism that make certain Asiatics dull and placid; it is both the cold and democracy which incline certain Europeans to be active both in body and in spirit. But Montesquieu treats these cases as no more than accidental. There is no such thing as a pre-established harmony between the geographical and the governmental factor. They may be sometimes in co-operation, but often they will be in conflict, the one tending to lead human thought in one direction, the other pressing it into an opposite development. We have seen already that Montesquieu is inclined to believe that among the savages nature holds supreme sway,[1] whereas in civilised communities such as Rome the maxims of government are far more important than geography (cf. II, 558). "There are some climates where *le physique* has so much strength that *la morale* can do almost nothing" (II, 514). But these are exceptional rather than the rule. Usually, there will be a tussle between the two tendencies. "Acquired taste," Montesquieu writes in his last work, the *Essai sur le Goût*, meaning socially determined

---

[1] Another situation mentioned by our author in which "the physical causes have the strength to act by themselves" is the case of people, who "are inhabitants of inaccessible mountains". Cf. I, 1303, fragment 1209, where, however, the influence of the physical factors is played down. All that Montesquieu admits here is that the physical causes "would sally forth and act in all their breadth", if "moral causes did not interrupt them"—but they do.

taste, "affects, changes, augments and diminishes natural taste, just as natural taste affects, changes, augments and diminishes acquired taste" (II, 1242). There is, then, a trial of strength, a contest for the mastery of men's minds, and the question arises which factor will usually emerge victorious. There is every indication that Montesquieu regarded this problem as the sore spot of his whole sociology of knowledge; if he did, he was certainly justified. Granting for argument's sake that there are two tendencies at work in the substructural sphere, it is surely incumbent on him who wants to elucidate the superstructural complex, its genesis and its content, to show in which way and to what respective degree they co-determine it. It is a weakness of Montesquieu's that he came to no assured and final solution of this difficulty. He was not bold enough to cut the Gordian knot. And this is all the more regrettable, as a solution, and a very sound one, is often approached and even sometimes expressed, but never with the assurance and insistence which would have been necessary to close the system of ideas at whose construction Montesquieu was working.

What is the evidence? It falls naturally into two groups of passages, the one seeming to ascribe the primacy to the geographical element, the other to government. The former have always been emphasised, and more often than not over-emphasised, by those who were themselves inclined towards a one-sidedly materialistic view of social life. Franck Alengry, for instance, a follower of the younger, still largely Spencerian, Durkheim, thought it possible to sum up Montesquieu's theory in the following words: "The positive laws of a country derive from the form of its government, but this [in turn] derives by necessity from the number of citizens living in society, from the volume of that society, from the nature of the soil which supports it and from the climate which environs it. Here we behold so many mechanical causes over which the human will has no power; for it must submit to them as to the other natural necessities, for instance to the necessities of astronomy and physics."[1] This interpretation of Montesquieu's thought is about as realistic as would be a description of the moon based exclusively on its appearance in the first quarter when it is as yet

[1] *La Sociologie chez Auguste Comte*, 1900, 392 *seq.* Cf. also 394 and 399.

a wan, thin sickle in the sky and not yet a shining rounded disc.

The passage which is invariably, almost automatically, quoted when an attempt is made to prove that Montesquieu was really and truly a geographical determinist, is a short sentence from chapter 14 of book XIX of *De l'Esprit des Lois:* "The empire of the climate is the first of all empires" (II, 565). Certainly, taken by and for itself, this terse formula seems to assert, and that unequivocally, the primacy of the geographical factors. But short sentences must never be taken by and for themselves. And if we read the paragraph of which this sentence forms the end, we see that it implies no argument in favour of geographical determinism; on the contrary. Montesquieu discusses in this chapter the innovations which Peter the Great was introducing into Russia, particularly the innovation in the field of manners—the introduction of women into society, the shaving of men's whiskers etc. "What made this change easier [to carry out]", he writes, "is that the *mores* of those days [i.e. before the reforms began] were foreign to the climate and had been imported by the intermixture of the nations and by conquests. Peter I, giving the *mores* and manners of Europe to a nation of Europe, found a facility which he himself had not expected. The empire of the climate is the first of all empires" (*loc. cit.*). How clear this passage is, and how unfavourable to geographical determinism! Let us note first of all that Montesquieu operates here with the concept of a "European climate" as if there was such a thing, as if Norway and Italy could really be thrown together. It is plain that no convincing argument can ever be built on such shoddy foundations. But let that pass. What Montesquieu really asserts is that when Peter the Great appeared at Moscow, the Russians' thoughts and feelings were other than one would be led to expect on the basis of geographical determinism; the words "*étrangères au climat*" allow of no other construction. Hence Russian society was clearly not under the "empire" of geographical conditions. On the contrary, so long as her life remained spontaneous, she followed, in freedom, foreign examples rather than indigenous tendencies. In fact, the geographical conditions of the country would not have asserted themselves at all and would not have come to dominate and to determine Russian life, unless a despot had helped them to come to influence. So it was not the climate that shaped the Muscovites' way of life but the will of their ruler, albeit that that will was helped in its enterprise by the tendencies arising from the physical subsoil and environment. This is just one of those "often" occurring cases noted by Montesquieu where "the physical cause has need of the moral cause in order to become effective" (I, 1303). Montesquieu would have done better—indeed, he would have come nearer to the essential content of this very chapter—if he had said, the empire of the climate is the second of all empires; for it appears here only as the helpmate of a stronger influence. But, then, this would not have made a flashy sentence; this would not have made high-falutin rhetoric. When our author was attacked by the Theological Faculty of the Sorbonne, he admitted, somewhat shamefacedly, that this sentence was "no more than a metaphorical expression" (II, 1173). But, surely, it was even less than that. A metaphor is, after all, a way of formulating the truth. But Montesquieu did not assert, in book XIX, that the climate's empire was the first either in importance or in operation or in any other sense. Not the first in operation, because it was not in evidence when Peter the Great arrived, not the first in importance, because it had to be helped into power by a stronger hand. The whole sentence is elliptical rather than metaphorical. But whatever it may be, it is no proof that Montesquieu—the sober, sound, scientific Montesquieu, the Montesquieu who disciplined his tongue and controlled his pen—really believed in the primacy of the geographical factor.

The subject of Russia is generally interesting in this context. Russia is nothing if not a northern country. Why should her cold air not have inspired democratic sentiments as it did elsewhere? After all, it is the heat that evokes dictatorship, not the cold. Montesquieu vaguely alleges *"causes particulières"* (II, 294). "Though the Muscovite nobility has been reduced to servitude by one of its princes," he says in another chapter (ch. 3 of book XVII), yet "one will always observe there are signs of impatience which the climates of the south do not arouse" (II, 526). Hence, here again, the climatic factor is demoted to a secondary position; certainly it is not accorded primary importance. It cannot shape Russian life towards the libertarian ideal, though this is its proper tendency,[1] but is confined to the causing of diffuse unrest—a mere nuisance to the despot, not a threat to despotism. Indeed, Montesquieu admits that even the Russian powerholders find it difficult to reduce their own power, notwithstanding the fact that geography should be on their side in their endeavour to introduce some measure of democracy into the country (II, 294). We are led to conclude that he does not regard its help to constitutional reform as particularly great; that it is not decisive is too obvious to need special emphasis.[2]

The one chapter in which the question which is stronger in its influence on the mind and society, government or geography, can be said to be directly and squarely tackled, is chapter 21 of book VIII, entitled "Of the Empire of China". China, Montesquieu explains, is essentially a despotic state, with fear as its constitutive principle (II, 368). Yet the missionaries speak with respect of the Middle Kingdom and call it "an admirable government". How can that be? How can, in that part of the world, an abominable root produce admirable fruit? Montesquieu tries, first of all, to show that the condition of China is not quite so fortunate as some reports would lead one to expect; but his essential argument is that the worst features of despotism are absent because geographical reasons have cut across

[1] In one chapter, Montesquieu says quite clearly that a moderate climate is no guarantee against the rise and the triumph of a despotic government and all it stands for. Speaking of Europe, he writes: "If, by a long abuse of power, [or] if by a great conquest, despotism should establish itself at a certain point, there would be neither *mores* nor climate which [i.e. whose influence] would hold fast; and human nature would [even] in this fair part of the world, suffer, at any rate for a time, the insults which have been inflicted on it in the three others" (II, 356).

[2] A geographical determinist might point out that Russia is a territory of great plains, and that this accounts for the absolutist set-up, the cold climate being over-ruled by another geographical element. But—apart from the fact that this argument has its own difficulties—Montesquieu does not fall back on this line of escape and it must be assumed that he disdained to do so. He is not enough concerned about the defence of geographical determinism to manœuvre himself into an extremist and over-dogmatic position. He is too wise to do so. Indeed, he expressly rejects recourse to the size of the territory with regard to China, where the first legislators are said to have established very good laws "in spite of the horrors which [as a rule] follow the too great extent of an empire" (II, 535). Cf. also II, 717: "It is the Christian religion which, in spite of the large size of the empire and the viciousness of the climate, has prevented despotism from establishing itself in Ethiopia . . ."

the political tendencies and deeply modified them. "The climate of China is such that it prodigiously favours the propagation of the human species . . . In spite of tyranny, China will, by dint of the power of the climate, always people herself, and triumph over tyranny . . . As, despite the exposure of babies, the population is always on the increase in China, indefatigable labour is necessary to make the earth produce the necessary food: [but] this demands great attention on the part of government. The government is at every moment concerned that everybody should be able to work without fear of being frustrated in his efforts. It must be less of a civil than a domestic government," i.e. it must be more paternal than imperial and imperious (II, 366 *seq.*). Hence it will be less distant, less selfish, less cruel than a despotic set-up generally. And there is a second (geographical reason for the comparative mildness of the Chinese imperial power. Where rice is the staple food, there famines will occur from time to time. But while a famine rages, robber bands will form which will roam the land in search of nourishment. Many of these bands will be exterminated; but some may survive, grow, become armies, and usurp the power in the land. Hence there is always a latent threat to the established authorities; the emperor is not quite so sure of his throne, and of his head, as other despots are. He not only inspires fear, he is himself under its shadow. "He will know that, if his government is not good, he will lose [both] empire and life" (II, 367). Thus the despotism of China is a modified, reduced, chastened, humanised despotism, though it is a despotism all the same.[1]

Let us note, first of all, in evaluating these passages, that here again geography appears only as a modifying factor. Certainly, it is so strong in its influence that it inhibits the free unfolding of those culture-forming and life-determining tendencies which lie embedded in the constitutional order. But it is, all the same, seen only as a secondary tendency, however strong (by accident) it may be. And, what is more, Montesquieu regards the case of China only as an exception that confirms the rule— the rule that the culture and the life of a land depend first and foremost on its politico-social constitution. His words are quite

[1] Cf. also chapter 6 of book XVIII (II, 534 *seq.*), where the same subject i discussed and the same conclusion is reached.

clear. "Particular, and perhaps unique, circumstances may bring about that the government of China is not as corrupt as it should be. Certain causes, drawn for the most part from the physical nature of the climate, have been able to overpower the moral causes in that country, and perform a kind of miracle" (II, 366). In view of these absolutely unambiguous sentences, it is difficult to see how anyone can assert that Montesquieu was a consistent geographical determinist, i.e. that he gave the environmental factor in principle the primacy over the political.

But we need no indirect and implied proof, however clear, for the fact that Montesquieu's sociology of knowledge was a cœnonic-holistic-constitutional rather than an ecologico-materialistic one: we have open and direct proofs *ad libitum*. Our author's best work falls into the fifteen years between 1732 and 1747: those were the years when the *magnum opus* of his life, *De l'Esprit des Lois*, was written. From the beginning of this period to its end, Montesquieu held to the primacy of the political factor as to a basic axiom. In December 1732, he read to the Academy of Bordeaux his *Réflexions sur les Habitants de Rome*. In it he investigated the question why the Romans, once so tough and gluttonous, had become so soft and abstemious. "I found several causes for this change," he writes, "the ones physical, the others moral". The decisive physical development consisted in a shift of the city from the Seven Hills with their subtle air to the plain along the Tiber "where the air is coarse". The main moral revolution was the replacement of a constitution which, with its frequent elections, made for a life of effort and excitement, by the papal rule which has rendered Rome "the most tranquil city of the world". There prevails now, around St. Peter's, "a reserved life which the constitution of the State makes necessary". Which of the two factors thus to be observed is the stronger? "Education, habitude, mores gain an easy victory over the strength of the climate" (I, 910–912). In May, 1749, the attitude is still the same. Congratulating David Hume on his "beautiful dissertation," he praises him because he had allotted "much greater influence to the moral causes than to the physical".[1] M. Dedieu rightly emphasises

[1] Cit. Dedieu, *Montesquieu, L'Homme et l'Oeuvre*, 1943, 148. For the text of the letter, cf. *Correspondance*, ed. Gebelin and Morize, II, 1914, 188 *seq.*

that this testimony to Montesquieu's true way of thinking is particularly valuable. Anyone asserting that the Baron de la Brède paid exaggerated lip-service to moral causes in his printed works because he was afraid of the Sorbonne, of the Congregation of the Index, and of obscurantist public opinion in general, is here shown to be mistaken. He is speaking privately, in the intimacy of a letter; and his addressee is an atheist. He can show his real opinion, and he does.

Nor is there any want of witness to the truth from other writings of the period. "The moral causes have a stronger formative influence on the general character of a nation and are more decisive for the quality of its spirit than the physical causes," we read in the *Essai sur les Causes qui peuvent affecter les Esprits et les Caractères*. And a little later on more decisively still: "The moral cause overpowers the physical cause"; and even, on the same page: "The moral cause destroys the physical cause" (II, 60 *seq.*). Two illustrations are offered here. One is the case of the Jewish "intellectuals", the rabbis. Scattered over all the world, born under every sun, they yet have all their heads full of the same nonsense. The reason is that their thinking is fed from the same source, wherever they may be, whatever the geographical circumstances under which they live. The Jews who returned from their exile were slaves, and sons of slaves. They could not even read, let alone understand, their holy scriptures. Thus they developed from their orally handed on stock of miracle stories, a rude, irrational, superstitious version of the sacred lore, and it was this which, congealed into a firm tradition, was imbibed by successive generations of Jewish "scholars", and ultimately broke all their thought into the same pattern.

The second example is perhaps not quite so clear. It concerns the contrast of north and south. The northerners have, from the geographical point of view, the advantage over the southerners because their climate leads them towards liberty, the greatest good, not towards slavery, the greatest evil. Yet the timid slavish peoples of the south, longing, as they are, for peace, learn to appreciate the values and enjoyments and life, whereas the brave and foolhardy freedom-born peoples of the north develop a certain thirst for martial glory which leads them to throw away those true values and enjoyments and thus makes them less rational than their brethren, even though they are favoured by the climate. "The moral cause destroys the physical cause, and Nature is so strongly falsified that the nations which she has destined to possess the better spirit have less sense, and those to whom she has given less sense have the better spirit" (II, 61 *seq.*).

Other passages of the same import can easily be adduced, (indeed, amassed). For instance: "That bellicose spirit which, once upon a time, the climate gave to the people of Rome, is [now], by [the action of] moral causes, restricted to the liking which it has nowadays for those combats that are to be seen in the theatres; and the climate which at one time made the people of Athens so turbulent, does no more [now] than to show us slaves who are perhaps a little less stupid [than slaves elsewhere]. Nature always exerts her influence; but she is overwhelmed by the *mores*" (I, 1328 *seq.*). She is overwhelmed, and she ought to be overwhelmed. We have seen already, how Montesquieu demands, time and time again, that freedom be introduced by the constitution where geography makes for unfreedom, be it in the form of public slavery, of private slavery, of the subjection of women, or of any other form of human degradation. His call for legislative action, reverberating as it is through the whole of the *Esprit des Lois*, would have been altogether nonsensical if he had not assumed—if he had not been convinced—that, in case of conflict, the clash between geography and government is the clash between an earthen pot and an iron one, the political constitution being the stronger vessel. It is as impossible as it is superfluous to quote all the available references here.[1] The proper reference at this point is simply: *passim*.

However, there is one passage from Montesquieu's pen which must be quoted in any discussion of the question to which of the two mind-determining factors he attributed the primacy, and that passage is most proper to form the last word in this whole investigation. It occurs in his *Réponses et Explications données à la Faculté de Théologie:* "It seems that the author of the *Esprit des Lois* should be the last person to be accused of ignoring the power of moral causes and, in consequence, of morality itself. As he has spoken a good deal of the climate in some books [of the work]

[1] Cf., however, e.g. II, 479 *seq.*, 495–497, 517 *seq.*, 532, 534 *seq.*, 644.

which had the climate for their subject, so he has spoken a good deal of moral causes in almost the whole of his work, because moral causes are under discussion there, and *it can be said that the book of the Spirit of Laws presents a perpetual triumph of morality over climate, or rather over the physical causes in general*" (II, 1173).[1] If these are strong words, they are no more than is justified. Attacked, Montesquieu did not wish—and had no need to—make his theory appear different from what it was. All he was concerned about was to show it, in all honesty, in its true colours.

This does not, of course, mean that he ever abandoned his conviction that mind-determining tendencies issue from the physical environment of a society and may even come to dominate its intellectual life, if, and in so far as, they are not countered by the stronger mind-determining influences arising from the socio-political, and, in particular, from the constitutional life. But as there is hardly a state without a constitution; as there is hardly a people without a will; as there is hardly a society without a desire for mental self-determination, the *esprit* of men can never, or hardly ever, be completely explained on the basis of an ecologico-materialistic sociology of knowledge. In another polemical writing, the *Défense de l'Esprit des Lois*, directed against the Jansenist organ, the *Nouvelles Ecclésiastiques*, Montesquieu spoke, while defending the reasonableness of his insistence that the climatic conditions must be brought into the picture, of geography as merely "apt to produce various dispositions in men's minds" (II, 1145); but dispositions are no dominants; they incline, but they do not coerce; men are free to follow them or not to follow them when they build the social, political and moral structure within which they mean to dwell; but, whether they do follow them or not, it is always the spirit behind the constitution of the state which they have made that will give its colour to their whole culture and culture-mentality.

This, then, is Montesquieu's theory of the "real" or "existential" bases of human thought, of the substructure underneath the mental superstructure. It has nearly, though, it must be confessed, not fully, conquered the facile rationalism of his young years. A handful of relapses into rationalism must be noted even in that maturest of all his works, *De l'Esprit des Lois*.

[1] Our italics.

Thus he says, for instance, that the Jewish and Mohammedan ban on the eating of pig's meat was due to the fear, prevalent and justified in such countries as Arabia and Palestine, of skin diseases which pork is supposed to cause or to make worse (II, 733 *seq.*); that the Homeric horror stories of the sea, Ulysses' encounter with the Sirens, his experiences between Scylla and Charybdis etc, were "fables . . . introduced by those sailors who, carrying on a *commerce d'économie*, wanted to frighten the other nations from taking after them" (II, 1087); that the talk of Ariosto of enchanted and hence irresistible arms or armour was originally the reaction of such peoples as the Lombards to the heavier armaments developed by the Franks whose efficacy they could not understand (II, 1115). But such lapses from grace are very rare; and it is perhaps characteristic that two of the three passages just summarised were not, ultimately, included in the printed version of the work. Montesquieu had learned to understand that superficially irrational ideas cannot, as a rule, be explained by equally superficial surface reasons; that they have often—and perhaps always—a deeper, hidden *raison d'être* which it is for the student to find and to expose.

While looking at the debit side of Montesquieu's account, we must also accuse him of not having applied his sociology of knowledge in a few cases which seem to call for its application. There is, for instance, the medieval ban on usury and hostility towards commerce. One would have thought that Montesquieu would have looked for the deeper, i.e. social, causes of this attitude. It is not too difficult to find them. But our author simply refers to Aristotle's teaching on the subject and to his influence on the "subtle minds" of the "ages of ignorance": "We owe to the speculations of the scholastics all the misfortunes which accompanied the destruction of trade" (II, 639, 641). In a similar way, Montesquieu fails to see the social antecedents of the reception of the Roman law into the legal systems of Continental Europe at the turn from the middle ages to the modern era. Chapters 42 and 43 of book XXVIII *De l'Esprit des Lois* make very disappointing reading for the sociologist of knowledge. In so far as he had any explanation at all of this important phenomenon, it is the survival of some Roman principles and precepts in such territories as Burgundy where the *codex Theodosianus* had once ruled and where, for this reason, the *codex Justinianus* could enter more easily when it appeared (II, 807)—a feeble explanation. What prevented Montesquieu from tackling these interesting questions in the spirit of the sociology of knowledge, was the narrowness of the theory which he had built up in his mind. It is plain that his ecologico-materialistic principle could never hope to shed light on such historical conditions; but his cœnonic-mono-genetic key did not fit these particular locks either. How bring the medieval control of economic life or the post-medieval re-direction of legal thought and practice under the triad mon-archy-honour, republic-virtue, tyranny-fear? It can't be done. Of course, Montesquieu could have used here the cœnonic-holistic approach which, as we have seen, is sometimes applied by him; but, then, it is applied only rarely, and by the time *De l'Esprit des Lois* was written, from which our two examples are taken, it had been virtually given up for the two-fold theory—geography and government—which we have studied with such application.

XI

THE PROBLEM OF THE MODE OF
DETERMINATION

WHILE there is, as we have seen, a good deal of detailed discussion in Montesquieu's works of the problem which in "The Sociology of Knowledge" we have called problem A—the problem of the determination of the substructure which underlies and explains the mental superstructure established in a society—there is very little on problem B, the question in which way the superstructure arises from the substructure, what exactly the links are between the two. It can hardly be said that this aspect of the sociology of knowledge was within the lighted circle of Montesquieu's consciousness. Nevertheless, it is possible to study his attitude to this complex of problems; for if it was never directly seen, it was yet dimly envisaged as a peripheral or background necessity and is sometimes dealt with in an oblique manner and by implication. Moreover, the basic problems of the sociology of knowledge are connected with each other by certain semi-logical links. Any thinker through whose mind there runs a strain of consistency must speculate, however half-heartedly, about them all, once he has tried to solve one.

There is one section (and, it would seem, only one) in which Montesquieu comes for a split second near to the theory of mutual selection or *Wahlverwandtschaft:* chapter 2 of book XXV. "The various religions of the world," we read in the first paragraph, "do not give to those who profess them equal motives for attachment to them: this depends a good deal on the manner in which they adjust themselves to men's way of thinking and feeling" (II, 735). But what follows this promising starting point is rather disappointing. We are not told how concrete religious systems fit themselves to, or into, concrete systems of opinion and sentiment. We are only treated to such generalities as that people like to see ceremonial, or pomp and circumstance; that a creed which conjures up the contrasting images of heaven and hell will impress more than one which does not, etc. etc. Indeed, the whole passage proved a negative point rather than a positive, namely that Montesquieu did not seriously explore the possibility of a progressive mutual adjustment or harmonisation of substructural and superstructural elements.

What about determinism in the technical sense of the word, the conception that ideas follow either geographical conditions or the governmental constitution as effect follows cause? Montesquieu has often been understood in this sense. It was one of his troubles at the time when the *Esprit des Lois* was under scrutiny by the ecclesiastical authorities that an Italian translation of the work had put a strong emphasis on the possible deterministic interpretation of its argument.[1] And, indeed, some passages can be quoted, both from the *magnum opus* and from minor writings, which seem to give colour to the suspicion that the Baron de la Brède was something of a mechanical determinist. "It is the different needs in the different climates which have formed the different ways of life," runs one sentence. "And these different ways of life have formed the divers kinds of laws" (II, 483 *seq.*). Another context seems to be even more deterministic in its import. Admitting exceptions to the strict rule, Montesquieu says: "I do not speak of particular cases: mechanics has its frictions which often change or inhibit the effects of theory: politics, too, has such" (II, 530). One of the *Pensées* is so outspoken that it seems to admit no doubt of our author's belief in a fatal concatenation of things: "Dr. Luther is taken for the starting-point of the Reformation. It was necessary that it should come. If it had not been Luther, it would have been somebody else. The sciences and the arts brought in from Greece had already opened the eyes [of all] to the abuses [in church life]. It was necessary that such a cause should produce some effect" (I, 1566). This fragment certainly expresses a deterministic and fatalistic mood. But was it more than a mood?

[1] Cf. Dedieu, *Montesquieu, L'Homme et L'Oeuvre*, 1943, 185.

Was it ever a mode of thought really established in Montesquieu's mind? Most certainly not.[1]

The truth is that Montesquieu was somewhat undecided about the nature of the ties which bind substructure and superstructure together. M. Dedieu rightly asserts that, for him, the laws are connected with such moral forces as the principles of government by "*rapports plus ou moins incertains*" (*loc. cit.* 188). Reviewing, in 1750, what he had written about "trade under the different forms of government", he felt that he had given these considerations too absolute, too deterministic a hue. He did not take back what he had said, namely that the "rule of one" produces the "*commerce de luxe*" and the "rule of a plurality" the "*commerce d'économie*". But he thought it necessary to append the following proviso: "I do not wish to say that there is any monarchy which is totally excluded from the *commerce d'économie;* but monarchies are less drawn to it by their nature. I do not wish to say that the republics which we know are altogether deprived of the *commerce de luxe;* but it has less connection with their constitution" (II, 588). These sentences not only put a negative on all attempts to interpret Montesquieu's thought as a whole in a mechanistic-deterministic vein, they also reveal, rightly understood, what theory concerning the links between substructure and superstructure was hidden in the depths of his mind.

But before we begin to plumb and explore these depths, it is

[1] In the fragments written for a projected book on *Jealousy* there appears also a certain deterministic mood. For instance: "It is not always Nature and Reason which govern men, but pure accident and . . . certain circumstances which do not at first appear important, influence them so much and act with so much force and regularity that they may give the whole of human nature a mental twist" (I, 1074). If the Mohammedans had conquered the world, everybody would think that women were of necessity and by nature slaves; if the Amazons, everybody would think the same of men (I, 1075 *seq.*). Although these passages express a belief in the strict concatenation of mental antecedents and consequences, they yet do not deserve to be considered in the text. The *Histoire de la Jalousie* is of early date and still steeped in rationalism. All Montesquieu really wishes to say is: see, how quickly certain irrational conceptions spread and engulf all!—The late *Défence de l'Esprit des Lois* cannot be quoted either in our present context. Montesquieu certainly says in it that "all effects whatsoever have causes: climate and the other physical causes produce an infinite number of effects"; but we have already seen that the "effects" here in question are only "dispositions". Dispositions do not force thinking into predetermined modes; hence there is no suggestion that the link between physico-geographic substructure and mental superstructure is one of one-sided and necessary, quasi-mechanical determination.

necessary to take note of a more superficial idea on the same topic which Montesquieu sometimes canvasses—the suggestion that the whole of a culture receives its specific tone and colour through a process of diffusion which starts at the socio-political centre and from there works outward towards the periphery. This theory (if a theory it can be called) is developed especially for the monarchy. Brought into a brief formula it asserts that the court is imitated by the country. As the court reflects the nature of the political principle of the monarchical constitution, as it surely must, so will the country at large, whose life, and especially whose ideas and tastes, will be modelled on it. (Montesquieu here anticipates some analyses later on attempted by Gabriel Tarde and E. A. Ross.) *"Seigneur,"* says one of the Troglodytes, Montesquieu's Utopians, to their king, "it will be you alone who decides whether riches are pernicious to your people or not. If they see that you prefer them to virtue, they will soon be accustomed to doing the same and in this your taste will regulate theirs" (I, 378). The same idea is at the basis of *Lettre Persane* CXLVI which is, *sub rosa*, an attack on John Law: the Scottish financier, sitting at the hub of power, had seduced and corrupted, in a short time, all France. But the clearest formulation of this whole doctrine occurs in the *Lettres de Xénocrate à Phérès:* "Heaven has done a great thing when it has placed a prince in so high a rank that all others have their eyes on him, that he is their example and their model; that he can, so to speak, give the tone to human nature . . ." (I, 517). Sometimes the capital city rather than the court is regarded as the centre of cultural radiation: "It is the capital which, above all, makes the *mores* of the nations; it is Paris which makes the French" (I, 1332; cf. also I, 1333, and II, 1076). The difference between the two versions is, however, hardly significant: the capital is simply an intermediate link in the chain of influences which binds the country to the court, the centre of everything.

Surveying the passages where this explanation of the cultural uniformity of a country is tried on, it is impossible not to be struck by the fact that they are all of early date. The *Lettres de Xénocrate*, for instance, where the whole conception comes out most clearly, are of 1723. In later works, there is little trace of this doctrine. A few lines in chapter 9 of book VII of *De l'Esprit des Lois* come perhaps nearest to it. "The women do not introduce luxury into the despotic States, but they are themselves an object of luxury. They must be enslaved to an extreme degree. Everybody follows the spirit of the government, and brings into his own house what he sees established elsewhere" (II, 341). It will be agreed that the suggestion that the political constitution determines the thought of society because it informs the centre of the state and from there spreads, through waves of imitation, to all the citizens, has become thin and shadowy here and is, in fact, no more than vestigial. For this reason we cannot regard it as more than a blind alley into which Montesquieu indeed peeped but which he never properly explored, let alone penetrated to the blank wall which forms its latter end.

But there are better turns of thought in Montesquieu's work even though they, too, remained only half-developed. Let us follow them out from the core of his system, the conviction that it is the basic principle of the political constitution which constitutes the life-principle of any ordered and organised society. The reader will remember that Montesquieu distinguishes the *principle* of a polity from its *nature*. The nature of a republic is to be ruled by all; the nature of a monarchy to be ruled by one tied by laws and traditions; the nature of a despotic state to be ruled by one not tied by laws and traditions, but free to follow his caprice. Montesquieu himself speaks of the nature of a governmental system thus determined as its definition (II, 239) and its specific structure (II, 250 *seq.*). The *principle* of a governmental system is something entirely different: Montesquieu, in a footnote, takes good care to underline that distinction and to stress its importance (II, 250). "There is this difference between the nature of government and its principle: that its nature makes it what it is, and its principle makes it operate" (*l.c.*). Immediately afterwards the principle of government is identified with "the human passions which make it move". The motor passion in a country ruled by all is, as we know, virtue; in a country ruled by a law-abiding and tradition-bound monarch, honour; in a country ruled by a tyrant, fear. In the *Réponses et Explications données à la Faculté de Théologie*, Montesquieu emphasises once again the fact that the principle of government in the specific sense he has given to the term is a principle of movement, of action, of life—not a principle in the sense of quasi-mathematical definition or static determination. "That political Virtue, which is the love of country or of equality in the Republic, is the spring which makes the republican government operate, as Honour is the political spring of monarchical government. What causes these political springs to be different is that in the Republic he who puts the laws into execution feels that he will himself be subject to them and will feel their weight. Thus it is necessary that he should love his country and the equality of the citizens in order to be inclined to put the laws into execution; and, without that, the laws will not be executed. It is not the same in the Monarchy. For the laws to be executed [there], it suffices that the Monarch wills them to be executed. Here you have principles of so great fecundity that they make up almost the whole of my book" (II, 1181).

What is the upshot of this important passage? Surely this: that the principle of a polity (unlike its "nature") is not a formal definition from which certain consequences can be deduced *more mathematico*—from which certain consequences follow as effect follows cause; but rather a vital essence or basic inspiration which demands certain complementary developments in order that the life which is expressed in and grouped around it, be possible, be healthy, be harmonious.[1] While we move, when we speak of the nature of government, in the Cartesian sphere of pure form, we go over, as soon as we turn to the principle of government, to the post-Cartesian preoccupation with embodied reality; while we handle, in the concept

[1] Durkheim's interpretation of Montesquieu seems the correct one. Montesquieu's dictum "that human laws spring from the nature of things", is, Durkheim points out, "an equivocal formula . . . which implies two [possible] interpretations. It may mean, either that the laws have followed from the nature of things, that is to say of societies, as the effect issues from the cause which brings it forth; or that they are simply the means which the nature of society demands in order to perfect itself, that is to say, to reach its end, means which may, however, not be forthcoming. In other words, should one assume that the state of society is the efficient cause of the laws or merely their final cause? Montesquieu does not even seem to suspect [the possibility of] the former interpretation" (*Montesquieu et Rousseau, Précurseurs de le Sociologie*, ed. 1953, 83). Durkheim severely criticises Montesquieu for not taking a more strictly "scientific"—i.e. deterministic, mechanistic—line in this discussion. It is certain that at the end of his life he would have judged Montesquieu's attitude very differently, and much more favourably, than in 1892 when this little book (his thesis) was written.

of the nature of a state, an abstract category of definition, we are confronted, in the concept of the principle of a state, with a concrete phenomenon of life; while the implications of the one can be brought out by simple logic, by ratiocination, those of the other must show themselves in practice, by spontaneous growth, by free development, by livingly unfolding themselves. In a word, at this crucial point of our analysis we find in Montesquieu's mind the germs of the organological doctrine so characteristic of the romantical approach of which Montesquieu (in spite of his occasional use of rationalistic language) was the pioneer. We are led to expect that the connection between substructure and superstructure will be treated in his sociology of knowledge as an organic tie, not as a mechanical concatenation; that a culture, a society, a state will appear to Montesquieu as a total configuration in which the parts constitute with each other an integrated and functioning whole and not merely a logically consistent scheme; that the ideas and feelings of a society will fall into such a pattern that they can harmoniously *work in* with the constitutional laws which make the polity concerned what it is. In these expectations we shall not be disappointed. Montesquieu does not, unfortunately, make his relevant conceptions quite explicit; in a way it would be surprising if he did, writing as he is in the rationalistic century which regarded even the organical whole *par excellence*, the human body, as a mechanism, as a machine; but though not explicit, the organological mode of thinking is clearly implicit in his works, and it is possible to bring it out.

Sometimes the very words of Montesquieu show his thought to be embedded in the bio-organismic, romantical matrix. "The life of States is like that of human beings. These have the right of killing in the case of natural defence; the former have the right of waging war for their self-preservation. In the case of natural defence, I have the right of killing because my life belongs to me, as the life of him who attacks me belongs to him: in the same way a State wages war because its preservation is in accordance with justice like any other preservation" (II, 377)—in accordance with justice, right and rightful like the preservation of any living thing. Thus the state is seen, in its external action, as a quasi-individual, as a quasi-organism. And the same is true of its internal processes: these, too,

Montesquieu regards as quasi-vital, quasi-organical. Speaking of England, the land of liberty, he has this to say: "All the passions being free there, hate, envy, jealousy, the eagerness to gain riches and distinction, will appear in all their power"; but "if this were otherwise, the State would be like a man laid low by sickness who has no passions because he has no strength" (II, 575).[1] A state is, and must be, endowed with vitality—that was clearly Montesquieu's opinion, however far he may have been from the organological doctrine in its fully developed and mature technical form, from the doctrine of a Bluntschli or a Spencer or an Izoulet.

But the near-organological philosophy of Montesquieu is visible not only in an occasional use of the organological simile, the comparison of body politic and body natural. It is discernible in and behind all his doctrine, as an underlying and inspiring basic conception. Assuming that the constitution— the formal "nature"—of a polity is, as it were, its anatomy, its bone structure—what physiology, what tissue, what assortment of organs, in a word: what vital "principle" will fit it so as to produce a total entity capable of life, survival, and development? Montesquieu answers: if it is the rule of all, only the life-principle of virtue; if it is the rule of one who deserves to be called a monarch, only the life-principle of honour; if it is the rule of one who must be pronounced a despot, only the life-principle of fear. These life-principles are necessary complements of the dead letter of the constitution, if that dead letter is to break forth from the textbook of rational definitions and give itself body on the stage of real life. They are in no sense logical implications or definitional aspects of it: they are much rather conditions of its incarnation in a historical phenomenon, in a concrete state, conditions of the process by which alone the word can become flesh and come to life.

Many of Montesquieu's most essential ideas are explicable only in the light of this interpretation of his central position. Anybody who has read him with attention will know that he is a confirmed traditionalist, an enemy of innovation, of experiment. Had he been a rationalist, he would have insisted on the

[1] Cf. also II, 354: "A monarchy is lost when a prince believes that he shows his power more by changing the [established] order of things than by following it; when he takes the natural functions of some [of his subjects away from them] in order to give them arbitrarily to others ..."

realisation of reason; had he been a mechanist, he would have recommended the reconstruction of the machine, the making of a better one. But he was neither. He was a vitalist, and as such turned towards development and growth; he was correspondingly averse to machination and artificial interference. He loved tradition because it was an organically grown whole, a spontaneous product of history. And he also loved it and defended it and thought every departure from it highly dangerous because it had proved its worth in terms of experience, because it had shown itself as appropriate to the needs of the nation carrying it, as a life- and survival-value. No democracy can survive without republican *mores*, i.e. *mores* of civic virtue; no monarchy can last without aristocratic *mores*, i.e. a spirit of honour in the sense of *noblesse oblige;* no despotism can exist without the *mores* of slavishness, i.e. the cringing fear of the underdog. This formulation brings out, perhaps better than any other, the true meaning of Montesquieu's distinction between the "nature" or formal definition of a polity on the one hand, and its "principle" or vital unfolding on the other.

We must also remember, in this connection, the highly important role which Montesquieu ascribes to the legislator, especially the original legislator, the man who—like Lycurgus —gives a society its first form. If laws arose more or less mechanically from certain substructural conditions, if they followed from them as warmth does the fire,[1] the role of the legislator would be humble indeed: all he would have to do is to put into words what was operating as law already, to make explicit what is implicit in the social life around him. But this is obviously not the idea which Montesquieu has of the function of the lawgiver. He sees him much rather as a creative spirit, as one who, in a sense, makes the society for which he legislates. Now this, in view of Montesquieu's "determinism", cannot mean that he may pour it into any shape, as one can pour water from a jug into a mug and *vice versa*. It can only mean that he creates in response to certain conditions, that he provides what is demanded by the situation. But that, too, is true creation—not indeed free mechanical creation where man asserts himself as the absolute master over matter, but rather an organic creation, the creation of what is fitting, of what is

[1] This simile is borrowed from Durkheim, *loc. cit.* 83.

appropriate, of what will harmoniously blend into the wider life, a kind of relative creation. The legislator is for Montesquieu the organiser of the polity in the specific sense that he introduces and institutes what will allow the society concerned to lead an organically integrated and harmonious life, and the greatness of the greatest lawgivers consisted in this, that they recognised what would be appropriate—a task which would be easy if laws could be calculated by a kind of rule of three, but which is in fact most difficult because organic developments are not univocally determined, are not predictable, and it is impossible to say with assurance what concrete detail will suit the general framework, what consequence will go with the antecedent, what flower will harmoniously fit the branch and stem and root. If we may use again the formula which we have used above, we can say that, for Montesquieu, the lawgiver is he who, in and for life, unfolds the basic principle of a state and society—he who realises the vital possibilities inherent in it, he who draws the fruit from the seed.

That we are supremely justified in our organological interpretation of the master's thought can be shown by one further convincing argument—the presence, in all his books, of the fear of involution which is, as he well knows, as possible, at any moment, as evolution. States, like all living things, are for ever suspended between the poles of health and disease, survival and death. If the relation of the principle of a state to its nature—the relation of its spirit to its definition—were one of logical implication, of rational inherence, of mechanical concatenation, then the two could never break asunder; then, above all, time could not bite and break into it and lead one half against the other, because time would not enter into the matter at all. But the fact, as Montesquieu sees it, is that the two can and, indeed, do, often break asunder and take up positions against each other. Time is the plane on which, and the medium in which, societies live and move and have their being, and although it is conceivable that "nature" and "principle" may continue in unchanged and unbroken harmony and mutual adjustment, it is—time meaning change—much more likely that rifts will develop between them and concord give way to discord. We may say—in the fullest assurance that we are faithfully representing Montesquieu's social philosophy—that he distinguishes the healthy community from the diseased and decaying state. In the healthy community nature and principle are smoothly functioning together as in the healthy body physical bone and flesh, unvital structure and vital parts, are perfectly co-ordinated and co-operative. In the diseased and decaying state the life-processes of the society loosen themselves from the basic pattern with which they should cohere and co-function; there is disintegration which will end in death. Why did republican Rome disappear from the stage of history? Because the Romans, developing all manner of *mores* inconsistent with the republican spirit—above all a desire for aggrandisement—abandoned that principle of virtue through which alone the form "democracy" can become a real entity, a "nature" incarnate in concrete historical shape. In such situations redress can only come from rejuvenation,[1] i.e. return to the pristine spirit of the community, the spirit truly appropriate to its specific being.

The relation between the basic defining pattern and the real life issuing from it is thus not a firm concatenation, assured of permanence by the unbreakable bonds of logic, but rather a link exposed, because of its organic character, to the dangers which threaten all that is organic—disease, degeneration, decay, death. "These are the principles of the three forms of government", Montesquieu writes at the end of book III *De l'Esprit des Lois*. "[All] this does not mean that, in a given republic, people are virtuous; but that they should be so. This does not prove either that, in a given monarchy, people have honour, and that, in a particular despotic State, they have fear; but that they should have it: without which the government would be imperfect" (II, 261). The same idea is also expressed, with a somewhat more practical twist, in a fragment finally excluded from the printed version: "When one sees the causes of prosperity in a State which does not prosper, famine reign when Nature had established abundance, a cowardly pride where the climate had promised courage, evils in the place of the good things which the religion of the country had led one to expect: it is easy to recognise that the aim of the Legislator has been abandoned. The difficulty is to know when, how, and in what way to get back to it" (II, 1038 *seq.*). The normative

[1] Cf. Dedieu, *Montesquieu, L'Homme et l'Oeuvre*, 1943, 158.

element is thus contained in the very root of Montesquieu's thoughts, and the norm and normality which it envisages are the normality of harmonious integration, of organic adjustment of part to part and part to whole, of the smooth functioning together of spirit and body, in a word, the image of health.

The study of the process of degeneration of social and political order which is apt to come over any historical society and consists essentially in a living away of the people concerned from their proper constitutional principle, occupied Montesquieu a great deal. He regarded it essentially and exclusively as a process of demoralisation, of human corruption. Near though he was to the organological tradition in sociology, he was yet far from those who consider society *à la* Izoulet or Spencer or Schaeffle as a living organism in the literal sense of the word and thus speak—like Lilienfeld—of a "social pathology". The organic adjustment which is lost when the citizens of a republic are no longer virtuous or the subjects of a monarch no longer careful of their honour or the slaves of a despot no longer fearful of his knout is a mental link, a moral congruence. (It was necessary to state this in order to avoid the impression that we are trying to push Montesquieu all too deeply into the biological camp.) Not only is the strain of consistency which we find running through a social order, not conceived by Montesquieu as a logical and mechanical link; it is not even considered to be a quasi-physiological link, a link comparable to the firm connection between the different parts of a coherent living tissue; but only as a moral link, a link which is rightly, if metaphorically, called organical because it shows the harmonious ordering and integration so characteristic of healthy organic wholes. The stricter, more materialistic, organicists who knew Montesquieu have for this reason not claimed him as their own. It is characteristic that Durkheim—or rather the young Durkheim; for later even Durkheim outgrew his excessive biologism—cannot come to terms with Montesquieu's doctrine of socio-political involution. How can society, *"un ordre déterminé"*, contain contingency, the faculty of falling away from its own nature? How can human beings—or any beings—ever act in opposition to the laws which regulate them and their co-existence? Are not diseases as controlled by objective laws as healthy states? Does not the Baron de la Brède betray his

soundest opinions and spoil his whole contribution to social
science by admitting, or even emphasising, that the regularities
of social existence can be abrogated by men simply by changing
their mode of behaviour, by relaxing their self-discipline and
falling into evil ways? Vainly does Durkheim try to make out
that Montesquieu treats moral degeneration, and the consequent
destruction of politics, as a marginal phenomenon, as a kind of
freak, an exception which confirms the rule, and that, even
according to Montesquieu, reality follows "most often" the
pattern of its inherent "laws".[1] The truth is that in Montesquieu's opinion ethical deterioration and moral downfall
threaten every society at every moment, as they do every
individual human being; that death lies in wait for every state,
as it does for all of us. His organicism is conceived in idealistic
terms, not in (philosophically) realistic ones. The organic
integration of a social life is for him a task, not a fact. A society
ought to be a healthy organism, or rather: *like* a healthy
organism; but it will come up to this ideal perfection only if its
members are constantly putting forward the necessary moral
effort to fit themselves into the ideal pattern, and this they are
hardly likely to do for any length of time. Montesquieu, let us
not forget it, was a disciple of Montaigne; he was deeply
influenced, too, by that Augustinianism which Port Royal had
revived in France after Calvinism had revived it for all the
world. Far from being marginal, the problem posed by the
brittleness of the bond between the political constitution (the
substructure) and the moral and mental life complementing
and implementing it (the superstructure), the problem posed
by the precariousness of the organic coherence of any and
every society, was central to his whole theory. Well was the
matter understood by the leaders of the French Revolution,
and above all by Robespierre. They had read the master with
deeper understanding than did Durkheim a hundred years
later. Not only did they wipe away everything to which the
monarchical sentiment of honour could conceivably continue
to cling: privileges, prerogatives, titles, down to ribbons and
medals. They also tried, with increasing desperation, to
introduce Roman virtue, republican manners, into the French

---

[1] Cf. *Montesquieu et Rousseau, Précurseurs de la Sociologie*, ed. 1953, 86–94, 100–102,
112–113.

Republic. It was the glories of Roman civic devotion that the painter *par excellence* of the Revolution, David, exalted on every canvas. Robespierre himself, with his forbidding sternness, with his incorruptible austerity, did nothing but to try and live the doctrine of Montesquieu which we are analysing here: the doctrine which asserts that a nation must fit its living *mores* to the letter of its constitution if it wishes its state with its inherent excellences to last, and which consequently implies that the bond between constitutional substructure and mental superstructure is an organic one as long as all is going well with the polity concerned—organic not in the narrow sense of a social somatology but in the more metaphorical sense of successful integration, of smooth functioning, of historical survival.

The detail of Montesquieu's doctrine concerning the corruption of states need not detain us here where we had simply to show that it is convincing proof of the domination of his mind by a non-materialistic, non-biological form of organo-logical thinking. It will be sufficient to point out that each of the three systems of socio-political organisation, being a distinct historical type, has also its own proper and characteristic way of degenerating. The republic, built as it is on equality, frugality and austerity, is doomed as soon as a taste for luxurious living creeps in: "It is necessary in republics that there should always predominate a [certain] general spirit. In the measure in which luxury establishes itself, the spirit of self-preference establishes itself also. People who need nothing but necessaries, can desire nothing but the glory of their fatherland and their own. A soul corrupted by luxury is hostile to the laws which always restrict the citizens. Why was it that the Roman garrison of Regium slaughtered the inhabitants at the instigation of Decius, their tribune? Because, during their stay at Regium, they had begun to fall into luxuriousness" (I, 1434). It is the same danger which today threatens the modern citadel of freedom, namely England; the fate of wealthy nations seems to attend her.[1] The monarchy, whose twin foundations are tradition and the hierarchical principle, is on the decline, as soon as the monarch develops a lust for unrestricted power which makes him impatient of the restrictions laid on him.

[1] Dedieu, *Montesquieu, L'Homme et l'Oeuvre*, 1943, 153.

"What ruined the dynasties of Tsin and Soui, says a Chinese author, is that, instead of restricting themselves, as did their forebears, to a general supervision, alone worthy of the sovereign, the princes wished to run everything directly themselves. The Chinese author gives us here the cause of the corruption of almost all the monarchies." "The monarchy is lost when the prince, centering everything exclusively upon himself, calls the State to his capital, the capital to his court, and the court to his own person"; when he robs the estates of their prerogatives; when he innovates where he ought to preserve; when he is guided by his fancies rather than by his reason; in a word, when he falls from the pinnacle of moral perfection and self-control which his princely office demands (II, 354 *seq*.). As for despotism, this, Montesquieu feels, can hardly be said morally to deteriorate since it is in itself the very epitome of moral deterioration. "The principle of despotic government corrupts itself incessantly because it is corrupt by its nature" (II, 357). This is a somewhat rhetorical flourish, characteristic of the fact that Montesquieu, in his love of liberty, can never keep calm when he comes to deal with tyranny. We can perhaps express the meaning behind his high-sounding phrase more soberly by saying that, in the case of despotism, involution has a positive rather than a negative sign: when despotism decays, human dignity, which it has held down, rises up. The case is different in the two other—the two "moderate"—forms of political organisation. It is, paradoxically, not moral deterioration, but on the contrary moral improvement that spells ruin for the despotic order. A tyrant can lord it over men who are less than men; he cannot, for any length of time, hope to control men who have come to men's estate.

This analysis of the specific processes of socio-political deterioration again shows up the characteristic idealistic and moralising organicism basic to Montesquieu's thought. The concrete principle of disease and degeneration springs, in each type of polity, naturally from its own proper principle of health and normality. Indeed, we see here the inner nature of Montesquieu's philosophy with particular clarity and convincingness. Surely, the principle of decay can never be logically or mathematically or mechanically implied in the principle of stability; if for no other reason, then simply because logico-mathematical and mechanical definition excludes time, excludes *a limine* both evolution and involution. It can only follow from it *more organico*, as the result of a process, taking place in time, of ebbing vitality, decaying power, and loss of vigour. It makes little difference to the organicism of the fundamental conception here that the vitality that ebbs away, the power which decays and the vigour that is lost are moral rather than material, of the spirit rather than of the body.

But the near-romantical, configurational character of Montesquieu's theories shows itself at this point in yet another essential detail. As social orders are organically coherent wholes, decay must of necessity be total decay, decay that will engulf the body politic in its entirety. "When the principles of government are once corrupt, the best laws become bad, and turn against the State; when its principles are healthy, the bad laws have the effect of good ones; the force of the principle pervades all" (II, 357).[1] The unifying, organising, dominating force of the vital principle pervades all, in the state no less than in the physical organism. The deviant detail is digested, so to speak, by the organic pattern, be its state healthy or diseased, and assimilated to it and into it. And Montesquieu emphasises once again that the decay of, as it were, more peripheral portions of the social whole does not follow the decay of its more central parts with absolute necessity, with the necessity with which logical conclusion follows logical antecedent or mechanical effect follows mechanical cause, but only as a natural consequence. "I do not say" he writes in a short, but important fragment, "that the [corresponding] change follows always and that, if political government is destroyed, civil government is at once destroyed [also]. I say that it would be natural if this were so . . ." (II, 1101).

In view of all that has gone before, there can be little doubt that only one theory concerning the relationship between substructure and superstructure can harmoniously fit into Montesquieu's system of ideas, and that is the theory of functional interdependence. "The spirit of the laws," writes M. Dedieu, one of our author's most penetrating students, "is it not the connection which exists between a legal text and the form of civilisation which has made it necessary . . .? If this

[1] Cf. *ib.*, chapter 12 of book VIII, for some illustrations of the point.

connection changes, the law changes and so does the civilisation, because the actions and reactions of these two elements condition and call forth each other".[1] In the same sense, M. Dedieu writes later on, summarising the gist of Montesquieu's *Romains:* "All transforms itself, all evolves, and in that evolution the laws create the *mores*, and new *mores* create new laws."[2] It is easy to show that this interpretation of Montesquieu is correct, that he sees substructure and superstructure in mutual dependence, in a synallagmatic relation. Let us take up one example which will stand for many others that would be equally adducible here. Where nature has created, by her rivers and mountains, a certain territory of middling size (such as, for instance, France or Spain), she has created the conditions and she calls for a limited monarchy as the appropriate political form to fill this physical space: the country will be too large to permit of democracy, which always presupposes a high degree of neighbourliness, and not large enough to make that concentration of power necessary which we find in despotic states. Now, here the substructure (which, in our example, comprises both the geographical and the governmental element in harmonious association) demands for its supplement a definite superstructure: all those virtues and vices, all those sentiments and ideas, which are grouped around the central mental characteristic of limited monarchies, attention to "honour". Say, now, that the king of France or the king of Spain abandons that spirit of moderation which alone is fitting and healthy in his position as law-abiding, constitutional monarch, and develops a lust for new conquests which pushes the frontiers of his realm outward until they enclose vast spaces, spaces as vast as those controlled by the typical oriental despots. Then, by a spontaneous process of adjustment, the substructure will settle into new shapes. Not only will the geographical basis of the state be altered, but the constitution, too, will be transformed. The king will become a tyrant, and society as a whole will slough off the characteristics of monarchy, will cease to be dominated by the principle of *noblesse oblige*, and will don the garb of despotism and be controlled, in all its aspects, by fear and lethargy and vice and all the other banes of the despotic

[1] *Montesquieu, L'Homme et l'Oeuvre*, 1943, 120 *seq.*
[2] *Loc. cit.* 131.

state. Here, then, the superstructure will have created, or at any rate tend to create, as its supplement a definite substructure. One will always condition the other: and that is precisely what we mean when we speak of functional interdependence.

As this whole problem was never in the focus of Montesquieu's mind, but remained permanently in its peripheral penumbra, we cannot expect to find many passages which show the conception which we have tried to extricate from the semi-conscious layer of his thoughts in complete clarity. Yet there are some which undoubtedly contain it. "As a particular form of government gives a certain turn and a certain disposition to the [citizens'] minds," one passage runs, what you do if you change abruptly your political system is that "you change the former without the latter [i.e. the minds] following you, you join the new government to the manner of thinking [characteristic of] the old; and this produces very bad effects" (I, 1460 *seq.*). In other words, change is only healthy if it carries along both substructure and superstructure, if it is so circumstanced that the two halves of the social order keep in step; because otherwise rifts appear and harmony is lost; because otherwise the social organism cannot function as it should. In another context Montesquieu praises the Romans for changing their penal laws when they changed their political constitution (II, 325): that great people had the sense of the essential unity of a state and a society, of the fact that the communal life will only function smoothly if all its parts are attuned to each other. Sometimes the emphasis is placed on the synallagmatic character of the relationship of the various elements, on the *mutuality* of dependence.[1] "Of the inertia of the soul [in hot climes] is born the Mohammedan dogma of predestination; and of that dogma of predestination is born the inertia of the soul" (II, 724). "The more the earth is devastated, the more will the empires grow in size ... The more the empires grow in size, the more is the country devastated" (II, 1095). "The love of the fatherland [inherent in a sound republican constitution] conduces to the purity of *mores*, and the purity of *mores* leads to the love of the fatherland" (II, 274).

[1] The term "synallagmatic" describes a system of structure which is strictly symmetrical. (Originally it was used to characterise contracts which imposed essentially reciprocal obligations.)

"As the equality of fortunes preserves frugality, so frugality maintains the equality of fortunes. These things, though different, are such that they cannot subsist without each other; each one of them is cause and effect; if the one disappears from [a] democracy, the other always follows" (II, 279 *seq.*). A similar formula is used in the opening paragraph of book V *De l'Esprit des Lois:* "We have just seen that the laws of education should be relative to the principle of each government. Those which the legislator gives to the whole of society, are in the same case. This connection of the laws with the appropriate [constitutional] principle controls all the links of the governmental system;[1] and the principle itself receives in its turn a new force from it. Thus it is that, in physical motion, action is always followed by a reaction" (II, 273). Perhaps this passage with its metaphorical allusion to mechanics is less fortunate in formulation than the one immediately before where everything within the social system is described as being simultaneously both cause and effect—a clear proof that Montesquieu regarded the relationships concerned as mutual, and hence as functional; but we must surely understand the latter quotation in the same sense. Finally, there are also one or two passages in which the great man shows that he is aware of the unpredictability of the reaction which will follow the action, that, in the sociology of knowledge, we know indeed that substructure and superstructure will always tend to adjust to each other, but that we cannot in advance delineate the nature of the adjustment. This is again an essential point because only where there is mechanical concatenation, is there complete predictability: mechanical effect must be equal to mechanical cause; but where the concatenation is basically conceived as organical, a reaction can logically be envisaged which goes beyond its cause: it is one of the outstanding features of the sciences of life in contradistinction to the sciences of matter that they regard the principle of causality as one according to which the cause indeed generates the effect but does not imply it because the effect is a growth, a development, a self-willed phenomenon as it were, as is all life. "A small change in the civil laws," Montesquieu writes, looking from the superstructure towards the substructure, "often produces a change in the constitution. It

[1] "... *tend tous les ressorts du gouvernement;* ..."

173

appears small and has immense consequences." And again, in a more sophisticated manner: "A government is like a sum of figures. Take one away or add one, and you will change the value of all. But, as one knows the value of each figure with exactitude, one is not deceived. In politics, on the other hand, one can never know what will be the result of the changes which one makes" (II, 1111 *seq.*).

We are fortunate to be able to wind up this whole analysis with a quotation which shows Montesquieu's opinion as clearly as can be expected in a case where the problem concerned is never directly confronted and the solution of the problem is never made explicit. It is a passage strongly reminiscent of those in which Montesquieu delineates his conception of the substructure on which the total life of a society rests[1] and must thus be ranked as one in which he presses forward towards a theoretical formulation, towards an adequate expression of what is really in his mind. After all that has gone before, we put it to the reader without further comment, knowing that its content and importance will not be lost on him: "The States are governed by five different things: by religion, by the general maxims of government, by the particular laws, by the *mores* and by the manners. These things all have a mutual connection with each other. If you change one of them, the others follow but slowly; and this spreads everywhere a sort of discord" (I, 1156 *seq.*).

[1] Cf. above, p. 58 *seq.*, and esp. II, 558, i.e. chapter 4 of book XIX *De l'Esprit.*

XII

THE PROBLEM OF THE DEGREE OF DETERMINATION

WHILE we have been able, with the help of diligent searching and a somewhat daring analysis, to collect together the rudiments of a solution of problem B, the problem of the character of the interconnection between substructure and superstructure, we are in a much more difficult position with regard to problem C, the question how far the influence of the substructure extends. It is clear from the foregoing discussion that Montesquieu admits the possibility of time-lags in the adjustment of ideas and sentiments to the basic constitution of the state, and in one context he gives a concrete example of such a situation: "It is possible that this nation [i.e. the English], having formerly been subject to an arbitrary power, should, in some respects, have preserved its style; so that one can often see, on the foundation of a free government, the form [characteristic] of an absolute government" (II, 580). But this pronouncement is really a further corroboration of our conclusions re problem B rather than an indication of a possible solution of problem C: it does not tell us very much, if anything, on the reach of the social determination of thought-processes assumed by the author whom we are studying.

Much more interesting is the following passage which occurs in the chapter devoted to the discussion of "education in monarchies": "Here honour, penetrating everywhere, enters into all modes of thinking and all manners of feeling, and governs their very principles" (II, 264). This sentence looks, on the surface, like a god-send to the searcher for Montesquieu's opinion on this head; it reads like the formulation of a theorem. But is it permissible to accept it as such? Are we confronted with a well-considered statement, or simply with a well-turned phrase which flowed from our author's pen without much consideration and was inserted in the text more for stylistical than for analytical reasons? It is impossible to give a confident answer to these questions, but we are not likely to go wrong if we regard it as an indication of a tendency on Montesquieu's part to ascribe to the geographical and governmental substructure a far-reaching influence. We have already seen that he regarded various highly abstract and philosophical or theological doctrines as definitely substructurally determined: the Mohammedan concept of destiny, for instance, and the Buddhist concept of Nirvana (cf. I, 1568 and II, 724; II, 479 *seq.*). We must take these more concrete applications of his sociology of knowledge together with the more abstract formulation quoted above, and then we find that Montesquieu was not inclined to impose a narrow limit on the area within which he saw thought determined by government and geography.

So much, then, for the objective delimitation of the sphere within which determination operates: it is, in principle, largely coextensive with thought itself, since it takes in even metaphysical speculation. But what about personal delimitation? Are all members of a society determined, in their mental life, by the two substructural elements, and are they all determined in this way to the same degree? And are all societies alike in the measure in which they control the thought-processes of their members, or are there significant differences from society to society? The *Essai sur les Causes qui peuvent affecter les Esprits et les Caractères* attempts to answer all these questions, and though its argument is not very systematic and sometimes confused, we can disentangle from it certain valuable insights and ideas.

This *Essai*, as the reader will no doubt recall, falls into two parts, of which the one deals with the *causes physiques*, the other with the *causes morales*. The separation is not fully carried out in form, but there are two separate theories in point of fact. As for the physical causes, Montesquieu strongly emphasises the undeniable differences between human bodies, between individual "machines". In so far as emotions depend on the response of the physical apparatus to a stimulation, there must be differences from human being to human being in the mental processes which result. For instance: two persons may hear the same sound or the same symphony, but the one will be deeply affected and the other not. Why? Because in the former, Montesquieu says, with the materialism so prominent in this particular essay, the sound waves will set up a reverberation which will go through all the parts of the organism, whereas in the latter a certain coarseness or sluggishness of fibre will damp down the reverberation and soon bring it to a halt. In this way it is possible to explain a good deal of the variations in thought and feeling observable in reality simply by reference to physique and physiology, and this goes particularly for the differences between unrefined and refined minds. "The more sensations are necessary for us, the more they are clear, strong, general. Thus the sense of sight, of hearing and of touch are very distinct. The nerves which are their organs strike and affect men in one climate just as in another. It is the small sensations which are useless for the welfare of the machine, that are not given to all but only to refined people. It was necessary that everyone should hear sounds; not that everyone should be sensible to the beauties of music. It is necessary that everyone should know how to express his ideas in words; but it is not necessary that all the world should think in a refined way. In a word, the strong and coarse actions of the senses are given to all men; the delicate ones are given to few" (II, 47). There is a good deal more in this style; and though it is justifiable in a discussion of the extent to which individual thought is determined by extra-individual influences, to point to the fact that individual differences in bodily structure alone will tend to refract these influences in their operation on concrete persons, it will be clear to all but the most confirmed materialists that it must be wrong to labour such an obvious point and that its discussion will end in platitudes and not in an enlightening theory.

Fortunately, there are better things in this essay. One important idea at any rate stands out in the half devoted to the physical causes such as climate: they operate on a broad front rather than in depth; they determine the outlines of the image of reality which the members of a society will form and have

177

in common, rather than the detail as it exists in personal minds; they make (to use the language of the Durkheim school) collective rather than individual representations. "These causes," Montesquieu writes, "become less unreliable [as guides to the understanding of the genesis of ideas] in the measure in which they have a more general effect. Thus we know better [through them] what gives a certain character to a nation than what gives a certain spirit to an individual, what [mental] modifications are shown by a [whole] sex group than what affects a man, what forms the genius of societies which have embraced a way of life than [what forms] that of a single person" (II, 39). Those artless sentences contain by implication a principle which can be made explicit by saying that the mind-determining power of the physical causes decreases as we advance from more general to more specific thought-contents.

The second half of the essay in which the influence of the moral causes is investigated, begins with the trite, but, in a writer of the eighteenth century, important statement, that the latitude of individual variations in thought depends on the stage of evolution which a given society has attained. "Those who are born among a barbarous people have, properly speaking, no ideas but those which are connected with their self-preservation; they live in an eternal night with regard to all the rest. Here the differences from man to man, from mind to mind, are less great [than in advanced—"polished"—societies]: the coarseness and the dearth of ideas level them in a manner" (II, 53). Furthermore, a truly civilised society will also tend to be a free society, and "the great liberty of saying all and writing all which exists in certain countries produces there an infinity of singular spirits" (II, 59). But the diversity and diversification of thought on a higher level of cultural evolution are not simply due to the fact that the stream of thinking is broader as it were and can flow more freely; they are also due to the further fact that it has two sources there, so to speak: the general education which we all equally receive in society at large, and the particular education which we personally receive in the smaller circle of the family. "Particular education consists: 1. in giving us ideas; 2. in proportioning them to the true value of things. Now, the different number of ideas, and the different degree of precision with which one relates them to these values, must produce great diversity of minds" (II, 54). These initial differences in the modes of thought are later on in life accentuated because the total individual life-histories diverge. Montesquieu emphasises more particularly two factors. One is the differences in our individual likes and dislikes, in the passions great and small which we experience. We like a writer whom we read or a man whom we meet, and impulses which come from them are at once given greater weight by us than by others; we love, and all is tinctured by our love; we hate, and all is tainted by our hate (II, 55 *seq.*): "Life is but a chain of passions, which are sometimes stronger, sometimes weaker; now of one kind, and now of another. It cannot be doubted that the combination of these passions during the whole of life, a combination different in every man, brings great variety of minds" (II, 50). The second factor which drives men *quâ* minds apart in their later lives is habitual occupation. We are what our work makes us to be: as our work is not the same, so our whole manner of thinking must differ accordingly (II, 63 *seq.*).

Would it be over-bold to conclude from these speculations that Montesquieu saw in the field of moral causes the same decreasing determination of thought-contents from the more general towards the more individual as in the field of physical causes? It would certainly be easy to sketch a theory of this import from the very materials of his thought: the general education which all men receive in society at large depends on the political form, on the constitutional frame of that society (that is stated in so many words in *De l'Esprit des Lois*); hence in their general outlook all members of a community are shaped to the same pattern. But the more specific formation which they severally receive inside the wider framework of the state, by closer and mutually exclusive agencies, will complement this general outlook by more personal ideas, thus adding variety in small things to agreement in great. Montesquieu nowhere develops ideas of this kind, and all we can do is to state that they would have fitted harmoniously into his system: both into the *Essai sur les Causes qui peuvent affecter les Esprits*, as being parallel to what he says there concerning the influence of the physical causes, and into his wider philosophy as it comes out most strikingly in the great work *De l'Esprit des*

Lois. There is only one passage from the *Spicilège* which proves that his mind was in fact definitely travelling in the direction here sketched out as appropriate to it: "Our thoughts", he writes, "all circle around ideas which are common to us; yet, through their circumstances, their turn, and their particular application, they may have something original [even] to infinity, like the [human] face" (II, 1281 *seq.*).

XIII

THE PROBLEM OF ABSOLUTE TRUTH

APART from the problem of the substructure, i.e. the question whether the primacy of influence belonged to government or to geography, no problem occupied Montesquieu so much, both on the conscious and on the subconscious level, as the question of the relationship between substructurally or socially determined ideas and eternal truth, that is to say, the problem of relativity. We have, in these pages, pleaded for an interpretation of Montesquieu's thought which sees him more as a predecessor of romanticism and historism than as a camp-follower of rationalism, and we have no reason now to abandon this opinion, for which we believe we have adduced substantial proof both in breadth and in depth. But this does not mean that we overlook the element of rationalism in our author. He was a rationalist, a believer in the existence of eternal truths but—to bring our interpretation into a short formula and to show its entire unity and consistency —these truths do not show themselves in reality but only behind reality, not in life as it actually is, not in phenomenal life, but in life as it ought to be, in noumenal life. As far as observable facts go, the mature Montesquieu knew very well that they are explicable in terms of historical relativity rather than in terms of rationalistic absolutism. But even the mature Montesquieu felt that there is a tension between the variety and variability of existence on the one hand and the rest and immutability of essence on the other, and he saw in this tension one of the most excruciating problems with which the philosophical mind is confronted. He never solved it to his own satisfaction; indeed, we see how it occupied him more by a certain vacillation in his argument concerning other things than by any direct discussion. But it was never far from the centre of this thought.

This is a point at which we can see with particular clarity how Montesquieu sloughed off his early rationalism—his rationalism concerning the Is and not only the Ought—as he grew up.[1] In the summary which he wrote himself of his address to the Académie Royale at Bordeaux on May 1, 1725 he expresses himself as follows: "The author [of the *Traité des Devoirs*] . . . shows that Justice is not dependent on human laws, that she is founded on the existence and on the sociability of reasonable beings, and not on the particular dispositions or volitions of these beings" (I, 109). The same line had already been taken in the serious and interesting *Lettre Persane* LXXXIII. "Justice," Usbek writes to Rhédi, "is a relationship of rightness which is found *réellement* between two things; this relationship is always the same whatever the being who considers it, be it God, or be it an angel, or, finally, be it a man . . . Justice is eternal and does not depend on human conventions".

All Montesquieu admits at this stage is "that men do not always see these relationships" and that "often even when they see them, they break away from them": "Justice raises her voice: but she has difficulty in making herself heard in the tumult of the passions" (I, 256). The word *réellement* which we have not translated, already foreshadows the later conviction that the eternal principle of justice belongs to the noumenal world of lasting reality rather than to the phenomenal world of shifting appearances; but the passage as it stands still implies that there is only one relationship of "rightness" which is known to all men everywhere *quâ* beings endowed with reason, and that they lose the vision of it only when they cloud their minds by allowing passion to get the better of them. There is not yet the insight that "right" may be one thing in one place and another thing in another—one thing (as Pascal had said) to the north of the Pyrenees, and another to their south.

It is no real concession to relativism if Montesquieu expresses the opinion in *Lettre Persane* LXXXV that "all religions contain precepts useful to Society" (I, 259), for apart from the fact that it is usefulness and not truth that is under consideration

[1] Cf. Dedieu, *Montesquien*, 1913, 177.

here, the historically given religions had been credited by almost all rationalists with some share in the "absolutely true" religion of deism. Yet there is a paragraph in the papers entitled *Continuation de quelques Pensées qui n'ont pu entrer dans le Traité des Devoirs* which show quite clearly how the principle of relativism is breaking into the Baron de la Brède's mind: "Accident and the mental turn of those who have concluded the social contract have established as many different forms of government as there are peoples: all of them good since they were the will of the contracting parties" (I, 1141). This passage is still steeped in rationalism, resting as it is on the rationalistic theory of the contractual origin of social life; yet it admits that rationality may have different forms all on the same level—that the solution of the social and political problem is not like the solution of a determined equation but rather like that of a diophantine equation which is equally fulfilled by several possible magnitudes.

In the work of Montesquieu's maturity such passages of relativistic import greatly predominate over those conceived in the spirit of absolutism. We have seen that the Baron de la Brède was above all a traditionalist in politics, a conservative. Now, the traditions of different countries are manifestly different; our philosopher knew this as well as anybody after his protracted travels. If he wanted to see them preserved and carried forward into the future, if he saw social reform not as a breaking of reality on the wheel of reason but rather as a return of each decayed socio-political system to its own individual and exclusive principle, this was due to the deep conviction that had grown on him that *every* development is informed by a kind of reason even though this reason is implied rather than conscious, and even though this historical reason is concrete and manifold and multiform rather than abstract and self-identical and univocally determined like the reason which operates in mathematics. Hegel's dictum: what is real that is reasonable, can without exaggeration be described as the key-thought of the *Esprit des Lois*. Even the detestable system of oriental despotism is not without *raison d'être;* even it corresponds to some need, even it is the appropriate solution of the problems posed by some given circumstances. If Montesquieu condemns it, it is because it offends against a higher, more than historical principle. Physically, it is justified; metaphysically it may be damnable all the same.

The relativism of the author of *De l'Esprit des Lois* has been emphasised by many competent observers.[1] Here we are only concerned to show, by a few quotations, its depth. He presses it, for instance, on the critic. "If one devotes oneself to the art of criticism and if one wishes to direct the taste or the judgment of the public, one must examine whether one has often been of the public's opinion when the public, after having considered the matter, has once taken up a decided position; for its judgments confirmed by time are almost always sound. Hence, if a man has no opinions but extraordinary ones; if he is usually alone in his attitude; . . . if the public speaks out and he does not speak out; if the public does not speak out and he does: then he is not fit for criticism" (I, 1229). "The terms beautiful, good, noble, great, perfect are attributes of objects which are relative to the beings who consider them. It is necessary to establish this principle in one's head: it is the sponge of most prejudices." The ancients as well as some moderns have failed in philosophy because they disregarded it (I, 1537). Montesquieu carries the same relativism also into religion. "In the measure in which Christianity freed itself of Jewish superstitions [—would it be allowed here to translate "*superstitions*" by "peculiarities"?—], it loaded itself with pagan ones, in the same way in which liquids lose the odour which they had contracted in a previous receptacle, to take that of the receptacle in which they now find themselves. If [the true] Religion ever establishes itself in China, the oriental [form of the] Christian Religion will be very different from the occidental" (I, 1563). This is a most interesting passage which exhibits several facets of Montesquieu's thought. It shows first of all that he sees not one Christianity but several possible Christianities (if this expression be allowed): by entering into a certain "container"—into a certain geographical-governmental system of life—religion must specify itself, as it were, without thereby losing anything of its identity. But the passage also shows how Montesquieu thinks this relativism arises: it arises through the intermixture of absolute (though transcendental)

[1] Cf. esp. Dedieu, *loc. cit.* 177 and 180 *seq.*, and Alengry, *La Sociologie chez Auguste Comte*, 1900, 396 *seq.*, and footnotes on 395 and 402.

elements with relative (i.e. phenomenal) ones—through the blending of heavenly gold and earthly dross. "We may consider God as a monarch," we read in another context, "who has several nations in his empire: they all come to bring him their tributes, and each one speaks to him in its own tongue" (II, 1097 *seq.*; cf. also I, 1551). He who hears is above relativity, absolute: he who prays is caught in the coils of relativity and must speak the language of his time and place. Who is not reminded, when he reads this passage and perceives this attitude, of Ranke's famous statement of relativism: "Before God, all generations appear with equal rights, and this is the way in which the historian too, must see the matter"?

This relativism asserted by Montesquieu is not only confined to the great values such as those of æsthetics and religion; it also affects vices such as cruelty and stupidity. We have already quoted one characteristic fragment: "It seems that there is hardly any people which has not its own particular cruelty; that each nation is moved only by that of the other nations, as if barbarism were a matter of usage like fashion and habit" (I, 1327). "I find in the *Lives of the Saints* that Clovis gave to a holy person [St. Germer] the power over a territory of six leagues of land, and that he wished him to be exempt from all jurisdiction whatsoever. I believe that this is a falsehood, but it is a very old falsehood; the backcloth of life and the lies [appearing before it] are connected with the *mores* and the laws of the time . . ." (II, 922). Each has its own.

This far-reaching relativism is not unconnected with the far-reaching (many would say, excessive) empiricism of Montesquieu's theory of perception and knowledge. We do nothing in thought: everything is done to us, and in our passivity we follow the impressions we receive—a Lockeanism run riot: "The ends of the fibres of our brain receive a small shock which produces in us a stimulation or sensation. This is sufficient to explain everything. For instance, we see a square for the first time. It suffices that we feel that we see it to have an idea of it: for, without it, one would hardly envisage the square." Universals are gained only through concrete sensations. When our "soul" has seen a number of squares and gets a little uncertain as to what it has really seen, "it makes use of an idea which corresponds to that of confusion and envisages many squares. In the end it may allow itself to be stimulated by all the squares it sees, but also by the squares which could be in the space behind. It then sees squares which do not exist but which are possible. It may envisage all these possible ones, and it will [then] see squares in general, that is to say, the square in so far as it is not placed where I have [actually] seen one. Forthwith, it will make an abstraction and will see squareness as, when it sees a circle in general, [it sees] roundness" (I, 1537 *seq.*). This is an extreme sensationalism and empiricism which, in strict logic, would imply a consistent relativism, different social settings providing, as they must, different basic stimulations and consequential concepts, just as the diametrically opposite doctrine of inborn ideas and rationalism must, in strict logic imply, and has in its best representatives always implied, a consistent absolutism and unhistorical attitude.

But Montesquieu is not happy about his own sensationalism, just as he is not happy about the relativism in which he, nevertheless, firmly believes. The epistemological statement which we have just quoted ends with the tell-tale question which is more than rhetorical: "But, if what I have just said is in fact true, why do animals not think like men?" (*ib*). Is there not in the human soul a fund of verities which may indeed be set aside or clouded over, but which are yet there, visible, in principle, to all men who want to see them?—verities universal in themselves, and so mortal to the theory of relativity? One of the fragments in the first volume of *Mes Pensées* shows real perplexity and uneasiness on this head: "The theologians maintain that there are no atheists in sentiment. But can one judge what goes on in the heart of all men? The existence of God is not a truth clearer than these: man is composed of two substances; the soul is spiritual. Yet there are whole nations who doubt these two truths. This is so because our inner sentiment is not theirs, and because education has destroyed it. It is true that these are evident verities; but there are blind people. These are natural feelings; but there are people who do not feel" (I, 1542). In this passage, absolutism and relativism can be seen locked in combat. "Our inner sentiment is not theirs" certainly strikes the note of relativism; "education has destroyed it", however, introduces the basic tone of absolutism, thus producing in the sentence a jarring disharmony. They— the heathens—see things differently from us; but this is so only because they are denaturalised. It can be seen here, how there is laid on, in Montesquieu's mind, a final solution of this difficulty, the giving of this sublunary world to relativism and the reservation of absolute truths for the empyrean of a higher sphere.

We see how deep the conflict of the two principles was in Montesquieu's mind when we hold against the opinion quoted above that the art critic must take his cue from the valuations current at the time, the following maxim which implies the exact opposite: "Of two parties, the one of those who do not follow the stream [of general tendencies] is usually the better" (I, 1414). And while he closes the showing up of the falsehood in the Life of St. Germer concerning Clovis and his alleged donation with the words: "The backcloth of life and the lies [appearing before it] are connected with the *mores* and the laws of the time; and it is these *mores* and these laws which we are looking for here" (II, 922), clearly implying that the historian is not the judge of the past because the past must be understood in its own terms, he sometimes takes the opposite view. Under the heading "The Usefulness of the Knowledge of Things past" he writes: "It is a certain principle that the general opinions of each century are always exaggerated. This is so because they became general only on account of the fact that they made a striking impression on the minds [of the people then alive]. Now, to replace them in the order of Reason, it is necessary to examine the figure which would be cut, in other centuries, by the opinions dominant in this: this can make them very useful, on the one hand by utilising the enthusiasm which they inspire and the activity to which they give rise, for the good, on the other hand by preventing them from spreading prejudices which are bad" (II, 1103). While this passage (which is perhaps not altogether clear) still implies a certain relativism—the past can correct the present, as the present can correct the past—it is yet basically rationalistic, (a) in its whole pragmatic attitude, and (b) in its insistence that it is justified to mix up the ideas of two ages as if they were one without a gap of time between them, and in the assumption that a given period or society can reduce itself to an absolute rationality by measuring itself against other periods or societies—that there is an objective *ordre de la Raison* (characteristically written with a capital *R*) in which men can "replace" themselves and others if they will.

Thus relativism and absolutism are two alternatives which make Montesquieu's mind swing up and down like a pair of scales when both sides are weighted. Yet we have maintained all along that ultimately the side of relativism proved by far the more heavy one, and we have no reason to revise this conviction now. On the contrary; we gain here new confirmation for our general representation and interpretation of the master's philosophy and sociology. The principle of relativity solidifies itself and gains the upper hand by congealing into the firm conviction that the ideas and institutions appropriate to one age or country cannot be automatically transferred to another; that any and every attempt in this respect is fraught with danger and tends towards disaster because it goes against the essence of things as they are in this our human historical world.

We have already emphasised that Montesquieu does not suggest that the two sets of institutions which he admires most and which, in his opinion, come as near perfection as it is possible for human things to do—the institutions of republican Rome and the institutions of liberty-loving England—be exported to other countries or aped by other ages. *Quod licet Jovi non licet bovi*. With regard to Rome, his words are so outspoken that it is appropriate to quote (or re-quote) them here, where we are concerned to prove his consistent relativism: "The Romans have drawn the World out of the most flourishing state in which it could be; they have destroyed the most excellent established systems in order to form of them a single one which could not maintain itself; they have extinguished the liberty of the Universe and then abused their own; [they have] enfeebled the whole World, as victors and as vanquished, as tyrants and as slaves . . . I give little thanks to the Romans for having destroyed the institution of almost all the peoples of the Earth in order to establish their own" (II, 1061). Indeed, at the end of his life, Montesquieu regarded the transfer of customs and usages and other parts of the social code to societies differently circumstanced as almost physically impossible. As a young man he had written, in the fragmentary *Histoire de la Jalousie:* "It requires hardly any effort to give to one people the prejudices of another", and his assumption at that time had been that *one* system of ideas, like that of Mohammedanism, might conceivably engulf the whole world (I, 1075). As an old man, however, he thought very differently: "Those religions (the Mohammedan and the Indian)," we read on a sheet of paper contained in the *Dossier de l'Esprit des Lois*, "which ordain that people should incessantly wash themselves, and which cause all men, women, children and animals to be constantly in the water, if they are transported into countries where there is little water and where in consequence it is easily fouled, cause fevers which are very difficult to heal and very dangerous diseases, as happens to the inhabitants of India, of Persia and of Urgel" (II, 1003). Not only is it, according to this reconsidered opinion, not easy "to give to one people the prejudices of another", but the attempt to do so may be mortal, and that not in a vague metaphorical, but in the definite physical sense of the word.[1] A transfer is possible only—and with this proviso Montesquieu does not modify his relativism but only brings it into line with his sociology of knowledge in general—where the receiving country shows the same basic characteristics as the model country, in particular where it has the same political constitution. "As the civil laws depend upon the political laws", the *Esprit des Lois* teaches, "because it is always for one society that they are made, it would be good, if it is desired to carry a civil law of one nation to another, to examine at the outset if they have both the same [fundamental] institutions and the same political [i.e. constitutional] law. Thus, when the laws concerning robbery passed from the Cretans to the Lacedæmonians, as they passed along with the [system of] government and the very constitution, they were as appropriate with the one of these peoples as they were with the other. But when they were taken from Lacedæmon to Rome, as they did not find there the same constitution, they always remained strangers there and had no connection with the other civil laws of the Romans" (II, 875).

This relativism in the specific form of the assertion that ingredients of one social system cannot, or at any rate should

[1] Cf. also *De l'Esprit des Lois*, book XXIV, chapters 24–26, II, 732–735.

not, be transplanted into another, comes to the surface at many points of Montesquieu's system of ideas. His doctrine of beauty is one such point. Fr. Claude Buffier had put forward a definition of the beautiful according to which it was "the collection of what is most common". "Father Buffier says that beautiful eyes are those of which there is the greatest number of the same sort; the same applies to mouth, nose etc. It is not that there is not a much greater number of ugly noses than of beautiful noses, but that the ugly ones belong to very different kinds; and each species of ugly ones is in much smaller number than the species of beautiful ones." In spite of its manifest crudity Montesquieu was inclined to accept this æsthetic theory which, somewhat illogically, equated excellence and average or normality; he accepted it because it seemed to account for the variety of æsthetic standards between different societies, their inability to appreciate or even to understand each other's artistic preferences, that is to say for the relativity of values. "When his definition is [rightly] interpreted", Montesquieu says of the learned Jesuit, "it is excellent because it makes sense of a very obscure phenomenon . . . This principle of Father Buffier is excellent for explaining why a French beauty is repulsive to China, and a Chinese repulsive in France." "Perhaps," Montesquieu adds, a little less certain of his ground, but still keeping to his relativism, "it is [also] excellent for explaining all the [preferences with regard to] beauties of taste, even in the works of the spirit. But this would have to be thought out" (I, 1256 *seq.*). In a similar vein Montesquieu tries to account for the fact that serious preachers of the fifteenth and sixteenth centuries, such as Maillard, Menot, Rolin and Barletta, appear both scandalous and comical in the eighteenth. "These men preached what they knew, and taught what had been taught them . . . Hence [if we want to understand and appreciate them], we must transport ourselves into the times when all that could serve for the instruction of the people was of a different nature from all the works which are at present in its hands. This [change in the general tenor of education and mental formation] was bound to make for a new style of preaching" (I, 1233).

One of the most interesting fragments of the *Pensées* concerns the congealing of artistic tastes into artistic canons, canons characteristic of a definite society at a definite period, and here again Montesquieu emphasises that every society has its own classics rarely acceptable to other societies of the same age or the same society at a different juncture. Why, he asks, is it so much more difficult for a Destouches or a Marivaux to succeed in the theatre than it was for Molière in his own day? Because, he answers, Molière could put on the stage the most character-istic figures of the society to which both he and the later drama-tists belonged, so that for the latter there remained nothing but the chaff. Once *le bourgeois gentilhomme* or *l'avare* was held up to ridicule, the greatest subjects of that period were canonised as it were, made into classics. New models will only come with new forms of social life. "A new language, new *mores*, new circumstances will produce a new body of tragedies." Likewise, "a new nation will be needed to create new comedies which will mix its own *mores* with the [basic] human characters". But the end will always be the emergence of new classical standards, of new canons. "The authors [of the future] will take from life what we have already taken from it . . . and soon they will exhaust themselves as we ourselves have come to exhaustion" (I, 1225). Every society has its own stock in trade which is as limited as it is itself.

This is pure relativism. And yet—is there not a hint of absolutism even in this last passage, consistently relativistic though it seems on the surface? New societies develop new classical canons, we are told, because they mix their own specific and exclusive, locally and temporally determined, *mores* with the *caractères des hommes*. Are not these *caractères des hommes*, like all Molière's unforgettable figures which Montes-quieu quotes, *le Médecin*, *le Joueur*, *la Coquette*, *le Jaloux*, *le Misanthrope* etc. as well as the miser and the upstart, eternal archtypes rather than passing shades? The jealous man and the flirting women occur in all climes and in all ages. Is not relativity then something partial, fractional, and confined, a relativity of aspects rather than a total relativity of essence? Is it not so that in reality the temporal and the local, the purely phenomenal, enters into a close intimacy and union with the more-than-temporal and more-than-local, with the eternal, with the absolute, with the noumenal? There is no doubt that questions such as these passed through Montesquieu's mind and remained in it working like yeast in a paste, even while he was formulating all his relativistic statements. He never gave assured answers to them; yet the directions in which he sought these answers can be seen, or at least surmised.

One element of the human world that manifestly remains unaltered in the passage of history and functions in a like manner in all parts of the globe, and of which Montesquieu could have made great use in specifying the aspect of constancy which he sensed even in socio-cultural reality, is the human body, the "machine" as he often called it in agreement with other eighteenth century writers. The point did not escape him. "Man, as a physical being", says chapter 1 of book I *De l'Esprit des Lois*, "is, like the other bodies, governed by invariable laws" (II, 234). But, somewhat surprisingly, little is made of this somatic factor in the rest of the work. Indeed, the only context in which it is used for the purpose of explaining a ubiquitous feature of our mental make-up, is chapter 12 of book XVI, discussing "Natural Modesty"—a phenomenon very near the borderline between the cultural and the physical. "All the nations have equally agreed to attach contempt to the incontinence of women : this is so because nature has spoken to all the nations. She has set up the defence, she has set up the attack; and having placed desires on both sides, she has put into the one temerity, and into the other, shame" (II, 517). The sentiment of modesty, then, should appear, at any rate on the part of women, as a constant and ubiquitous feature, a factor beyond modification by historical forces as rooting in the sub-cultural biotic sphere. But it is significant that Montesquieu, having mentioned this absolute element in life, at once modifies his attitude by bringing in the cultural and moral aspect. "It is of the nature of intelligent beings to feel their imperfections: therefore nature has laid into us modesty, that is to say shame for our imperfections" (II, 518). Who does not see that the somatic is here again put out of doors, after it had only just been drawn in? Since men as well as women are imperfect beings and ought to be ashamed of it, the "naturally" different attitudes to sex satisfaction—"attack" and "defence" —are no longer seen as decisive causes of the sentiment of modesty, but the sentiment of modesty is raised to a higher, ethical and spiritual level. And at once Montesquieu explains that there are certain countries where people are not as modest as they ought to be, and calls upon the legislator to step in, where this is so, and to enforce the canons of decency. Clearly, then, Montesquieu makes next to nothing of the constancy of the physical outfit of man when he wishes to break away from his own relativism which seems to him excessive. "It is not true," he writes (*l.c.*), "that incontinence follows the laws of nature; on the contrary, it violates them. It is modesty and self-control which follow these laws." This sentence opens a deep insight into Montesquieu's thought in general and into his thinking about the absolute element in cultural life and the limitations of cultural relativity in particular. Though modesty may have a physical side to it and be, in this sense of the word, "natural" and at home in every society, it is yet essentially a norm, a desideratum, a duty, something that roots, not in the animal, but in the higher nature of man, not in his body but in his dignity, something that belongs to the Ought rather than to the Is. If there are features in social reality which appear untouched by historical and geographical diversification, they are not due to the identity of the biotic substratum underneath all societies, to the fact that all men are made of very much the same matter, of flesh and bone and blood and muscle, but to the entirely different fact that above all societies there thrones the same code of absolute and immutable values which they all have to realise, as far as it may be, each in its own circumstances of age and place and concrete conditioning. Contrasting, in fragment 1228, the "vain glory" of an Alexander with the true glory of an Epaminondas, i.e. with a glory "founded on the principles of duty, of virtue, of zeal for the Prince and love for the Fatherland", Montesquieu describes the former as ephemeral, the creature and accidental feature of a day, the latter, rooted in the eternal Ought, as lasting. "The one, as real, is or should be of all the nations and all times; the other, as chimerical, is subject to the same revulsions as prejudice" (I, 1307). So also it is with continence and incontinence. Continence belongs to the demands of the code of "natural" law which is as august and as permanent as the stars, incontinence to the catalogue of human actions, the actions of an imperfect being, which are all as perishable as the flowers of the field. But the "laws of nature" which incontinence violates and continence fulfils, are not physical laws; they are moral ones:[1] the "nature" of man is not his physis but his reason, that ray of the Eternal Light.

This brings us to a second element which Montesquieu might have used on a large scale to argue in favour of a static ingredient within changing reality, in favour of a constant factor running through all social systems: reason and its self-identity. He might have insisted that man is above all a rational creature; that rationality is mathematical in character and hence as immutable as the proposition that the square root of 9 is 3; and that, consequently, all men of all times and of all

---

[1] The same conclusion will emerge from a study of chapter 14, book XXVI, discussing "in what cases, in marriages between relatives, the laws of nature should be followed; and in what cases the civil laws should be followed". Montesquieu emphasises first of all, that, in point of fact, every conceivable custom is found in the world. As for the Ought, a distinction is made between mother/son marriages on the one hand, and father/daughter, brother/sister and cousin-german marriages on the other. The former are unnatural because the mother will be out of her period of sexual activity when the son enters it; "unnatural" here means literally "against physical laws". But at once the moral factor is brought in and given the limelight: what really makes us recoil from son-and-mother marriages is the fact that they create an ethically unacceptable situation. "The son owes boundless respect to his mother, the wife owes boundless respect to her husband; the marriage of a mother with her son would overthrow both in the one and in the other their natural [i.e. morally fitting] status" (II, 763 *seq.*). Nevertheless, though such marriages ought to be abhorred by all men as "unnatural", Montesquieu assumes not only that they occur, but even that there are societies where they may become respectful and religiously meritorious, "The Assyrians . . . the Persians wedded their mothers" (II, 765). One sees how little uniformity even the "natural" disgust of mother-and-son incest brings into the world! As for marriages between fathers and daughters or brothers and sisters, Montesquieu bases their prohibition by the "natural" law exclusively on moral considerations. The home must not become a field of amorous exploits: it would be destroyed if its life were to be riddled with lusts and attempts at seduction: "Marriages between fathers and children, brothers and sisters, are forbidden for the sake of preserving natural modesty in the house" (II, 766). There is in this way not really a "natural" (in the sense of physical) basis to the whole system of incest-regulation. Montesquieu opines that the ban on intermarriage within the narrowest circle of parent and offspring ought to be universally accepted. This "prohibition of the laws of nature is invariable because it depends on a thing which is invariable; father, mother and children dwell necessarily in the [same] house" (*ib*). It is obvious that "necessarily" does not, and indeed cannot, mean here "of physical necessity"; it can only mean "normally", "where things are as they ought to be", "where people act in accordance with the inner fitness of things". We see how true this is when we take the next step in Montesquieu's argument and consider first-cousin marriages: "There are peoples among whom . . . the cousins german are regarded as brothers because they ordinarily dwell in the same house; there are others where this usage is not known. Among these [former] peoples, marriage between cousins german should be regarded as contrary to nature; among the others not" (*ib*). As can be seen, the "nature" of M. de la Brède is one which accommodates itself to social conditions!

places, when and in so far as they acted rationally, acted in accordance with a pattern independent of time and space, and free of any and every specification. He might then have proceeded, as so many did, to transmute that self-identical reason into an ideal law "of nature", and might have demanded that the positive law of every society be brought into line with it, thus bringing to the surface the eternal groundwork of all social ordering. It would be wrong to deny that Montesquieu's mind was near to this mode of thinking; there are passages which can commodiously be interpreted in the spirit of that philosophical and legal rationalism which filled the common places of the eighteenth century; yet if he had been fully and truly in the grip of that system of ideas he would not have become the great forerunner of historicism as which he stands before us. The philosophy of the law of nature and of reason lies like a fragrance over his work, but it is no longer firmly established in it. If the passages are examined in which the *droit naturel* or the *loi naturelle* are discussed, for instance fragment 171 from the *Dossier* of the *Considérations sur les . . . Romains*, fragment 1935 from *Mes Pensées*, and chapters 3–7 of book XXVI *De l'Esprit des Lois*, we find them surprisingly nontechnical; we find them simply human; indeed, one might almost say that there is about them a certain emotionality. After listing the worst cruelties inflicted by the Romans on their slaves, Montesquieu exclaims: "Why degrade a part of human Nature?" (II, 220). This *cri du cœur*, so deep-felt and so genuine, is not only characteristic of the man, but also of the thinker. The Romans offended less against a definite set of laws, however unwritten, than against the duties of kindness and humanity which are more than legal in any sense of the word: they sinned less against the rights of their slaves than against their human dignity. In one of the passages in which he rates the Spaniards for their brutality towards Montezuma and Atahualpa,[1] Montesquieu shows very clearly that he thinks in terms of a higher, more-than-earthly morality, not merely in terms of a mundane natural law, however august: "When all is said and done," he writes, "the history of a Christian nation should be the applied morality of Christianity" (I, 1380). It is true that in fragment 1935 there is much more of the current

[1] Cf. also I, 1142 *seq.*

law-of-nature jargon and argumentation of the age. The very
first sentence proves it: "Slavery is against natural right,
according to which all men are born free and independent"
(I, 1467). But this passage is altogether unoriginal: in it,
Montesquieu is less himself than the mouthpiece of a common
opinion which he certainly shared, but which occupied only a
marginal position in his own philosophy. It is as if he wished to
make out in this passage a rational case for the law of nature,
whereas his usual practice is to press it on men in the name of
fairness, of decency, of kindness and of love. The argument here
is clever rather than vital: it is devoid of that full-blooded
humanitarianism, of that deep-rooted humanity which Montesquieu everywhere shows where he speaks with his own authentic
voice of slavery and all other institutions which degrade man
and violate his dignity.

We hear that voice much more clearly and authentically in
the appropriate chapters of the *Esprit des Lois*. A law passed
under Henry VIII, we read there, "which condemned any
girl who, having had illicit intercourse with somebody, did not
admit it to the king before marrying him, violated the defence
of natural modesty: it is as unreasonable," Montesquieu
comments, "to constrain a girl to make this declaration as to
demand of a man that he should not seek to defend his life" (II,
752 *seq.*). While the principle that a young lady who had fallen
should be allowed to keep her guilty secret is here hitched on
to the supposed "natural right" of self-defence which belonged
to the usual stock-in-trade of the natural-law-philosophers of
the eighteenth century, it is obvious that Montesquieu really
bases it on humanity rather than on legality: if she is forced to
expose herself to shame and to bring humiliation on her own
head, she is not so much attained in her rights as in her dignity:
the magistrate is not so much *ultra vires* as he is unkind. Similarly, Montesquieu writes this: "Gondebaud, king of Burgundy,
wished that the wife or the son of him who had committed
robbery be reduced to slavery if they had not revealed the
crime. This law," he says, "was against nature. How could a
wife be the accuser of her husband? How could a son be the
accuser of his father? To avenge a criminal action, one still
more criminal was ordained" (II, 753 *seq.*). How far are we
here from the Kantian cry (so thoroughly rationalist!) of *fiat*

iustitia, ruat coelum. "This law was against nature," Montesquieu writes. Must we not understand him to mean: This law was against humanity, against human affection, against love?[1] It is not rational principle by which Montesquieu goes—rational principle which is in its very nature unbending—but human understanding, indeed, *caritas.*

It is also characteristic that Montesquieu does not allow the theories of natural rights to go very far beyond life, liberty and the pursuit of happiness, but reserves the solution of concrete problems to positive law, different from land to land. A case in point is the regulation of successions. This field has been a happy hunting ground of the natural rights theorists who had attacked the traditional rules and regulations descended from the feudal past with great vigour and on a broad front, and had in particular assailed such principles as primogeniture or the exclusion of women. Montesquieu, in chapter 6 of book XXVI, orders the innovators and reformers off this pitch. He calls the chapter unambiguously "That the Order of Successions depends on the Principles of the Political or Civil Law and not on the Principles of the Natural Law" (II, 755), and when we read his disquisitions here we find that they are thoroughly relativistic. One actual country is better served by this law of inheritance, another by that: "nature" has nothing to do with the matter, which is one of human decision: "Natural law orders the fathers to feed their children, but it does not oblige them to make them their heirs. The division of goods, the laws concerning that division, the succession after the death of him who has had [a part in this] division: all this can be regulated only by society, and consequently by the political or civil [i.e. positive] laws" (II, 755 *seq.*). And Montesquieu hastens to give a number of practical examples which show how "reasonable" and, indeed, how "natural" it may be for certain states to deviate from the apparently most "natural" procedure to allow all children to take an equal share of their father's goods and chattels and to keep more distant claimants out. Perhaps the clearest illustration is the following: "It was the rule under

[1] Cf. also what Montesquieu says on p. 753 concerning divorce: "It is against nature that [the right of] divorce be put into the hands of a third party". What he means, and what emerges from the subsequent text as his opinion, is simply this, that it would be cruel to empower an outsider (like e.g. the Roman *pater familias*) to separate two marriage partners who wish to stay together.

several dynasties of China that the brothers of the Emperor succeeded him and that his children did not succeed him. If it was desired that the prince should have a certain amount of experience, if one feared minorities, if it was necessary to prevent the eunuchs from placing one child after another on the throne, such an order of succession could well be established" (II, 756). It could be established without sinning against nature, and without offending against reason. Indeed, Montesquieu clearly implies, it should be established in the given circumstances for the benefit of the state. We are obviously back here at our author's general sociology of law and of knowledge: legal enactments as well as legal ideas depend, not on reason, but on the exigencies of the state—not on "nature", but on the "nature" of the political constitution.

If we now raise again the question from which this discussion started—the question whether Montesquieu ascribed to the self-identity of formal reason an absolute element in life which goes unchanged and unchanging through all the periods of history and extends unmodified to all the corners of the globe— the answer cannot be in the affirmative. Near though he was to the rationalistic and natural law theories of his age, he was yet out of step with their emphasis on the absolute and basically mathematical character of the human intellect. "Reasonable" did not mean, for the Baron de la Brède, as it did for the rationalists proper, one and only one thing, namely "rational", "fully rational", "rational" in the sense of rational mechanics. It meant much rather three different things: (a) in accordance with common sense; (b) in accordance with the demands of human kindness and compassion; (c) in accordance with the needs of a concrete situation, appropriate, purposive. For all three meanings it is possible to give chapter and verse. "To condemn to slavery a man born of a certain woman [i.e. a slave or bond-woman] is a thing as unjust as the law of the Egyptians which condemned to death all ginger-haired people" (I, 1469). Here we have an instance of the first meaning. In so far as men are reasonable, they will not do things that are utterly absurd. This is, as it were, a negative definition of reasonableness or rationality, and as such altogether different from the very positive definition used by the mechanistic rationalists. For the problem of relativism *versus* absolutism it means nothing. That all men, *quâ* members of the species *homo sapiens*, have a tendency to avoid absurdity, does not in itself mean that their minds are filled by identical concepts. "Knowledge makes men kind; reason inclines to humanity" (II, 493). This statement, so clear and so crisp, illustrates the second meaning. One could almost call this the sentimental definition of rationality; in any case it is a thoroughly non-technical one, *toto coelo* different from the *ratio naturaliter mathematica* of the Cartesian tradition. Again, it means nothing in the problem of relativism *versus* absolutism. That all men, *quâ* beings endowed with the light of reason, are potentially human and humane, does not imply that they all think alike. So there remains the third definition which equates rationality with purposiveness. Men think and act reasonably if they fit their thought and action to the situation with which they are confronted. This definition certainly does mean something in the problem of relativism *versus* absolutism, but its weight is altogether on the side of relativity. The situations with which men find themselves face to face are different from age to age and from country to country. To be reasonable, then, does not signify to apply everywhere the same formula, as it does in mathematics and rational mechanics; it is much rather a willingness on the part of reason to accommodate itself to the things it sees before it, to particularise itself, to enter into creative synthesis with the diversities of this our world.

For this opinion, that reason, as it works itself out in life, is a particularised and concretised reason rather than a self-identical *ratio*, we can give a very good illustration from the chapter on the laws of succession quoted a little while ago. "Since it is clear," Montesquieu says, "that the order of succession should derive from the political or civil laws, it is for them to decide in which cases reason demands that the succession be conferred upon the children, and in which cases it must be given to others" (II, 756). This is a formulation as clear as we could possibly wish it for the purposes of our argument: reason is seen here as operating in different ways, or at least as leading to different results, in different societies: it is seen as working in subservience to the political and civil laws, laws, that is, manifestly and necessarily diverse: it cannot, therefore, account for any static element in life, for any stability of social institutions or mental conceptions amid the flow of history and the variations of geography.

We are thus led to a negative result. But perhaps it is not altogether negative. We have seen, both in our discussion of the part played by the body and in that ascribed to the role of reason, that Montesquieu takes his stand on the postulate that all men should treat each other in all circumstances with charity and consideration. Is this postulate not perhaps a pivotal point from which we can penetrate, through all the relativities of reality, to an absolute core—absolute not in a metaphysical sense, but absolute in so far as it is found wherever we see a human face? The element which goes unbroken through all societies though it is covered over and hidden from view in each of them, is not the *physis* of man nor yet his *ratio*, but his humanity. The absolute substratum for which Montesquieu is searching underneath all relativity is a certain common humanity, the simple quality of being man.

This is a conception from which the Baron de la Brède never broke away, which he held as firmly in his young years as on his dying day. It is a content of the heart as much as of the head, a conviction of the man as much as or more than an opinion of the author. "The heart is a citizen of all lands," Ibben writes to Usbek in *Lettre Persane* LXVII. "In whatever country I have been, I have lived there as if I had to pass all my life there: I have had the same predilection for virtuous people, the same compassion or rather the same tenderness for the unfortunate, the same respect for those whom good fortune had not made blind . . . Everywhere where I meet men, I shall choose myself friends" (I, 228). In the same spirit Xantippe says to Xenocrate: "I bind myself to all human beings" (I, 509). And, speaking directly of himself, and not hiding behind Ibben or Xantippe, Montesquieu confesses: "If I knew anything useful to my nation that would be ruinous for another, I should not propose it to my prince, because I am a man before I am a Frenchman, (or) because I am man by necessity and Frenchman only by accident" (I, 980).

It is because of this belief in a common humanity that Montesquieu eagerly welcomes all ideas and especially all precepts which are upheld by men of good will in more than one society. "One sees with pleasure," he notes, "that Christian charity does not demand of us anything but what the Pagans felt that humanity and love of the common good demanded of them" (I, 1548). Is not this, we can complete the statement, a proof that both ancient virtue and medieval are incarnations of a virtue that is higher than either, and yet in a manner identical with either, incarnations or concrete embodiments of a virtue that is eternal?

But the faith deep down in Montesquieu's heart that all men are in a sense brothers or should at any rate treat each other as such, poses a problem not only on the ethical but also on the epistemological level. If there is a common human substratum underneath all contingency, concreteness and relativity, does not this substratum also contain certain basic ideas or conceptions that are common to all men? This problem is confronted in two contexts, once in the late *Essai sur le Goût*, and once in the very much earlier fragmentary *Réflexions ... contre ... M. Bayle*. In the *Essai sur le Goût*, the existence of a common human area of artistic enjoyment is taken for granted because a *goût naturel* is confronted with a *goût acquis*. "The soul has, independently of the pleasures which come to it from the senses, also some which it would have independently of them, and which are proper to it: such are those due to curiosity, the ideas of its greatness, of its perfections, the idea of its existence as opposed to the experience of nothingness, the pleasure of encompassing the whole of a general idea, that of seeing a great number of things etc., that of comparing, connecting and separating ideas. These pleasures lie in the nature of the soul independently of the senses because they belong to all beings who think" (II, 1241).[1] In the *Réflexions ... contre ... M. Bayle* Montesquieu does not come to so positive and so neat a result. He sees here the common feature of thinking which exists in all societies merely in a common starting point, but not in a common content. "The first idea which presented itself to the mind of the Pagans, as it does to our own, was that of matter" (I, 1173). But the following discussion shows that the sages of antiquity fell already at the very first step beyond this "natural" point of origin of all speculation into some opinions which were peculiar

---

[1] The question whether these pleasures belong to the soul *qua* "substance united with the body" or *qua* substance separable or "separate from the body" is not further tackled as being "very indifferent".

to their age and, Montesquieu feels, are unacceptable to his own. They did not attempt to delimit what is material and what is spiritual: they assumed, in a child-like manner, that matter was all. Thus they came to the belief "that God is material", and from this "principle" they (quite logically) deduced certain consequences which are definitely not generically human but decidedly specific, specifically ancient. They gave to the deity human form because they knew nothing more beautiful than the human body and because they saw reason as inherent only in the human body, and the deity must be both beautiful and endowed with reason; they ascribed to god sex because they knew no human being without sex, and so they refracted the one god into many; they also refracted him into many minor agents because, fixing their minds too firmly and too exclusively on man and his necessary limitations, and making the creator too similar to finite man, they could not imagine that one God could possibly rule the vast, wide universe. This whole theology appears absurd to us, and rightly so. Yet the common human starting point is there, and if the man in the street imagines his Maker as an old man with a beard, or if a philosopher like Cudworth imagines Him ruling the world, as Jupiter was supposed to do, through other "natures" under him, he is simply taking the same turning at the first step beyond the basic conception common to all men as did the thinkers of antiquity, say, a Velleius.

Is there a big discrepancy between the two passages we have studied? By no means. On the contrary; a common conception emerges from both if they are rightly interpreted. It is more clearly expressed in the *Réflexions*, but it is contained in the *Essai* also. The common human content of the mind is only the uttermost limit of speculation, its inception, its jumping-off point. It does not reach into the detail, and yet concrete thinking is always thinking in terms of detail. All men, the *Essai* teaches, are alike gratified when they compare, connect or separate ideas: but these ideas themselves are not the same in all societies. All men are curious, yet the knowledge which alone can assuage that curiosity is different in different human situations. It is not claimed that Montesquieu expressly held these opinions; but it is claimed, and it follows from an integral view of his position, that they were in and behind his thought.

Men are alike not only because they are all capable of experiencing joy and sorrow—a fact which ought to determine our attitude and mode of action towards them; they are alike also in so far as certain common endowments lie buried in the depths of their being, and in so far as their thinking has to start from certain common experiences like that of the material world and the materiality of this world; but this does not mean that their minds are filled by the same concrete contents. The concrete is always specific; it has its own proper place somewhere in the field determined by the great ordinates of space and time, and is thus not common human but exclusive, exclusively spatial and temporal—exclusively social.

We are thus driven to the same result as before. As the body does not bring a static element into the human sphere, and as the intellect fails to do so, so is our common humanity caught in the coils of relativity. And yet, our common humanity does bring, on the limit of the field of vision, as it were, an inkling at least of the absolute into the picture. Our common basic endowments and our common basic experiences are the pledges, so to speak, of a sphere of the absolute which stretches beyond the confines of both our endowments and our experiences; it is like a light beyond the horizon: we know it to be there; we see its rays which travel towards us; but we do not behold the source of those rays, which is outside our ken. We are reduced here to imagining, to divining and to hoping. We are in face of a metaphysical problem, a problem posed on the very limit of the knowable. Among the philosophical fragments of *Mes Pensées* there is one which, however terse, shows us what was in Montesquieu's mind, and also shows that our interpretation of him is correct: "When one says that there are no absolute qualities, this does not mean that no such exist, but [only] that no such exist for us, and that our spirit cannot grasp them in their concreteness" (I, 1537).[1]

This conviction that absolute laws which we do not know, or at any rate do not know fully, hide behind the relative laws which we find positively established in individual societies and which are all that we do know adequately, is particularly clear in the central portion of Montesquieu's system, in his philosophy of legislation. The following passage is not altogether

---

[1] "*. . . ne peut pas les déterminer.*"

happily worded, but it proves that he thought of justice as a value that is both transcendental and this-worldly, both eternal (in its essence) and temporal (in its concrete appearances): "Almost all the virtues consist in a particular relationship of a certain man to another; for instance: friendship, love of country, pity, are particular relationships. But justice is a general relationship. Hence all the virtues which destroy this general relationship are not [really] virtues" (I, 1304). Patriotism, so we may interpret our author here, is purely phenomenal, a virtue in a sense, but a virtue confined as all human things are and must be, a virtue tainted by the imperfection of relativity; justice is noumenal, an absolute value that looks down upon us from a higher sphere like the eternal stars, a value of the supremest purity which attaches upon us not as citizens of this state or that, but simply as men, as beings made in the image of their Maker, as beings endowed with a share of Reason, of the Eternal Mind.

When the *Esprit des Lois* was attacked because of the strong dose of relativism which it contains, Montesquieu, not unnaturally and not unreasonably, defended himself by saying that, unlike for instance Hobbes, he was not a pure relativist, but a thinker who tried to hook on the relative values of our fallen world to the eternal values of the world above. "The author," he writes, referring to himself, "has had the intention of attacking the system of Hobbes, the terrible system which, making depend all the virtues and all the vices on the establishment of the laws which men have made for themselves . . . overthrows . . . both the whole of religion and the whole of morality. Against this, the author has affirmed, firstly, that there were laws of justice and of equity before the establishment of positive laws: he has proved that all beings had laws; that, even before their creation, they had laws *in posse;* that God himself had laws, that is to say [in this case] laws which he had made for himself" (II, 1123). That Montesquieu was quite justified in taking up this line of defence can be seen from the sketch of a polemic against Hobbes written perhaps twenty-five years before the *Défense de l'Esprit des Lois:*[1] in it, Montesquieu

---

[1] This came out in 1750, whereas the *Traité Général des Devoirs de l'Homme*, in connection with which the passage to which the text refers was penned, dates from 1725.

discusses the hypothetical situation posited by Hobbes in which two savages meet each other for the first time—the situation which, Hobbes was sure, would at once give rise to conflict because *homo homini est lupus*. Montesquieu, as we have seen already, denied that this was the necessary outcome to the encounter. War and peace, hostility and amity, would be in the balance. It would depend on the circumstances to which side the balance would incline. Montesquieu, as can be seen, is even more relativistic here than Hobbes, in so far as Hobbes knows at any rate one absolute necessity, namely the war of all against all. But though all depends on the circumstances down here below, the two savages are yet not free from all "legal" bindings, when they meet in the thicket of the primeval forest or on the desert plain, as Montesquieu sees things. There is present *un principe de justice* which is above and before men, even though men may deny it allegiance (cf. I, 1139 *seq.*).

It is only by applying our thesis that the terms "natural law" or "eternal law" as used by Montesquieu describe a metaphysical reality and not a physical one, a noumenal and not a phenomenal entity, a set of values-in-themselves and not a set of values which actually operate in this our workaday world, that we can reconcile the contents of chapter 1, book I, of the *Esprit des Lois* with the rest of the work. "Individual intelligent beings may have laws which they have made; but they have also laws which they have not made. Before there existed intelligent beings, they were possible; hence they had possible relationships, and consequently possible laws. Before there existed made laws, there existed possible relationships of justice. To say that there is nothing either just or unjust but what is ordained or forbidden by positive laws is tantamount to saying that before a circle was traced out, the radii were not all equal. Hence relationships of equity anterior to the positive law establishing them must be admitted: as, for example that, supposing there were human societies, it would be just to conform to their laws; that, if there were intelligent beings who had received some benefit from another being, they should be duly grateful for it; that, if an intelligent being had created an intelligent being, the creature should remain in the dependence in which he had been from his inception; that an intelligent being who has inflicted evil upon an intelligent being deserves to suffer the same evil, and so forth" (II, 233). It is clear from this passage first of all that the laws which men have not made but which they find ready-made, and which in consequence must be regarded as not relative but absolute, are "anterior" to the positive and hence relative laws, not in any temporal, but in a definitely metaphysical sense: they are as anterior to concrete enactments as God is to man. Indeed, the whole argument has an unmistakably theological flavour. Of the four concrete instances of absolute law which Montesquieu adduces, the third—that the creature should remain dependent on the creator—is altogether theological; it is impossible to apply it to the father-and-child relationship on the human level, since children grow up and the Baron de la Brède would have been the last to demand that they should be kept for ever in leading strings. Of the other three, the second—stressing the duty of gratitude—is at least predominantly theological. The gratitude of gratitudes is man's thankfulness to his maker, and just because the thankfulness of man to his human benefactors is put on the same level by Montesquieu, the whole law remains on the metaphysical level also. The first instance—laws should be obeyed—seems to refer to positive laws rather than to divine commandments; we are here consequently on the mundane plane. But our philosopher teaches no more here than an absolute duty to obey relative enactments; he says nothing of these relative enactments themselves, and least of all that they are anything but human or anything but relative. But perhaps most instructive is the consideration of the fourth and last item, the *lex talionis*. It is, in principle, always and everywhere just that he who has inflicted pain should also suffer it himself. Here we seem to be right in the middle of human law; here we seem to have a positive legal principle, not a metaphysical one; here we seem to hear Montesquieu talk with the voice, not of the relativist, but of the rationalist *à la Kant*. But appearances are deceptive. If we turn to chapter 19 of Book VI we find that this "absolute" principle actually operates in the world differently in despotic states and differently under moderate governments (II, 330). It is handled mercilessly in the former; it is applied mercifully in the latter. The index of the *Esprit des Lois* says of the *peine de talion* that it "derives from a law anterior to the positive laws" (II, 1726). The term "derives" seems to be the operative word in this clause. Both the penal codes of despotisms and the penal codes of democracies, in so far as they apply the *lex talionis*, are in agreement with that absolute law anterior to both of them: but that does not prevent them from being different—from working out the one principle in two contrasting ways. We can see then that even the *lex talionis* is not really an *absolutum* of this world (in which, indeed, it appears never otherwise than in refracted forms, in forms broken asunder by the political media in which and through which it operates) but an *absolutum* of a higher world—the world of things-in-themselves, the world of God.

What Montesquieu here says about the *lex talionis* applies in his opinion over the whole field of law. The *lex talionis* is part and parcel of natural equity; it is, in a sense, part and parcel of the code of reason, of *absolute* reason, of that reason which rests in itself and has only a faint and fitful influence on this our unreasonable world. The *whole* code of transcendental reason is somehow behind human legislation: but men, however much they may "derive" their positive enactments from that code, cannot help breaking it into dissimilar forms and shapes when they set about the business of law-making, so that in the end the common background and source of all positive legislation becomes lost to sight, indeed, becomes utterly unrecognisable. The absolute is smothered under the relative; more than that: the absolute is dissolved into the relative. It is and remains the absolute in itself, metaphysically: it is none-the-less transmuted into the relative when it concretises itself, when it enters the social sphere. "The law, in general," Montesquieu writes in chapter 3, "is human reason in so far as it rules all the peoples of the earth; and the political and civil laws of each nation should be nothing else but the particular cases in which that human reason is applied" (II, 237). In their source, therefore, all systems of right and wrong are one: but when they flow out of their source, when they assume body and shape, when they enter into their earthly dominion, they must diversify themselves, they must become relative and even irreconcilable. How near Montesquieu is, with this conception, to the great neoplatonist tradition! The laws, he goes on to say, "should be so proper to the people for which they are made that it is a very great accident if those of one nation may suit another. It is

necessary that they should be in accordance with the nature
and the principle of the government which is established or
which it is desired to establish; be it that they constitute it as do
the political laws; be it that they maintain it, as do the civil
laws. They should be relative to the physical nature of the
country; to the climate, ice-bound, burning or temperate; to
the quality of the territory, its situation, its size; to the way of
life of the peoples, [whether] tillers of the soil, hunters or
herdsmen; they should accommodate themselves to the measure
of liberty which the constitution may admit; to the religion of
the inhabitants, their inclinations, their wealth, their number,
their trade, their *mores*, their manners . . . It is in all these
aspects that they must be considered" (II, 238). Thus it is that
relativity breaks in from all sides and breaks up the absolute.
And the process of relativation goes far, very far indeed. "The
civil laws depend on so many things that they may have useful
faults and necessary imperfections" (II, 1030). It will not do to
judge them by the rule of reason, however much they may have
sprung from that rule. One cannot judge man as he is by the
image which was in the Divine Mind before he was made and
thrust out into this world of imperfection and mortality.

The same relationship between the eternal and the temporal
as in the law obtains also, according to Montesquieu, in
religion. There exists a "true" religion which he conceives,
somewhat vaguely, as a christianized deism or a deistic
Christianity,[1] but its kingdom is not of this world. In this world
every kingdom has its own specific religion; we find in practice
no definite form of the true religiousness but only confined
creeds and particular churches, all of which are in varying
degrees "false", even though all are at the same time, in a
sense, manifestations of one fundamental belief which is part
and parcel of a necessary and unassailable common meta-
physic—the belief in the existence of God. "It is the nature of
human laws," Montesquieu writes, "to be subject to all the
accidents which occur, and to vary in the measure in which the
wills of men change: the nature of the laws of religion, on the
other hand, is never to change. Human laws pronounce about

[1] Montesquieu's attitude to religion is faithfully reflected in his letter of May,
1754, to William Warburton, Bishop of Gloucester, and in his conduct in the face
of approaching death. Cf. for the former, *Correspondance*, ed. Gebelin and Morize,
II, 1914, 527 *seq.*, and concerning the latter, *ibidem*, 572–575.

the good; religion about the best. The good can have different objects because there are different kinds of good; but the best is but one and so cannot change" (II, 751). Yet although, or because, the true religion is one, eternal and absolute, it cannot become active in the world in its pure form; the relativity of all human things forces it through the prism of relativity so that its light shines in different directions and appears to have contrasting colours. There are passages in the chapters on religion which not only repeat or rather re-apply the assertion quoted above concerning "useful faults and necessary imperfections" but put even greater emphasis on the inescapability of the relativation of the absolute. "The truest and most holy doctrines may have very bad consequences when they are not tied in with the principles of society; and, on the other hand, the falsest doctrines may have admirable consequences when things are so contrived that they are in accord with these same principles" (II, 728 *seq.*). Must we not all then worship before idols? The question seems inescapable. Montesquieu answers it, keeping to his essential relativism as far as this world is concerned: "I do not throw doubt on the saintliness of Charlemagne, because I do not know of any end to the [divine] mercy for those who have offended against the laws of the Gospel by following the laws of their country" (II, 1113).[1] The true God beyond is approached by us, the creatures of circumstance, only through the less-than-true images which we form of Him in our age and place and general limitations.

Even the analysis of the passages, then, which mark Montesquieu's nearest approach to the natural law philosophy and deistic theology of his age, leads to the result that he indeed asserted the existence of absolute laws and eternal verities, but denied—and that is decisive—their direct and uniform operation in space and history. If they bring any absoluteness into the field of relativity which is coterminous with the field of human existence in the broadest meaning of the term, it is only by acting as a reference back from the relative to the absolute. "It is an admirable idea of Plato's," Montesquieu writes, thinking of book IX, chapter 13, of the *Republic*, "that

---

[1] Cf. also II, 1145 *seq.*, where Montesquieu, even under severe pressure, refuses to renounce this relativism, while strongly emphasising the absolute character of the "true" religion or religion-in-itself.

the laws are made in order to announce the commands of Reason to those who cannot receive them immediately from her" (II, 1042). This is a passage which goes as far as any that has come from the pen of our philosopher towards asserting rationality of concrete laws; yet even it insists at the same time on the unknowableness of the Absolute Reason which is hidden behind the relative reasonableness of our human rules and regulations.

The conviction that men's vision is limited belongs to the innermost core of Montesquieu's doctrine of man and gives it a decidedly tragic turn: "He must be his own guide; yet he is labouring under limitations." It is because of these limitations and disabilities that, in a kind of blameless guilt, "he violates without ceasing the laws which God has set up, and changes those which he himself has instituted" (II, 234). While our intelligence puts us in one way above the lower creation, in another it degrades us beneath it. To know without knowing all is to be fallible. There are both laws of nature proper, laws which rule the physical universe, and "laws of nature" of human life, laws which ought to regulate the affairs of men. But whereas the former work themselves out uninhibited, unrefracted and unbroken among molecules and atoms and plants and beasts, the latter are only a vision in the sky far too high above us to recognise their outlines. "Though this [intelligent world] also has laws which, by their nature, are invariable," Montesquieu writes, "it does not follow them with constancy as the physical world follows its own. The reason for this is that individual intelligent beings are limited by their nature, and consequently subject to error; and, on the other hand, that it is in their nature to act of themselves" (II, 233). Men, in other words, cannot focus the eternal verities even though they may realise that such exist; and men are *causae secundae* who have to build their own world. It remains a duty on their part to try and bring the world which they are making, as best they can, into agreement with the eternal verities; but the fulfilment of this duty must, in the nature of things, consist in a painful groping among the uncertainties of the twilight that encloses us on all sides, for the true light shines beyond and only the dimmest of rays penetrate to the valleys where we humans have our abode.

INDEX

211